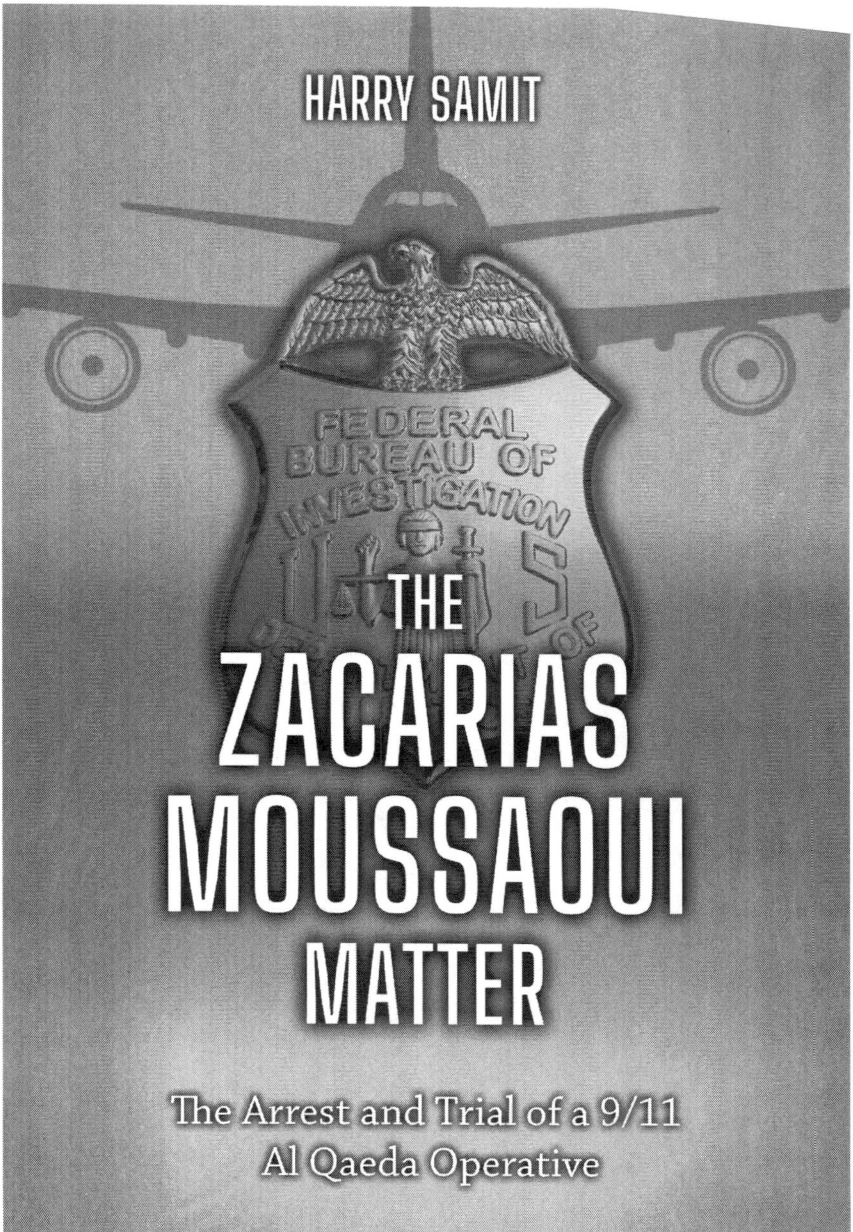

STONE TOWER PRESS

The Zacarias Moussaoui Matter:
The Arrest and Trial of a 9/11 Al Qaeda Operative

In accordance with my obligations as a former FBI employee and pursuant to my FBI employment agreement, this book has undergone a prepublication review for the purpose of identifying classified information or prohibited disclosures, but it has not been reviewed for editorial content or accuracy. The FBI does not endorse or validate any information that I have described in this book. The opinions expressed in this book are mine and not those of the FBI or any other government agency.

Stone Tower Press
7 Ellen Rd.
Middletown, RI 02842
stonetowerpress.com

ISBN: 979-8-9992313-4-5

Cover and text design by: Amy Cole, JPL Design Solutions

Printed in the United States of America

To Terri, Matt, Jake, Anna, and Tommy—I am aware of the sacrifices the events in this book required from you, and for them, and most of all for your love, I am eternally grateful.

CONTENTS

A Note About the People Discussed in this Book ix

Foreword 1

Preface: The Most Terrible Day... 4

1. FBI Minneapolis 7
2. Casework 10
3. The JTTF Matures 13
4. The Call 15
5. The Investigation Begins 19
6. The Witness 23
7. Flight School 29
8. Flight Instructor 33
9. Contact 39
10. The Monster 46
11. The Companion 52
12. Al-Attas' Story 56
13. The Prayer 61
14. The Last Will and Testament 68
15. Encounter With the Monster 75
16. The Tale 80
17. The FBI 90
18. More Lies 95

19. A Second Arrest 102
20. More Lies 108
21. Go For Broke 116
22. Next Steps 122
23. In Jail 127
24. Requests 130
25. Denied 136
26. France to the Rescue 142
27. The Intelligence Angle 148
28. Support from Langley 152
29. Finally, FISA 157
30. Plan C 161
31. Squashed 165
32. CIA Again 169
33. More Terrorist Connections 174
34. Our Big Shot 180
35. The FAA 185
36. Catastrophe 195
37. Finally 200
38. Another Delay 203
39. His Belongings 208
40. Losses 212
41. A New Threat 217
42. New York 221
43. Ground Zero 227

44. More Connections 234

45. Money from Germany 238

46. Blamestorming 243

47. Small Men in Big Jobs 247

48. The Legal Team 255

49. Criminal Charges 260

50. 15 Minutes of Fame 263

51. What Was His Mission? 269

52. Star Witness 275

53. The Defense 278

54. Embarrassment 283

55. Office of the Inspector General 286

56. Guilty Plea 293

57. Trial Prep 297

58. Penalty Phase 302

59. Direct Examination 305

60. Cross 313

61. Eligible for Death 320

62. Verdict 325

63. The Final Meeting 330

64. Day 1, Again 336

65. Day 2, Again 344

66. The Last Chance 347

The End of the Case 351

About the Author 353

A NOTE ABOUT THE PEOPLE DISCUSSED IN THIS BOOK

I have chosen to use aliases for some of the people connected to this case. A list of these follows to allow the readers to keep track. Where a person mentioned in the text does not appear on this list, then their real first name was used. All employees of U.S. Intelligence Community Agencies other than the FBI which are discussed in the book were given aliases to maintain security.

"Roland"—The Section Chief of the International Terrorism Operations Section at FBI Headquarters in 2001

"Devin"—The Unit Chief of the Radical Fundamentalist Unit at FBI Headquarters in 2001, Devin worked for Roland

"Martin"—A Supervisor in the Radical Fundamentalist Unit at FBI Headquarters assigned to program manage certain terrorism cases in Minneapolis in 2001, Martin worked for Devin

"Rosa"—An FBI Intelligence Analyst in the Radical Fundamentalist Unit at FBI Headquarters, Rosa worked for Martin

"Malcolm"—The head of the FBI's National Security Law Unit (NSLU) at FBI Headquarters, Malcolm was not a Special Agent

"Harold"—A non-Agent attorney assigned to the National Security Law Unit (NSLU) at FBI Headquarters, Harold worked for Malcolm

"Shari"—A non-Agent attorney assigned to the National Security Law Unit (NSLU) at FBI Headquarters, Shari worked for Malcolm

"Jeb"—A Supervisor in the Iran Unit at FBI Headquarters in 2001

"Celia"—The Chief Division Counsel (head attorney) for FBI Minneapolis

"Derek"—An Assistant United States Attorney assigned to prosecute Zacarias Moussaoui after the 9/11 attacks

"Marge"—An FBI New York Supervisory Special Agent assigned to manage the PENTTBOMB team investigating the 9/11 attacks

"Dana"—An FBI Intelligence Analyst in the Usama Bin Laden Unit at FBI Headquarters, during the trial Dana wrote a document attempting to discredit Moussaoui's admissions

FOREWORD

I began writing this book in the Autumn of 2001 when I realized that my colleagues and I on the Minneapolis Joint Terrorism Task Force (JTTF) were participating in historical events relating to the attacks by Al Qaeda on the U.S. on September 11. During the first months and for many years after, the writing simply consisted of a few bullets here and there, hastily typed into a Word document, often at the end of a long and wearying day working cases as an FBI Agent. I knew that the details and emotions of the moment should be preserved, but I did not have the time to fully document them. I was trying to leave prompts which would later serve as the framework of a narrative memoir about significant counterterrorism investigations.

When I retired from the FBI in April 2020, I at once began to knit what I had into a coherent document and one year later submitted my proposed manuscript to the FBI's Prepublication Review Office (PRO). I did so to honor my agreement with the FBI, signed when I first entered on duty, that I would not publish anything about the Bureau or my work as a Special Agent without first obtaining their permission.

At the end of a busy year of writing I had what I felt was a draft of a book which accurately portrayed events from my perspective while also protecting classified information and the sensitive techniques used by the U.S. Intelligence and Law Enforcement communities. In this I was helped by the fact that very few of the events discussed in the book occurred after 2007, meaning these happened 15–20 years in the past. Also, the case discussed in the proposed text went to trial, meaning the main facts were already in the public domain.

When I submitted the manuscript to them on April 1, 2021, I was cautiously optimistic that despite my criticisms of the FBI, PRO would diligently and in good faith apply itself to doing its job and provide authorization for publication. How wrong I was!

After more than a year of cordial yet formal back-and-forth with PRO, it became clear that the FBI did not, in fact, intend to allow me to tell the story as I wished (or at all), and I asked my congressman for help. Whatever request his office sent to the FBI merely had the effect of causing PRO to slow and then stop responding to my emails altogether.

I then, reluctantly, sought the advice of an attorney who specialized in First Amendment cases, and he told me what I already knew: "The FBI will only respond to a lawsuit." And sadly, that is how I wound up suing my former employer. Not surprisingly, the day the suit was filed the Unit Chief of the PRO called me—incidentally, marking the very first time ever I had a phone conversation with someone from that organization, to inform me they were working hard to clear my book for publication!

Months later, I received their proposed edits and saw that these made the book unreadable and the story unrecognizable. Furthermore, analysis of much of what PRO considered classified showed many of their edits to be absurd. To give just one example, they removed an entire storyline regarding two subjects (from 2001!) who we identified while reviewing footage from a business' security camera. When I naturally objected to this, citing this technique's showcasing on nearly every cop show on TV, I was told, "You've been gone from the FBI for years now. You don't know what is and is not sensitive."

And PRO's tactics were relatively mild compared to those of attorneys working on the case in the Civil Division of the Department of Justice. They resorted quickly to baseless accusations, claiming, among other things, that I "reproduced 30–40 pages of classified material" in my manuscript (a falsehood) and levying unreasonable security conditions on me for times when I visited my old FBI Office to have meetings with PRO to negotiate changes.

In the end, the FBI and I were finally able to reach an agreement, a process "shortened" to only 3+ years by my expensive lawsuit and with the help of some former colleagues in the Counterterrorism Division at FBI Headquarters who were able, at last to prevail upon the PRO to understand that much of what they proposed removing was no longer sensitive and belonged in the public domain.

I explain all of this so the reader will understand first the process that any former rank-and-file employee of an intelligence community agency must go through before their memoirs see the light of day. While senior figures have their submissions fast-tracked and approved in a matter of months or even weeks, if you are a frontline worker whose writing exposes cracks in the bureaucracy, you should expect to wait years and invest thousands of dollars in legal fees.

Second, it answers a question I have long wondered about: "Why are there so few firsthand accounts from FBI Agents going back to the Bureau's founding in 1908?" Anyone interested in military history can find memoirs of Soldiers, Sailors, Airmen, and Marines from every conflict of the 20th and 21st centuries, including the most recent Global War on Terror. Until my own battle with the bureaucracy, I did not understand why so few of my FBI colleagues, past and present, took up their pens, typewriters, and keyboards to record what they experienced during some of the most consequential moments in our nation's history.

I get it now.

PREFACE

THE MOST TERRIBLE DAY...

8:00 a.m. (CST) 9/11/2001, Twin Cities, Minnesota

Unusually for a weekday, I was home with my family at breakfast time. I was an FBI Special Agent and normally by this hour on a Tuesday I would have been at work at the Minneapolis Division of the FBI where I was assigned to 5 Squad. Another name for 5 Squad was the Joint Terrorism Task Force, or JTTF. I had been on this squad since arriving in Minneapolis a week after my graduation from the FBI Academy 2 ½ years before. The function of a JTTF was to investigate acts of international terrorism. In the words of the FBI's mission statement, the goal of our investigations was to "identify and neutralize" terrorist threats to U.S. interests, worldwide.

I was home that morning because one of my collateral duties in addition to my primary assignment as an investigator, was to fly as a Bureau Pilot. I was scheduled for a late afternoon surveillance mission piloting an FBI Cessna 182(RG) aircraft, and it would probably go well into the evening hours. Because the regulations governing the FBI's aviation program set limits on the number of hours a pilot can work and fly per day, I was heading into the office late. It was a nice opportunity to have breakfast with my two sons, Matt (5) and Jake (2), and my wife, Terri, who was five months pregnant with our daughter Anna at the time.

I am sure everyone in the United States who was old enough to grasp the enormity of the tragedy remembers where they were when they heard the news. I was, undramatically, in my kitchen cooking breakfast for the kids, wearing boxers and a tee shirt. Because I was planning to go in late, Terri had taken the opportunity to sleep in that morning but woke up right at 8 a.m. and turned on the radio as she came into the kitchen. As usual, it was tuned to KS95, the Van and Cheryl show. The kids were chattering, Terri and I were talking, when, at the edge of my consciousness, I heard Van Patrick, one of the DJs say very matter-of-factly that an airplane had just hit the World Trade Center in New York.

It was, I knew, what I had been waiting for and dreading over the last 3½ weeks. However, because of what Van Patrick said next, I indulged in one little moment of continued denial. He said that the plane which struck the World Trade Center was a Cessna, a category of aircraft which conjured up visions of a small, high-winged private aircraft of the type that orthodontists flew on weekends. A Cessna did not fit with the scenario I had been anticipating. Still trying desperately to remain secure in my self-deception that the nightmare had not begun, I continued to eat my bagel, although I was no longer hungry. My uneasiness turned to alarm when Patrick announced that while he and cohost Cheryl Kay watched in horror on a television in their radio studio, a second plane hit the undamaged other tower.

When Terri went down to the family room to turn on CNN, I followed with growing trepidation. What I saw on the screen froze my blood and left no doubt that my nightmares (which I had literally been having for the last few weeks) had come true. The image on the screen showed a Boeing 767 airliner, and it was headed for the undamaged south tower, standing next to its furiously smoking twin. While Terri and I watched the replay, the aircraft flew towards the tower. At the last minute, the pilot flying the airplane put on an abrupt left angle-of-bank to correct his path to ensure that the plane would strike the building. The horrible image we viewed left me no doubt that a recent case of mine just developed in the most tragic fashion imaginable.

Terri certainly anticipated my next words, which I barely choked out, "I have to go to work!" She nodded. Within minutes, I was headed into the office. I told my family that I did not know when I would be home. Terri and I had been married for 8½ years, and she had come to expect such occurrences. She was the glue that held the family together in situations like this.

Once in the car, I made some phone calls and got the word out to the rest of the JTTF.

CHAPTER 1

FBI MINNEAPOLIS

When I reported to the Minneapolis Division of the FBI in the Spring 1999 as a brand-new Agent fresh out of Quantico, I was assigned to 5 Squad, which was the catch-all for international and domestic terrorism cases as well as Foreign Counterintelligence matters. The office did not yet have a Joint Terrorism Task Force, or JTTF. Several other offices already did, beginning with New York, which organized theirs during the 1980s.

Our squad supervisor Chris was aware of this when he reported to Minneapolis from FBI Headquarters, and he did not like it. He realized that more offices were starting JTTFs, and he wanted Minneapolis to be among that number. By late Summer of 1999 the Minneapolis JTTF was formed. At its birth, we original members little realized that our Task Force would have such stunning success combating terrorism. One reason for that success was an Agent named Joe, who'd arrived in Minneapolis from Quantico less than a year before me. Joe was a former Air Force officer with dark hair and the muscular build of a wrestler. Behind his outward genialness, Joe was a first-rate investigator. He knew international terrorism and was extremely proficient at satisfying the administrative requirements so cases would move forward.

In addition to being successful, 5 Squad was a happy group. At least for me, the situation was terrific. There was a young and aggressive supervisor, knowledgeable senior Agents, and a small number of guys close to my age who were eager to work. Things seemed set to foster my development as an investigator.

The Immigration and Naturalization Service (INS) Agent who was assigned to the JTTF had been working terrorism issues with the FBI for a few years already and was respected by everyone on the Squad. John was a stocky, blonde Wisconsin native in his early 40s who was an outstanding investigator familiar with immigration law and able to apply it to virtually any situation where people connected with our investigations were citizens of foreign countries. Most subjects of international terrorism cases were born outside the U.S. and John was creative and skilled in his application of immigration laws. He could always be counted on to find a solution to a case where none previously existed. He was also an outstanding interviewer who could usually tell quickly if a subject was lying. His expertise would prove invaluable in the coming years.

There were certainly enough terrorism subjects in Minnesota to keep us busy. The Twin Cities by the late 1990s was home to the world's third largest population of Somalis (after Mogadishu and Toronto). These were people displaced by decades of violent civil war in their own country. Somalia is an exclusively Muslim country and some of the refugees who reached Minnesota brought radical Islam with them. There were also radical Muslims from other parts of the world living in the Twin Cities. And Minnesota was also home to several prominent and violent White Converts to Islam.

In addition to learning the ropes as an Agent and someone new to the Twin Cities, one other part of my education during this period concerned the relationship between FBI Headquarters, and the field. FBIHQ has a culture all its own, organized along hierarchical lines. And, of great significance to this story is the fact that people there think and act differently from the rest of the FBI working cases in the field. At the top of the FBI is the Director, appointed by the President. Despite an often humorously erroneous depiction on TV and in the movies, no Agent has ever worked his or her way up through the ranks to become Director. Louis Freeh, the FBI Director when I entered on duty, *had* been an Agent for a few years early in his career, but at the time of his appointment was long out of the FBI, having served as a federal prosecutor and then a judge. The sad truth is all FBI Directors are drawn from the ranks of attorneys working for the Department of Justice and very few of them have the background or experience needed to lead the Bureau well.

Under the Director are various Supervisory Special Agents (SSAs) ranging in rank from the lowest "desk supervisors" all the way up to the Deputy Director, the most senior Agent in the FBI.

The SSA position is the first rung on the promotion ladder which could lead them to the rank of Deputy Director. Because one specific SSA at headquarters is crucial to this story, it is worth looking at this role a little more closely.

Most of Minneapolis' terrorism cases were overseen by the Radical Fundamentalist Unit (RFU) at FBIHQ. This team was headed by a Unit Chief we will call Devin and oversaw cases involving Sunni extremist groups other than Al Qaeda itself. Under Devin was the person with whom Minneapolis dealt most often, and he played a central role in the events which followed. The desk supervisor assigned by Unit Chief Devin to manage Minneapolis cases was a Supervisory Special Agent (SSA) we will call Martin.

I did not know Martin personally when he arrived in RFU, but I can say that his reputation as a terrorism supervisor was poor. People in our office with whom he dealt had not formed a good opinion of him. The word I heard from Chris, and others more experienced with Martin was that he was excessively cautious and very preoccupied with protecting his own career. This was a problem because *we needed Martin's assistance* to obtain permission to employ some investigative techniques. A number of these could be approved right at FBI Headquarters by an official in the FBI chain of command. Some required the approval of the Department of Justice. A few required an order from a federal judge. But no matter what level of approval was required, Martin was the first stop.

CHAPTER 2

CASEWORK

In the summer of 1999 Chris assigned me my first real terrorism case. That meant my name went on the case file, and I was responsible for all that happened with the investigation. Other investigations soon followed, and from them I learned not just how to work a terrorism case, but also about the shadowy and violent world of the terrorists.

Although my and the FBI's collective knowledge of how Al Qaeda operated would grow significantly after the 9/11 attacks, even in those days we knew that Usama Bin Laden and his murderous leadership cadre were sheltering in Afghanistan under the protection of the equally violent Taliban. We also understood that they were running training camps for frontline fighters and terrorists, some of whom they were sending to the West to murder innocent people. That's what we were trying to prevent.

As my experience grew, I also made some connections to people in the Bureau who I believed could help me advance any unusual or complicated investigations. These included a non-Agent attorney we will call Harold, who worked in the National Security Law Unit (NSLU) at FBI Headquarters. Harold's supposed expertise was in the Foreign Intelligence Surveillance Act (FISA).

In a lecture I attended, Harold explained that all the FBI had to show to obtain permission from a judge to utilize techniques under FISA was that someone was acting as an "Agent of a Foreign Power." He defined a foreign power as a foreign government, a foreign company, or any other group or organization not comprised primarily of U.S. persons. The techniques we could use under FISA included performing a physical search of someone's property or conducting electronic surveillance of their telephone or email communications. The key was that the subjects had to be acting as an *agent of a foreign power* before we could employ FISA. The definition "foreign power," Harold explained, also covered terrorist groups. He concluded his lecture by telling us that if we ever needed assistance applying for a FISA, we should contact him at FBIHQ.

One investigation also brought me into contact with FBI representatives in foreign countries, members of the FBI's Legal Attache (LEGAT) program. As happens everywhere, some Agents assigned to the LEGAT program were great, and some were not so great. For this story, two assistant Legal Attaches (ALATs) with whom I worked during 2000 and 2001 are important: Jay, an extremely competent and aggressive Agent assigned to the U.S. Embassy in Paris, and a much less stellar example assigned to the embassy in London. Although we have never met face-to-face to this day, Jay proved to be a staunch friend and ally whose assistance would prove critical in the months to come.

The LEGAT Offices became involved anytime someone in a field office in the U.S. wanted to share information with a friendly foreign service about a case. It was the job of someone in the LEGAT office to pass the documentation to the right person in the foreign government and because Jay's responsibility in Paris included the counterterrorism program, all leads from a JTTF to the Government of France went through him. He was terrific at making connections and getting results in Paris and would play a crucial role in the coming months.

Unfortunately, his counterpart in London was less impressive. An older Agent who spent much of his career in New York, the counterterrorism ALAT in the UK was much less interested in helping when connections led to British shores. His responses, when they came at all, were sluggish and showed a distinct lack of enthusiasm. The ALAT in London also made it clear to me that he regarded my requests as unwarranted and the case I was working on unimportant. It did not bode well for the next time we needed something from our British allies, which we soon would.

CHAPTER 3

THE JTTF MATURES

By the late Summer of 2001 the team on the Minneapolis JTTF had worked enough cases that we were confident in our ability to handle most issues as they arose. The squad was functioning well together, and we had a lot of recent hard-won experience, both with investigating Al Qaeda, and in understanding how hostile Martin was to the idea we would advance any investigation. A few cases along the way confirmed he was averse to doing *anything* which in his mind posed a risk to his reputation.

During this time the Minneapolis Special Agent in Charge (SAC), a nonentity as far as we on the JTTF were concerned, retired. He was replaced by Ray, who was an Assistant Special Agent in Charge (ASAC). Ray was a nice guy who had been around for a while and seemed to have a lot of contacts.

We also had a promotion on the squad when Chris learned he was being advanced to ASAC for his good performance. What was unusual was that Chris was not transferred to another office as was common practice. In Chris' case, the SAC liked him enough to allow him to move up to ASAC while keeping him in Minneapolis. The one stipulation was that he would be moved to oversee the criminal programs in the office, not the terrorism cases he recently supervised. Thus, although he would still be in the Minneapolis Division, Chris was no longer in my chain of command.

Because every squad in the FBI must have a supervisor, Greg, a new arrival to Squad 5, was selected to serve as an acting SSA until a permanent supervisor could be appointed. He was my age—we both graduated from college in 1990, whereupon he opted to go into law enforcement, serving as both a police officer and as a trooper on the Minnesota State Patrol before joining the FBI. Greg was smart, experienced, and polished and he knew how to navigate the system well.

Therefore, by late summer 2001, the Minneapolis Division of the FBI had an affable and experienced acting SAC, an ambitious but capable acting SSA on the JTTF, a terrorism experienced ASAC who had no role in overseeing terrorism cases, and a very new but skeptical case Agent: me. In my defense, I will say that on the road to disillusionment I *had* worked quite a few terrorism investigations and learned a great deal in the 2 ½ years since I graduated from Quantico. I understood how to recognize a radical Muslim when I encountered one and I knew about Al Qaeda's methods for selecting and training its operatives before sending them to attack us.

The stage was now set for the biggest challenge the young Minneapolis JTTF would face up to that time.

The Summer of 2001 passed as all Minnesota summers do, quickly, in a welter of family outdoor activities that are not possible during the long winters. That summer Terri and I learned to our delight she was pregnant with our third child, due in January. We loved being parents and wanted more kids. It was very welcome news.

As summer wound down, we had the usual commitment to travel to Pennsylvania for Terri's annual family reunion. Because I was busy at work and had a significant backlog of paperwork, we decided that she would attend with our two sons, Matt, and Jake while I stayed behind in Minnesota. Terri and the kids were scheduled to fly out early on the afternoon of August 16, 2001, and spend about ten days away. I would miss them but resolved to work late each night they were gone until the backlog on my desk had been eliminated.

CHAPTER 4

THE CALL

Wednesday, 08/15/2001

At around 10 a.m. I was sitting at my desk trying to catch up on paperwork, a never-ending battle in the FBI. Our new Agent, Dave, sitting a few desks down from me in the squad area had complaint duty, his first ever shift as a "Duty Agent." Every FBI office has one or more Agents assigned to this job daily, and in Minneapolis we usually drew the duty once every few months. The Duty Agent had to be dressed in a suit and prepared not only to answer calls from the public, but also to meet with anyone who might walk in.

As any Agent who ever had the duty can tell you, most people who call, and an even greater proportion of those who walk in tend to range from the mildly misguided to the profoundly mentally ill. It is uncommon for members of the public, however well intended, ever to have useful information to report to the FBI. It is not unheard of, but it is rare enough that experienced duty Agents start each encounter with a measure of skepticism.

I remember it was a sunny summer morning, with bright light pouring into the squad area. Greg was in the supervisor's office and the other members of the squad were in the "bullpen," our nickname for the squad area, chatting or doing paperwork. In short, it was a normal day in the FBI. At around 10 a.m. I was sitting at my computer banging away on some report, when Dave came up to my desk holding a notepad. He wore a puzzled look on his face. Dave said, "I just had a call about aviation, and I don't know what to do with it."

I looked up. "What do you have?"

Dave explained that the caller worked for Pan Am International Flight Academy, a flight training center in Bloomington, Minnesota. The caller told Dave Pan Am used flight simulators to train aircrews on various types of airliners. He was concerned about a student at the school who was behaving strangely. The student paid several thousand dollars for training on the Boeing 747–400 aircraft using the school's simulators. Management at the school believed he was odd, so they asked the caller, one of the managers there, to contact the FBI.

"Uh huh," I said, waiting for the punchline.

Dave delivered it, right on cue. "The weird thing is the guy doesn't have a pilot's license. He would need that, wouldn't he?"

That got my attention. "Yep. He'd need a license and an ATP rating to fly an airliner." I added that it certainly would be weird for someone without a license to pay for training he could not use. I did not know much about the 747–400 or airline pilots since my area of knowledge was primarily military aviation, but what I did know was this:

The Boeing 747–400 was a big airliner, possibly the largest in the world. It could carry more than 300 passengers and cost hundreds of millions of dollars a copy. And I was 100% sure that the pilots who flew them all had licenses.

On top of that, I was pretty sure anyone who would be allowed behind the controls of a 747–400 would also need a type rating, meaning they would have passed a check ride in the specific aircraft type they intended to fly. Once armed with a license, ATP rating, and an appropriate type endorsement, they would then need to secure a job with an airline. Therefore, it certainly did not make sense that someone would be paying for training on the largest and most complex airliner in the world when he had no license and therefore no prospect of obtaining a type rating. He would have none of the required qualifications to apply for a job as an airline pilot. The expensive road he was on led nowhere. Now interested, I asked Dave for more.

Dave had done a good job gathering necessary information on the call and had the guy's name and date of birth. The name sounded foreign: Zacarias Moussaoui. Flipping through his notepad, Dave reported the caller believed Moussaoui was French because the administrative people at the school had seen his French passport.

Dave and I went into Greg's office to tell him what we had. Greg was also a pilot, so the story sounded as odd and compelling to him as it did me. Greg authorized a case to be opened on Moussaoui immediately, and I completed the opening form as we talked.

In filling out that form, I already tried to manipulate the situation a little, nudging our newly opened case away from Martin and his unit. One of the items of information that goes on the form is the investigative classification. This one, two, or three-digit number, usually followed by a letter, tells every FBI employee who sees it the type of investigation it represents, whether a kidnaping, a bank robbery, or a terrorism case.

In the days before 9/11 terrorism cases opened to collect intelligence were identified by the number 199, followed by a letter. The letter identified the terrorist group with which the subject was associated. More significantly for me, it determined which unit at FBI Headquarters oversaw the case. That is why this one letter made such a difference to me. Under normal circumstances, since we did not know Moussaoui's group affiliation, or whether he was linked to a terrorist group at all, his case should have been classified 199M, which stood for "International Terrorism (Other)."

I was reluctant to classify the case as 199M. All of Minneapolis' 199M cases were overseen by the RFU in the person of none other than Martin. I was sure that he would react true to form and do everything he could to squash the case and any investigative initiatives we proposed. It is not that I knew at 10:30 a.m. on the morning of 08/15/2001 that the Moussaoui investigation would turn into the major case it did, I just wanted to give the very new investigation the chance to progress without being stillborn. That chance lay with some other unit, *any* other unit.

I had to find a reason to pick another unit. As soon as I received Moussaoui's name and date of birth from Dave, I ran him through the

FBI database. No one known to the FBI matched the name exactly, but one person with a similar last name was listed in our records as being associated with the Lebanon-based terrorist group, Hizballah.

I therefore wrote *199Q* on the opening form signifying that we believed that the subject might be working for Hizballah and Iran. Although I did not believe it was likely, this did ensure the new case fell under the responsibility at of the *Iran Unit*, not the Radical Fundamentalist Unit. I was shamelessly shopping for a supervisor at headquarters who might be less obstructionist than Martin.

I knew a supervisor in the Iran Unit and was hopeful that he would support our case. SSA Jeb had been a contemporary of Chris' back in Los Angeles before they both became supervisors. During an interaction with the Iran Unit on other cases that spring, Chris had referred me to Jeb, indicating they knew one another in LA. Jeb had been pleasant to deal with, although we had not really asked him to do anything complicated or hard. Still, he was someone I knew in that unit, and he had to be better than Martin.

As we left Greg's office, I asked Dave to call Pan Am back with a list of questions. I had a few theories about what might be going on and some ideas of how to proceed with the case, but I needed info.

First, I needed to know more about the 747–400. I vaguely remembered that the -400 series of the 747 was the most modern variant of this line, making it easier to fly because the sophisticated avionics did much of the work.

In addition to questions about the 747–400, I also asked Dave to get as many additional details as possible about Moussaoui himself. I wanted the number on his French passport, if they had it. I was also looking for any financial data the school had on him as well as any telephone numbers or e-mail addresses he provided. Finally, I needed contact information for Moussaoui's instructors. I wanted to hear their observations. They dealt with him directly and would be in the best position to give their expert opinion as to what he might be up to.

CHAPTER 5

THE INVESTIGATION BEGINS

Dave went off to ask these questions while I went back to my desk to complete the case opening paperwork. He returned in a few minutes. Someone at the flight school confirmed that the 747–400 *was* one of the airliners with a two-person cockpit and greater automation. Dave also provided the name and phone number of Moussaoui's flight instructor, a pilot named Rich.

I called Rich to obtain his impression of Moussaoui. Although very friendly and helpful, Rich was a dead end. He explained that he was scheduled to be Moussaoui's instructor once he finished ground school and moved into the simulators. Because that was not supposed to happen until the following evening, they had not met yet. Rich indicated that the instructor with whom Moussaoui had been spending time was his ground school instructor, Clancy. Clancy was the person at the school who raised concerns about him.

I thanked him for his time and hung up. Since he had not met Moussaoui, that was about all we needed to discuss. I then called Pan Am and on the advice of Rich, asked for Alan, Manager of Pilot Training for Pan Am's Minneapolis office. Alan proved to be helpful and confirmed that Clancy was the person who spent the most time with Moussaoui. He also provided Clancy's telephone number.

I was planning to call Clancy next since he was the person who spent the most time with Moussaoui, and speaking to someone with firsthand knowledge was important. Greg and Dave had come over to my cubicle and while I was briefing them on what Rich said, I was thinking to myself that there was not much we could do to stop Moussaoui if the facts began to suggest he was up to no good. Nothing we had so far constituted evidence of criminal behavior and we needed more options in case things grew any more alarming with Moussaoui's conduct.

While we chatted, a head popped above the cubicle wall a few seats down. John looked at me and asked, "What's going on? Anything immigration can do to help?" Although I did not know it yet, John's involvement in this case would soon prove decisive.

Walking down the row towards John's desk, I quickly explained. Upon hearing that Moussaoui was a French citizen, he asked, "What's his status in the U.S.?" I did not know the answer to that. I had not thought of it, but thankfully Moussaoui's immigration status was first and foremost in John's mind. We had no information on how Moussaoui had entered the U.S. and what his reason was for being here, but John could find out quickly.

I about-faced and walked back to my desk to retrieve the notepad with Moussaoui's date of birth and French passport number. I passed these to John, who immediately got on the phone to his office to request that Moussaoui's name be run through INS databases.

While Greg and Dave and I continued to discuss our options back at my desk, John popped up again. He beckoned me over. "Your boy may be subject to arrest," he said.

Excited, I asked, "Why?"

John explained his checks revealed a Zacarias Moussaoui with the same date of birth and French passport number entered the U.S. at Chicago's O'Hare Airport on February 23, 2001. The important point, John explained, was that he entered the U.S. under the *visa waiver* program. The visa waiver program exists so that citizens of most countries in Europe and a few in Asia may enter the U.S. without having to go through the full visa application process, provided that the purpose of the visit is tourism, not work or education. Most importantly for our case, people who enter under this program sign an agreement that they will depart the U.S. in *90 days or less.*

Under the visa waiver program, a French Citizen like Moussaoui was permitted to arrive at a U.S. airport (like O'Hare) with a roundtrip ticket, provided the ticket had a return date in 90 days or less. He could then fill out an I-94W form, and be admitted to the U.S., provided nothing else appeared amiss.

And that is what he did.

Fortunately, the key part of the visa waiver program is the 90 days. As John pointed out, we were now far past 90 days from Moussaoui's entry date of February 23, 2001. He was, in INS jargon, an "overstay," and therefore *probably* subject to arrest by them.

I say "probably" because one was never sure with INS. As any Agent of the overworked but vital immigration agency could tell you, the rules and regulations governing whether aliens in the U.S. are subject to arrest grew increasingly complex during the 1990s. By 2001, there were all sorts of loopholes and measures aliens could take to avoid arrest, however egregious their violation of immigration law. It had become an accepted though unwelcome rule that when we went out to apprehend someone INS believed was subject to arrest, we waited to handcuff them until the INS Agents interviewed the subject first and gave them the opportunity to produce documents which might trump taking them into custody.

Still, John said he believed the rules governing the visa waiver program were written in stone. To get a second opinion, John called over the other INS Agent on the JTTF, a new arrival named Steve. Steve had recently been sent by INS to augment John. Steve was a real Minnesotan, blonde, tall, lean, and friendly. He had been with INS for significantly longer than his youthful appearance would indicate.

After some research, Steve confirmed John's opinion that there was no flexibility in the visa waiver program. After conferring for a few minutes, our two immigration specialists were as close to certain as they could be in their business that Moussaoui could be arrested on sight.

I breathed a little easier. Thanks to John and Steve, we now had at least had a way to neutralize the threat should our investigation show one existed. They were also certain that once arrested, a visa waiver overstay could be kept in custody until he was removed from the U.S. That was helpful too. They agreed to continue researching the issue. I also asked Steve to come in on the case, to which he immediately agreed. He was a very solid investigator, and I figured we might need his help. As it turned out, Steve proved to be critical.

CHAPTER 6

THE WITNESS

With that settled, I dialed the number Alan provided for Clancy. He answered his cell phone right away. I introduced myself as an FBI Agent looking into the suspicious student Pan Am had been training. "Yes, you mean Zack," he said. "He sure is odd." Clancy had a succinct, to-the-point way of answering questions, perhaps formed by years of flying airliners in busy airspace, during which controllers and pilots communicated in clipped verbal shorthand, lest any one of them tie up the radio for too long.

Clancy went on to acknowledge that he had asked the management at the school to call us after spending several hours with Moussaoui. Clancy met Moussaoui after Pan Am assigned him to conduct the ground school portion of the training. It was his responsibility to introduce Moussaoui to the various systems of the Boeing 747–400 and to train him on the procedures for safely operating this complex airliner. Clancy informed me that he at first assumed that Moussaoui was a rich "nut" who was willing to shell out money to have the chance to pretend to be an airline pilot.

Over the course of several days, however, Moussaoui had applied himself to the study of aviation and the 747–400, subjects about which he knew little, with significant and unexpected enthusiasm. Instead of just focusing on the more fun aspects of flying the 747–400 around the imaginary sky, Moussaoui was interested in *everything* about the airplane. This made Clancy suspicious.

Clancy also told me he was not sure where Moussaoui was from. He claimed to be French, but his complexion was dark. He spoke English with a heavy accent which Clancy could not identify. Although he was not certain, Clancy had begun to suspect Moussaoui was from somewhere in the Middle East. When I asked Clancy whether he heard Moussaoui speak any language other than English, he answered that he had not. Despite the accent, Clancy had no problems communicating with Moussaoui in English.

As Clancy began teaching the complex systems of the 747–400, he quickly realized Moussaoui had almost no knowledge of aviation. He began to ask himself, "What are we doing here? Is it right to give this guy from off the street so much info?" Clancy added that Moussaoui informed him had been taking flying lessons recently, having acquired around 50 hours in the Cessna 152.

Clancy went on to say that although Moussaoui had been quite personable and genial when they spoke, he was also very evasive when it came to discussing himself. Moussaoui informed him he ran an import-export business in London, where he was currently residing. Very few additional details were forthcoming. That sounded odd to me, chiefly because most people like talking about themselves.

Clancy went on. Once he became suspicious of Moussaoui, he began paying closer attention, so he was able to tell us quite a bit more about him. For starters, Clancy saw Moussaoui in the company of another man. Clancy described this guy as dark skinned and dark haired and reported that he dropped Moussaoui off at the school in a gold-colored Subaru sedan with a license plate which was green and white in color, and which contained the numbers 686.

Clancy added that when he was done for the day, Moussaoui had not been picked up by this man but had ridden with Clancy and the other students and instructors in the school's shuttle van which took them back to their hotels. This gave Clancy the chance to observe that Moussaoui was staying at the Marriott Residence Inn, in Eagan, Minnesota. Clancy indicated it was normal for students and instructors to stay at this hotel as it was close and relatively inexpensive.

Talking to Clancy, even briefly on the phone, spiked my already high interest in Moussaoui. Nothing he said about this strange student made sense and I realized it would be valuable to sit down with Clancy in person to get more details from him. I asked him whether he was available the following afternoon, to which he replied that he was. He had completed the three-day portion of ground school instruction of Moussaoui earlier that day and was open. He was not sure when Moussaoui was scheduled for his first simulator session, but believed it was not until the following evening. We agreed to meet at Clancy's hotel at 2 p.m. the following afternoon, which would be after I dropped my family off at the airport.

There were several things we could ask to be done outside the Minneapolis Division, and I was planning to request them right away. They consisted of checking with other agencies in the U.S. intelligence community to see whether they ever heard of Moussaoui. In addition, since Moussaoui was French, I was planning to send a lead to Jay, in our LEGAT office in Paris, to ask him to query French law enforcement and intelligence agencies to see whether Moussaoui was known to them. I knew from recent experience Jay would pass the lead to the French authorities promptly and get us an answer to our questions about Moussaoui.

Just after lunchtime, things had calmed down enough for me to make another important call and send an e-mail. Because we knew Moussaoui had only been in the U.S. since February and his name was not in FBI databases, it was clear that the key to learning more about him was overseas. That meant the Central Intelligence Agency (CIA).

Using a secure telephone, I called a friend I knew at CIA Headquarters who was an experienced case officer and understood terrorism from tours in the Middle East. I explained what we had so far on Moussaoui and asked him to see whether CIA was aware of the guy. Like us in Minneapolis, my friend found the fact pattern suspicious and agreed to quickly run checks to see whether CIA had heard of Moussaoui.

Hanging up the phone, I returned to my computer and began typing an e-mail to Jay in Paris. Although official requests required a document called an Electronic Communication (EC) from Minneapolis with attached leads to go through formal channels, I had developed a very solid working relationship with Jay on the Ali case. Therefore, I decided to short-circuit the system slightly and send a combination "heads-up" and *unofficial* request in the form of an email, which I would follow up with an EC later. I didn't know much about Moussaoui other than his highly unusual activities in Minnesota plus his name, birth date and French passport number, but Jay had proven to be an aggressive investigator, so I dashed off an email to him on what I referred to as Moussaoui's "whole (weird) story." It read:

> "Jay,
>
> Minneapolis has a short notice check request for info on a French citizen. We don't really know what we have here, but here's the (weird) story.
>
> Our duty agent received a call from a company that does flight simulator training for Boeing 747 Series 400 pilots. They are now training a student who just showed up to learn to fly the 747. He has no pilot's license and minimal previous flight experience (in any aircraft type). He paid between $6000 and $8000 dollars to essentially learn to take off and land the 747–400. His excuse is weak: he just wants to learn how to do it! That's pretty ominous and obviously suggests some sort of a hijacking plan.
>
> He's in the U.S. since 02/2001 on a visa waiver from the UK, where he claims to reside. He's traveling on a French passport, although the flight instructor who has been with him for the last few days believes he's Middle Eastern. Indices show that his last name is Lebanese. [Redacted by the FBI].
>
> I'm not even sure if you can run checks on French citizens, but if so, here he is:

Zacarias Moussaoui, DOB 05/30/1968
French Passport 00AE27016

Can you determine if he is known to the [Redacted by the FBI] French? I will do an EC to follow up if you need one, but we're working on fairly short notice since his training is only scheduled to go for a few more days and we don't want him to depart this area. Our INS guy on the JTTF is pretty sure we can arrest him on a visa overstay, but we want to get all we can on him first.

Thanks in advance for anything you can do,

Harry Samit" [1]

Given Jay's aggressiveness and his track record of fast responses, I hoped to have information back in the next few days since things with the case had the potential to begin moving quickly.

By now it was now getting late in the day. I had been planning to get home early to help Terri pack, but as usual she had to handle that burden pretty much on her own. I checked out with John and Greg, making sure to tell them I needed to take my family to the airport in the morning. John replied that he would take Dave and Steve out to the Residence Inn in the morning to locate the vehicle described by Clancy. They would just scope things out for later and wait for me and the interview with Clancy. We knew Moussaoui had completed the ground school portion and that his first simulator session

1 This email is Defense exhibit 326 on the EDVA website. Many of the documents I and others in Minneapolis authored in the days between the opening of the investigation and the 9/11 attacks were subsequently declassified for use at Moussaoui's trial. These documents were used as primary sources for writing this portion of this work. Following Moussaoui's trial, the U.S. Attorney's Office placed electronic versions of these documents on their website at **https://www.vaed.uscourts.gov/101cr00455-trial-exhibits**. As of the date of this writing, they are still available there.

was not scheduled until sometime the following evening, so we were unlikely to run awkwardly into him at the school before 6 p.m.

When I arrived home, Terri, as usual, had things under control. The kids' bags were packed for the trip and were ready to be loaded in the van. After a quick dinner, we put Matt and Jake to bed. We then chatted as Terri packed. I was preoccupied by the case as this was certainly the strangest thing I had seen so far in the FBI.

CHAPTER 7

FLIGHT SCHOOL

Thursday, 08/16/2001

I did not sleep well that night and Terri was up early so she could get Matt, Jake, and herself ready to go. Unusually, I was not hungry at breakfast, just keyed up and eager to resume working the case. When I got dressed, I made sure I had three extra handgun magazines and two pairs of handcuffs on my belt. That was more ammunition and restraints than I usually carried, but I did not know what the day would bring. I wore my tan cargo pants (part of the required uniform for trainees at Quantico), Columbia hiking boots and a loose fitting, short-sleeved cotton shirt. It seemed smart to make sure I could blend in with the public and run and fight if need be. While the attire so beloved of FBI management, a business suit, might be appropriate when interviewing a bank president, I wanted to be able to blend more easily and be ready should things become dynamic.

I remember the morning clearly, probably because subconsciously I was aware that something significant might be happening. We arrived at the airport, and I walked my family *to the gate*. Those pre-9/11 days seem so far off now, but back then people did not need a boarding pass to be able to walk right to the jetway to see people off. By the time I took the kids for lunch at Burger King on the concourse, my Nextel began beeping. It was John calling to tell me he had located the car. It was a Subaru with a green and white license plate, just as Clancy had said and the license plate it bore was from Oklahoma. They ran the plate, and the results were waiting for us back in the office. It was good work by them and would help us plan for later that day.

When I arrived at the office a little after noon, John was waiting. He handed me a printout from our NCIC (National Crime Information Center) operator. The license plate on the car that brought Moussaoui to Pan Am each morning, Oklahoma tag YPM 636 (Clancy was close) came back to a 1991 4 door Subaru Sedan, registered to a Hussein Al-Attas, born 01/23/1978 or an Abdulla Al-Attas, with an address of P.O. Box 19205, Oklahoma City, OK.

I ran a check in the FBI database which was negative for both Hussein and Abdullah Al-Attas. John ran his own checks and reported that Hussein Al-Attas, a citizen of Yemen, was listed in INS databases as having entered the U.S. on a student visa. He was currently a student at the University of Oklahoma, so the license plate on his car made sense.

John, Steve, Dave, and I crowded into Greg's office for a final discussion before it was time to head out to begin our first round of interviews. It was clear that the arrest option which INS provided offered us significant flexibility. Because we were not likely to get checks back from CIA or the French in the next 30 minutes, we only had the information we could gather in Minnesota to help us make critical decisions.

The most important question we discussed in Greg's office was whether we would allow Moussaoui to continue with the training or arrest him prior to 6 p.m. that evening. Because we would have no way of monitoring his training in the simulator once it began, we decided that unless the interviews at the flight school and with Clancy somehow convinced us this was a big mistake and that Moussaoui was harmless, we were going to arrest him to prevent his getting into the simulator. As pilots Greg and I both understood that in the flight training world there is a huge difference between the theory taught in ground school and the learning which occurs when a pilot gets his hands and feet on the controls of an aircraft or a highly realistic simulator.

While it has been discussed by virtually every group of experts and amateurs which later examined the 9/11 catastrophe, one action we did not consider was allowing Moussaoui to receive the simulator training while we conducted surveillance on him over the next few days. Monday morning quarterbacks have theorized that this could have led us to the other hijackers, some of whom Moussaoui might, they reasoned, have met before the attacks. The supposition is that if we had done so, the FBI might have identified additional participants in the plot.

We did not choose this course for several reasons. First, was manpower. Prior to 9/11, the Minneapolis Division did not have dedicated surveillance squads. Therefore, when needed, surveillance was conducted by members of 5 Squad itself, working around-the-clock shifts to cover the targets. While television dramas would have us believe otherwise, proper physical surveillance requires large numbers of skilled personnel for *each eight-hour shift*. Using fewer people risks detection. Because of this, attempting surveillance with inadequate numbers was worse than no surveillance at all.

We also at that stage were not aware of what later became known: that there was a major terrorist group behind Moussaoui. That afternoon, all we had was one subject and his friend. Although our interviews and information added by the French and the CIA would paint a much more detailed and ominous picture in a few days, at noon on August 16, 2001 all we had was one guy, his buddy, and an unusual fact pattern. And the smarter and safer course argued against allowing him to receive any additional training before we had the chance to speak with him.

Also, each negative fact we gathered on Moussaoui made letting him walk free increasingly less likely from a bureaucratic standpoint. As everyone is aware, the media makes its money second guessing the U.S. Government. Headlines criticizing INS for allowing illegal immigrants to roam free while committing crimes against innocent Americans had been in the press lately. Therefore, they would be very reluctant to delay taking Moussaoui into custody, especially when the next few days would be those in which he was learning to fly a 747–400.

When the meeting was finished, John and I headed to Pan Am International Flight Academy with Dave in tow. We wanted to get a copy of Moussaoui's flight training schedule so we understood where he would be, and when. We also planned to talk to the staff there to get their impressions of Moussaoui. Once we were done at Pan Am we would interview Clancy at his nearby hotel. This plan was calculated to allow us to collect as much information as possible before we encountered Moussaoui.

When we arrived at the flight school, located in Eagan, Minnesota, we were ushered into an office where we met Alan, the manager of flight training. When asked, he handed us a computer-generated syllabus, which showed Moussaoui had several sessions scheduled for 747–400 simulator #7. A quick glance confirmed his first session was scheduled for that night at 6 p.m.

The other thing that leapt out at us was that there was a gap in the training that Friday: no ground school, no simulators. Nothing. A complete day off. I asked whether this had been done to accommodate Pan Am's schedule, or at Moussaoui's request. The manager replied that the day off was scheduled at Moussaoui's request, reason unknown.

This was another clue. Taking Friday off might represent the reluctance of an observant Muslim to work on Islam's Sabbath. John and I filed this away. If we uncovered additional evidence that Moussaoui was a fundamentalist or radical Muslim, this would be another data point to add to our list of concerns. Glancing at my watch, I realized our interview with Clancy was scheduled to start in about 10 minutes, so we thanked the manager and excused ourselves.

CHAPTER 8

FLIGHT INSTRUCTOR

John, Dave, and I arrived at Clancy's hotel to find him waiting in the lobby. Tall, distinguished, and serious, he looked like the retired airline pilot he was, with white hair, military haircut, and clad in khaki slacks and a dress shirt. It was obvious that we were talking to the right person after Clancy confirmed he spent the most time with Moussaoui at Pan Am. First, however, we had to overcome his reluctance to talk to the FBI. While he was sufficiently concerned by Moussaoui's unusual behavior to make several requests to his supervisors that they contact the FBI, Clancy was still not certain Moussaoui's eccentricity warranted getting him into "trouble."

We gave Clancy the usual explanation to allay his worries, informing him our job was not to pass judgement on anyone, but simply to investigate. We would then go where the facts led us. If Moussaoui was not up to anything illegal, he would be okay. I also informed Clancy I was a pilot and that from what I knew of Moussaoui's behavior so far, things sounded fishy.

Pronouncing himself satisfied, Clancy then agreed to proceed. He told us that he was a retired airline captain with Northwest Airlines. When I asked, he acknowledged with modesty that he had tens of thousands of hours of flight time, much of it in the 747. He was currently working as a contract employee of Pan Am who traveled to the Twin Cities when his services were required and had been doing that for several years.

Moussaoui was unlike any student Clancy ever encountered. He told us Moussaoui informed him he was paying for the simulator training because he had an interest in becoming a pilot but that did not make sense to Clancy. He knew Moussaoui had a mere 50 hours or so of dual instruction in light aircraft, had no pilot's license, and had not yet even flown solo, making this training useless to him in advancing his goal of an aviation career. Moussaoui also told Clancy that the schools in the UK were too severe in their training methods and too expensive.

I agreed with Clancy. Little of this made sense to me either. Moussaoui's reasons for opting out of flight training in the UK were strange. While it *was* more expensive to get a pilot's license in the UK, the cost was not prohibitive. I was also aware flight schools in England cranked out plenty of private pilots who proceeded on to advanced training as commercial pilots. The only real factor which sent pilots to the U.S. from Europe was cost, and Moussaoui claimed he was a wealthy businessman based in London. It seemed to make more sense for him to train in the UK in the evenings and weekends while tending to his company.

Also, the fact that Moussaoui had not received his pilot's license (or even soloed) after 50+ hours of flight time was odd. There were sixteen-year-olds who already had their licenses with that amount of flight time in their logbooks. Maybe he was a slow learner? But paying $8000 for instruction in the 747–400 at this stage of his aviation training made no sense. Clancy likened Moussaoui's presence at Pan Am to being like someone who had not finished kindergarten (and was having trouble learning to color) paying to take PhD classes in astrophysics. And paying handsomely.

If Moussaoui's lack of qualifications sparked Clancy's concern, the legwork he did regarding his payment fanned the flames. He went to speak to the controller at the company and asked how Moussaoui paid. Clancy learned that Moussaoui arrived at the school to pay the balance of his fee in cash, with a large stack of $100 bills to be exact. It was not common to pay nearly $7000 in cash, no matter who you were.

Once Moussaoui arrived at Pan Am, Clancy began his ground school instruction as he usually did, by using Northwest Airlines' teaching materials, including a series of PowerPoint presentations. These lectures began with instruction on the various aircraft components, including the electrical system, hydraulics, flight controls, etc. He informed us that, although Moussaoui was extremely interested in the briefings, the block of formal instruction he usually utilized with students was useless because of Moussaoui's complete lack of previous experience with sophisticated aircraft systems.

Clancy noted that there were aspects of the 747–400 in which Moussaoui was particularly interested. Moreover, Clancy believed Moussaoui *studied these in advance of their meeting* since he knew about them when he first arrived. Moussaoui was particularly focused on the aircraft's Mode Control Panel, or MCP. Clancy explained the MCP was the system which gave the 747–400 the ability to fly, navigate and land in a full automated mode. Although I did not know it at the time, this same piece of equipment was in the cockpits of nearly all late-model Boeing airliners, including the 757 and 767, the two aircraft types which would be used in such tragic circumstances 3 ½ weeks later.

Moussaoui's interest in the MCP raised a flag with me. As a pilot, I also wanted to try my skills in a 747–400 simulator. However, because we would be in a box on the ground with no lives or expensive aircraft at stake, my inclination would be to turn off all the automated features and try to fly the thing the same way I would fly a Cessna 182, an F-4 Phantom II, or a Sopwith Camel. Real pilots want to test their abilities by flying an aircraft through challenging maneuvers, the key word being "fly." Sitting in the cockpit inputting data into the MCP and watching as computers smoothly and obligingly controlled the aircraft is not any pilot's idea of fun.

It would be one thing if Moussaoui had been a real airline pilot with an ATP certificate who was looking to pick up a 747–400 type rating as a means of getting hired by a new company or advancing his career with his current employer. Had that been the case, then given that the standard airline procedure is to use the MCP, Moussaoui had a strong incentive to learn the MCP. But Moussaoui was not an airline pilot. He was supposed to be on a rich man's joyride. And there is no joy in the Mode Control Panel.

Clancy told us he spent Monday, Tuesday, and Wednesday with Moussaoui and observed him closely. In addition to the classroom work, Moussaoui had been allowed to sit in on a simulator session with real students, observing as they went through a simulated flight.

Clancy confirmed that the simulator in which Moussaoui would be training later that day was of extremely high fidelity. To my surprise he explained that many new pilots do all their airliner training in these simulators, including obtaining their FAA type rating in them. I was astonished to learn that many new airline pilots fly real airliners for the first time with passengers in the back on regularly scheduled flights. Of course, these flights are supervised by experienced captains, but it does speak to the realism of the simulators that the ultra-strict FAA allows new pilots to obtain their type rating in a simulator before ever actually flying a real airplane.

Clancy described Moussaoui as being Middle Eastern, between the ages of 30 and 40, 5'9"-5'11" in height with a heavy build and a trimmed beard. Clancy told us Moussaoui spoke English fluently, but with a heavy accent. Moussaoui informed Clancy that he was born in the south of France but had been living in London. So far, so good. That certainly tracked with what we knew.

Clancy also noted that Moussaoui was very amiable, with one noticeable exception: he was reluctant to share details about himself. Although he gave Clancy a broad outline of his life, Moussaoui was very vague on specifics. After being asked about his business, a topic which most people are usually eager to discuss in greater detail than others want to hear, Moussaoui told Clancy that he worked with family and friends in an import-export business. He provided no details, not even elaborating enough to name the company or describe the products they imported and exported.

And there was more. Clancy explained that what really peaked his concern and made him decide to raise the issue with Pan Am management was a conversation which started innocently enough. Commenting to Moussaoui on how unique what he was doing really was, Clancy remarked that he would soon be able to fly a 747. Stroking his ego, he went on to say that if he were ever on a 747–400 where the pilots were served a bad meal and became unable to continue with their duties, he would have the ability to safely land the airplane and be a hero.

Upon hearing this, Moussaoui had looked at Clancy and then remarked that he would rather take a parachute and jump out to safety than try to land a real 747–400. Clancy laughed and then corrected him by explaining the aircraft doors cannot be opened in flight. Moussaoui seemed surprised by this and asked questions about why this was.

Clancy explained that once the aircraft was pressurized, the doors, which opened inward, could not be moved against the force of the air inside the cabin until someone in the cockpit took steps to depressurize the interior. As is very typical among pilots, Clancy went on to describe to Moussaoui a real-life accident related to this. The incident happened years before aboard an airliner chartered to fly people to Saudi Arabia for Hajj. During the flight, passengers in the back of the airplane lit a fire to brew tea. Predictably, the fire spread out of control. Although the plane was either on the ground when this happened or landed soon after, in their panic the crew failed to depressurize the aircraft and many people in the cabin perished because the passengers were unable to open the doors against the force of the air pressure inside the fuselage.

While Clancy's understanding of Islam was fuzzy, he understood that the Hajj was something Muslims did. When he finished his story, he said to Moussaoui, "Hajj, what is that? Do you know? Are you Muslim?"

Shaking his head, Clancy recounted that when he was asked that question, Moussaoui looked shocked. His face clouded, and he responded with far more emphasis than their casual conversation warranted, "I am nothing!"

We agreed with Clancy that this seemed significant, and we thanked him for the observation. Most Muslims in our experience are willing to disclose that fact and to discuss their religion should it come up in respectful conversation. In fact, it is considered a religious duty by observant Muslims to discuss Islam with those outside the faith as a means of educating them.

In response to additional questioning, Clancy informed us that Moussaoui wanted to train to a level where he could fly a simulated flight from beginning to end. He told Clancy that he would "love" to fly a simulated flight from Heathrow Airport in the UK to John F. Kennedy Airport in New York. Moussaoui wanted to learn all the necessary skills to allow him to fly the plane while navigating and communicating with ground control. He gave no explanation as to why he wished to fly this route. And again, learning how to do what was needed to accomplish a flight under these conditions would not be conducive to having fun. The flight would involve a series of mundane steps, none of which would involve manually maneuvering the aircraft.

Clancy noted that Moussaoui also mentioned to him he felt he would need additional simulator sessions after he completed the four for which he was initially scheduled. He informed Clancy he planned to book several more sessions extending into the following week. In response to my question, Clancy answered that he did not believe that Moussaoui would be able to safely fly the 747 at the end of his first four sessions, but with good instruction, the extra week of training might make the difference.

We thanked Clancy for his information and for being so persistent in persuading his bosses to call the FBI. He nodded, and we headed for the door.

CHAPTER 9

CONTACT

John and I agreed we had heard enough. We were going to arrest Moussaoui when he emerged from his hotel room to go to his 6:00 p.m. simulator session. Moussaoui raised enough flags with Clancy, and with us, and we were simply unwilling to allow him to go forward with his simulator training. If he truly were just some rich nut and this was a big misunderstanding, we would talk to the school and try to get him a refund when INS sent him back to England. But if no innocent explanation came to light it was simply too great a risk to let him acquire skills he would begin to obtain that evening.

A look at my watch showed it was about 3:30 p.m. and we intended to be in place for the arrest by 4:00 p.m. The plan was for John, Dave and me to meet Steve at the INS Office and then go to Moussaoui's hotel to wait for him to come out. If the Subaru was gone when we reached the Residence Inn, Plan B called for us to arrest Moussaoui at Pan Am when he showed up for his training. Either way, he was not getting into that simulator.

Steve was waiting in the INS garage when we arrived and I hopped out of John's car and got in with him, leaving John and Dave together. John and I previously agreed we would pair up this way, so there would be at least one experienced JTTF member in each vehicle.

I briefed Steve on the way and told him that we were going to head for the Residence Inn and set up in a place where we could observe Moussaoui's vehicle. When he came out in time to get to Pan Am for his 6:00 p.m. simulator session, we would arrest him. Steve nodded as he followed John out of the garage and onto I–494.

After a few minutes, Steve's brow furrowed. "You know," he said, "There is no guarantee we can arrest him. We have to check his documents first."

My heart jumped. I had forgotten the INS curse. Because of the vagaries of immigration law and the chaos of the INS record-keeping system, we might be facing a worst-case scenario. If we approached Moussaoui he still might be able to trump us by pulling out a document which proved he was legally able to stay here but which had not been in INS records.

I had seen that happen.

We understood that if we had to let Moussaoui go, we would still need to follow him and track his movements. If we were successful in persuading him it was just an INS error, he might relax again once we left, allowing us to mount a useful surveillance. It would give us a fighting chance at figuring out what he was doing.

It was not much of a backup plan, but it was the best we had.

When we arrived at the Residence Inn, Steve took us to the south end of the parking lot, past the Subaru with the Oklahoma tags. He expertly backed into a spot from which we could see the car. As we went past, we saw no one was in it. John and Dave were parked to the north, out of our view, but also able to see the target vehicle. My first thought was that there were a lot of rooms, and therefore many possibilities where Moussaoui was staying.

My Nextel beeped. John, obviously thinking this same thing, asked me what I thought of the idea of him and Dave going into the lobby of the hotel and asking the desk clerk what room had been assigned to Moussaoui and his friend. It was standard fugitive hunting practice to do this and would certainly help, since we did not know from which of the several buildings at the hotel he would emerge. I considered this for a second and then told him I thought it was a good idea. That would also help because we did not know what either of the two men looked like.

I glanced at my watch and saw it was about 4:45 p.m. I figured if Moussaoui had to make a 6:00 p.m. simulator session, we would see him sometime after 5:30 since the school was only 10 minutes or so from the hotel.

It was the end of the workday and Steve and I watched as motel guests returned to their rooms. We looked at each of them to see whether Moussaoui might be among them. No one resembled Clancy's description of him.

A few minutes later John told us Moussaoui and his friend were in Room 1414. Even though the building containing that room was to our left front, Steve and I could not see the door to 1414 from our vantage point. John could, so he and Dave would be able to see Moussaoui as soon as he came out and would let us know he was headed to the car. We agreed that when the arrest was initiated, both drivers would approach and position their vehicles to block the Subaru and then get the people under control. We did not want to risk a car chase in the crowded Residence Inn parking lot because that would put members of the public in jeopardy.

More time passed.

A few minutes after 5, my phone rang, this time not the brief chirp of the Nextel "direct connect" feature, but a phone call. Glancing at the screen of my phone, I saw it was a number with a "202" area code: FBI Headquarters. I was then inexperienced enough that I answered, something I would NEVER do in that situation later in my career. Once I got more time under my belt and became a more seasoned veteran of operations on the street, it became obvious that there was nothing anyone at FBI Headquarters could do to help our situation. Thus, I should have ignored the call.

Not this time, though. "Hello?" I answered.

"Agent Samit, this is Jeb at FBI Headquarters. I spoke to your acting supervisor, and he told me you're out trying to arrest this guy who is taking the flying lessons?"

"Yes..."

Consistent with nearly all FBI Headquarters supervisors, Jeb spoke too much and listened too little. Supervisors at headquarters were accustomed to directing Agents in the field, even though in this instance he was 1200 miles from the scene of the action with absolutely no understanding of what was happening. In his defense, Jeb was better than most. He was not overbearing or directive, but he believed, wrongly, that he knew better than us what should be taking place.

Jeb began firing questions, one after the other, without pausing long enough to hear my answers. I was replying quickly, my eyes darting between the Subaru and the building with Room 1414. Jeb seemed to have a strategy all figured out for the case. As what he was saying began to sink in, my mild irritation at being interrupted while on surveillance changed to alarm when Jeb told me that we were *not to arrest Moussaoui*.

"I'm sorry?"

"Don't arrest the guy. We're going to put together a surveillance team and get them out there to see what he's up to."

After a long and fruitless back and forth, I informed Jeb that we had already talked to the hotel staff, and he grasped the significance of that immediately—they could and probably would tell Moussaoui law enforcement asked about him. Thus, surveillance would not work, because he would be alerted by a civilian to our interest.

There was a long silence while Jeb considered that. I filled it by saying something that was not strictly accurate but that was designed to end the call and Jeb's on-the-fly brainstorming from the J. Edgar Hoover Building, "Jeb, I think they're coming out. Gotta go!"

Jeb replied at once, "Okay. Do what you have to! Good luck." I hung up.

We settled down to wait some more.

It was another five minutes before my Nextel chirped again. This was it. As always, John was completely professional, despite the tension all of us felt. Speaking in a measured tone, he announced someone was coming out of Room 1414.

After a few seconds that seemed more like an hour, I saw a small, dark-skinned man walking down the sidewalk from our left. He was headed toward the Subaru. As we watched, he casually opened the driver's side door and got in. There was no doubt about it now, we were looking at one of our subjects.

As John passed the arrest signal over the Nextel, Steve put his car in gear, and we smoothly glided to block the Subaru in from the car's right rear. John and Dave approached from the other direction. All four of us got out of the vehicles quickly. I drew my gun and trotted the ten feet to the rear of the car and watched the driver through the back window as John spoke to him. I held my Glock 23 in both hands with the muzzle angled down, a position the FBI calls "low ready." If a deadly force situation arose, all I needed to do to begin shooting was to bring the gun up and put the front sight on my target before pulling the trigger.

I was looking for a weapon or some move which would indicate the driver intended to hurt us or escape. I knew that if the guy made a move for a weapon, John would be shooting down into the car at him through the open driver's side window. For this reason, I was behind the car. That way, if I had to shoot too, John and I would not be in a crossfire situation. His bullets would be traveling down and straight across the car and exiting through the front passenger's side door. My bullets would come from the rear. If we were disciplined with our shooting, we would both hit the driver without endangering one another.

The driver just sat there with his hands on the steering wheel looking at John as he identified himself as an INS Agent and asked him to step out of the car. He was a dark haired, olive-skinned man in cargo pants and a t-shirt. As John's words sunk in, he complied and opened the door. As he stood up next to John, I noticed that he was short, around 5'2", chubby, and young, in his early 20s. He had a neatly trimmed goatee and short hair. He looked slightly awkward in the new T-shirt and rugged outdoor style cargo pants he was wearing, and I got the impression this was not his normal style of dress.

John grabbed the man's arm and spun him around, so he was facing away from him, towards the front of the car. John then proceeded to pat him down, while asking him whether he had any weapons. The man replied in accented English that he did not. John finished the search and turned him back around.

John asked the driver his name and he replied in accented English that his name was Hussein Al-Attas. I recognized the name as the registered owner of the car and realized we were speaking with Moussaoui's companion. Once John had determined Al-Attas was unarmed, I holstered my handgun. By now I had moved over to the driver's side and was listening to John's quick interview. In less than a minute, John learned Al-Attas was traveling with a friend named "Shaqil" from Oklahoma. Al-Attas and Shaqil were on their way to an appointment, and Shaqil would be coming out of their hotel room any second. Given Al-Attas' claim that they were on their way to an appointment, Shaqil was almost certainly Moussaoui, but we had not heard that name yet.

In a truly varsity move born of John's experience in law enforcement and his skill as an investigator, he casually asked Al-Attas for consent to search his car. Al-Attas nodded his agreement, and Dave and Steve began searching immediately. While this was going on, John continued his discussion with Al-Attas. Since I knew Moussaoui would be coming shortly, I kept one eye on the door to room 1414, which I could see clearly now to my left. By listening to John's conversation with Al-Attas I learned he was a student at the University of Oklahoma and that his friend Shaqil was taking classes there as well.

Dave, who was searching the driver's side of the car, stood up with a folding-blade knife in his hand. I could see that it was silver with a red handle. Dave asked Al-Attas if the knife was his. Al-Attas shook his head and replied the knife was Shaqil's. Dave told me he found it under the driver's seat and stuck it in his pocket for safekeeping.

When John asked Al-Attas why they had been keeping a knife there, Al-Attas replied that Shaqil put the knife under his seat for personal protection since there was a lot of crime in the U.S. In response to a question about whether he had any other knives or additional weapons in the car, Al-Attas answered that there were none. He stood there looking a little lost. From listening to the conversation and studying his features, I guessed Al-Attas was from the Arabian Peninsula and that he was a native Arabic speaker. His English was good, though.

Steve had been searching the passenger's side of the car, including the glove compartment. He showed me a small green pamphlet that he found and then turned to Al-Attas and asked if it was his. Al-Attas acknowledged that it was, though I sensed a degree of hesitancy or nervousness about this reply. Most of his previous responses had been relaxed, so I walked around the rear of the car to join Steve so I could try to determine why Al-Attas was concerned. When Steve handed me the pamphlet, I saw it was an English-language guide to preparing a proper Islamic Last Will and Testament.

Although we had been in contact with Al-Attas for less than two minutes, what Steve and Dave found in the car already raised my suspicions. First, there was a knife under the seat of the car being driven by two foreign college students from Oklahoma. The presence of the pretty wicked-looking knife was odd, as was Al-Attas' explanation for it. It was not as if we were in a bad neighborhood in Eagan, Minnesota. I also assumed Norman, Oklahoma, where the university was located, was safe, too. Why did they feel they needed a knife?

On top of that, one of the two men was carrying a document on drafting a Will. However, both were young and the guy we were talking to looked perfectly healthy. It is unusual for young men to draw up wills under normal circumstances. I knew, however, that people engaging in jihad drew up Wills for themselves on the reasonable assumption that they might be killed in battle. Because a battle death was what many hard-core radicals were seeking anyway, it was prudent for them to prepare a Will specifying the disposition of their worldly possessions and the treatment and burial of their remains. While not the only explanation, it certainly might be one reason why Al-Attas might be drawing up a Will at his age.

CHAPTER 10

THE MONSTER

I was mulling this over when, over the top of the roof of Al-Attas's Subaru, I saw a man emerge from room 1414. I asked Steve to come with me and we moved towards this man, stepping up onto the sidewalk from the parking lot as we did so. I nodded at John, still engaged in his interview of Al-Attas, letting him know Steve and I would handle the newcomer.

As Steve and I got closer to the man and I could see him more clearly, I hesitated, thinking there must have been a mix-up. The guy at whom I was looking and rapidly approaching looked like a light-skinned African American. He was stocky and wearing olive cargo pants, a dark-colored tee shirt, leather jacket and a ball cap with a Nike "swoosh" on the front. As he got closer, I observed he had a neatly trimmed goatee and short hair, at least on the sides. He was carrying a book bag over his left shoulder. The guy appeared unconcerned and looked very much like a businessman on his way to a meeting. I had been expecting someone who looked less American, and for an instant thought we might have the wrong guy.

Steve clearly had no such doubts, and he stepped right up to the man, causing him to slow, and then halt. Steve asked, "Mr. Moussaoui?"

The man replied, "Yes?" He was clearly unsure of why we were there, or how we knew his name.

Steve then produced his INS credentials and badge and indicated that he was a Special Agent. He explained we were investigating to determine whether he was in the U.S. legally.

Moussaoui's demeanor changed immediately, from relaxed and mildly confused, to angry. He informed us loudly and in an annoyed manner that he had a very important appointment, and he had no time to talk to us "at the moment." For the first time, I heard Moussaoui's distinctive lisp, mingled with his heavily French-accented English.

Steve was unmoved by Moussaoui's protests and informed him we were there to verify his status and the legality of his remaining in the U.S. While Steve explained these facts, I relieved Moussaoui of his bag and looked inside. There, I saw an aviation headset, a flight manual for the 747–400, and a checklist for this same aircraft. He was on his way to the simulator session, alright.

Moussaoui continued to protest. Watching me rummage through the contents of his book bag, he obviously felt more of an explanation was in order. "I have spent a great deal of money on some very expensive flight training! I must get there and do not have time to speak with you!"

Steve explained to Moussaoui that this was not possible. He informed him that he was an immigration official who had reason to believe Moussaoui was in the U.S. in violation of immigration law. Until this was cleared up, Moussaoui was not free to leave.

On hearing this, Moussaoui brought his tone down a bit. Bluster had not worked so speaking slowly and calmly and looking back and forth between the two of us, Moussaoui stated he took care of the paperwork and renewed his visa. Steve and I were standing so that we formed the letter "V", with Moussaoui at the point, as is standard law enforcement procedure. Each of us had our bodies "bladed" so that the hips on which our guns were holstered were away from him. Both of us were alert, and ready for anything he might do. When I heard his claim that his expired visa had been taken care of, my heart skipped a beat, fearing the immigration curse.

Steve then informed Moussaoui that we would require some proof his visa had been renewed. Moussaoui replied that the paperwork was in his hotel room and he turned to walk back there. We were close behind, both to ensure he did not attempt to flee, and to make sure didn't produce a weapon. Moussaoui used his key card to enter room 1414 with Steve and myself just behind and on either side of him. Upon entering, Moussaoui halted and began rummaging through a pile of documents located on the kitchen counter. After a short time, he made a noise of triumph and handed Steve an official-looking document which he pulled out of an envelope. From where I was standing, I could see the INS seal at the top of the letter.

As Steve read it, I began to worry, and to sweat. That paperwork looked legit. In my mind's eye I could already picture us having to let Moussaoui go.

Although I was having a mini panic attack, I noticed Steve looked unconcerned. He was the one who had thoroughly researched the visa waiver and concluded there was no way Moussaoui could avoid arrest. Steve read the letter for a second and then shook his head. "No," he said, tossing it back on the pile, "This is just an acknowledgement that they received your *request* to renew your visa waiver. There is no way to renew it without leaving the country, so you're still here illegally." With that, my relief must have been visible as I said, "Well, Mr. Moussaoui, you're under arrest. Place your hands behind your back."

After the shortest hesitation, Moussaoui complied, lowering his head, and meekly putting his hands behind his back. Steve swiftly stepped behind Moussaoui and snapped handcuffs on him. As soon as I was sure his hands were under control, I stepped forward and began searching him. Under the law, people being arrested can be searched by law enforcement officers "incident to arrest." My first purpose was to locate and remove any weapons or other dangerous items for our safety. The second purpose was to obtain more information about who Moussaoui was and what he was up to.

As soon as I put my hands on Moussaoui, I noticed he was muscular. Although his clothing was somewhat baggy, I could feel that he regularly lifted weights and observed that his shoulders were broad. As I searched, I was careful to stay behind Moussaoui to complicate things for him should he decide to fight, even now.

I started with Moussaoui's pockets, quickly locating a short dagger in a sheath in his left front pocket. The sheath was attached to a black and red nylon lanyard which read "Oklahoma—2000 National Football Champions." The dagger, which had a large plastic handle, was held in the sheath by a thumb-activated release, which I depressed. Pulling the short weapon from its sheath, I observed that it was razor sharp and serrated across the top of the 3" blade. Nasty. On the ring at the end of the lanyard was a single car key, presumably to Al-Attas' vehicle. After returning the dagger to its sheath, I placed it in the pocket of my cargo pants. Moussaoui obviously would not be getting that back while in custody. Resuming the search, I located a large wallet in Moussaoui's back left pocket. This contained his French passport, a UK driver's license, and some other documents. Moving up to his waistband, I discovered Moussaoui was wearing a money belt containing several thousand dollars in cash. This, too, was removed.

Although Moussaoui was surprised that showing us the INS document failed to win his release, he quickly recovered and while we were still searching him, began to protest, loudly, that we were making a mistake. As we concluded our search, Moussaoui explained that the flight training which he had scheduled was important, and we were causing him to miss it. During his angry protests, I looked around the room and realized it contained luggage as well as plastic bags. In some of the bags were clothing, while in others there were notebooks and loose papers. These notebooks and documents were in addition to the large pile of papers on the counter in the kitchen. I also noticed a laptop case leaning against one of the armchairs in the room.

While Moussaoui was speaking, John came into the room. He smiled at me when he saw Moussaoui in handcuffs and then hardened his expression at Moussaoui's continued angry words. Grabbing Moussaoui's cuffs, he turned him around, pointed him towards the door of the room, and began walking him out. As we neared the door, I asked John to stop for a second and turned to Moussaoui, still vocally protesting his arrest. Moussaoui looked back at me and stopped talking. “Sir,” I said, attempting to sound polite and helpful, “Is it possible you have another document in your room which might prove you are correct?”

Moussaoui shook his head and replied that the one he gave us was the only one.

I then asked, “Maybe there is another one? We could help you look for it. Maybe that would help you prove you are here legally? Maybe it’s on your laptop...”

On hearing that, Moussaoui shook his head vigorously. His eyes widened, his body tensed, and he nearly shouted his reply: “No! No! I do not give you permission to search my things! You do not have permission to look on my laptop!” Moussaoui was obviously concerned about what we might find among the documents scattered around the room or on his laptop computer. Denying us permission to search was his right, although it certainly was not normal behavior for a legitimate businessman anxious to rectify an immigration mix up. However, the law was clear: without a search warrant, we could not legally search any of Moussaoui’s things, including his laptop.

Once buckled in the back seat of Steve’s car, Moussaoui’s tantrum had progressed to where he claimed he could not breathe and told us he was going to be sick, Adopting my most soothing tone, I informed Moussaoui that he was going to be okay, that he had been arrested on a minor immigration violation, and that usually these matters could be cleared up quickly. This seemed to have a calming effect. Moussaoui’s breathing slowed and he stopped rocking, though he was still looking at me. I moved around to the front of the car and knelt on the front seat to speak to him.

Seeking to keep the conversation going, I asked in my most cheerful and friendly voice, “So, you’re a pilot? Me, too.What do you fly?”

Moussaoui shook his head quickly and began breathing rapidly again. He shot out a quick answer, “Cessnas,” only he pronounced it, “Cezznas,” and resumed huffing and puffing. Moussaoui looked like he was working himself up again.

I tried once more, "I fly Cessnas, too. What model?" No reply. "How many hours do you have?" No reply, just rocking and breathing. I abandoned this attempt at rapport building, reasoning Moussaoui needed time to calm down. "I'll see you in a little bit, Mr. Moussaoui. Until then, don't worry."

With Moussaoui's departure, John and I turned our attention to Al-Attas, still standing on the sidewalk next to his Subaru. He was shifting nervously from foot to foot as John addressed him with a smile, "Well, Mr. Al-Attas, so you say you're a student?"

Al-Attas nodded slowly.

John continued, "Do you have any documents in your possession which will allow us to verify that?" Al-Attas replied that he did, in the hotel room. He offered to show us, and we accompanied him back there.

CHAPTER 11

THE COMPANION

When we reached room 1414, Al-Attas used his key card to open the door. Before entering, we asked Al-Attas whether he was staying in this room with Shaquil. He replied that he was. We then asked him for consent to search the room, specifically his items. Al-Attas agreed to this, so we asked him to sign a consent form, which John produced from his notepad. Once he had done so, we asked Al-Attas to stand in the doorway while we conducted a sweep for weapons and dangerous items. Even though he was such a meek and forlorn little character, we did not want him to produce a knife like we encountered already, or worse, a gun.

There was a mix of luggage and clothing in the room, as well as the paperwork and laptop computer I previously noticed. The room seemed cluttered and the volume of stuff in there seemed high for just two people, but for the most part it was clothing, food, and materials pertaining to Moussaoui's flight training.

There were some items in the room, however, that certainly were not normal. John and I noticed there were two sets of fighting gloves and shin guards in the room. The gloves were not exactly boxing gloves, they were more like those martial artists wore, made of black nylon with red lettering that read "Century" across the back of each. The shin guards were red, white, and blue, and looked like those soccer players wore, with hard plastic fronts and elastic straps to hold them in place. They might have been for playing soccer, except there were no soccer balls or shoes with cleats in the room. There were, however, two sets of heavy work boots, made of light tan leather with thick soles. Both pairs looked new, like they had never been worn. There were also binoculars and a bag from Best Buy which contained a copy of PowerPoint 2002 software. We did not see anything which could be used as a weapon, so John asked Al-Attas to step into the room and provide us with some proof he was still enrolled as a student.

After a quick rummage through a backpack, Al-Attas pulled out a folder. From the folder he took a document which he handed to John. As I glanced over his shoulder, I saw it was a transcript from the University of Oklahoma, with Al-Attas' name at the top. I noted the transcript showed Al-Attas had been enrolled in classes at Oklahoma for several years, with the last semester of record being Spring 2001, which ended in May. I also noticed the grades were good, all A's with only a few B's, many of which were in some hard-sounding math classes. Since the Fall 2001 semester was not scheduled to begin until later that month, Al-Attas met the requirement of his student visa: he was enrolled full-time at an accredited school. John verified with a nod that this document would suffice to keep him out of custody. Al-Attas was "in status," to use the INS term.

Since Al-Attas gave us consent to search the room, John began to do so. While this was happening, I asked Al-Attas to have a seat at the kitchen counter, across from me. He complied and sat there looking uncomfortable. There was a large pile of documents between us. I knew at least some of the documents were Moussaoui's since this was the pile from which he retrieved the paperwork he showed to Steve. When I asked, Al-Attas replied that some of the documents in the pile were Shaqil's, some were his.

I wanted to keep the pressure on Al-Attas so that he understood the seriousness of the situation and told him it was unlikely Shaqil would be returning from custody. John piped up from behind him and asked Al-Attas what he was planning to do now. Al-Attas turned around to face John and replied that he would probably return to Norman, Oklahoma the following day.

Recognizing a golden opportunity to preserve what might be important evidence, John jumped on this and asked Al-Attas whether he would give consent for us to remove Moussaoui's property from the room since he planned to leave the next day. John explained this was a good idea because this would allow INS to return his belongings to Moussaoui when he was deported. Al-Attas agreed to this and offered to show us exactly which items were Moussaoui's, and which were his. He also obligingly assisted us with carrying the suitcases and plastic bags and loading them in John's car.

Before we started taking Moussaoui's stuff to the car, John called Steve, already at the INS office with Moussaoui. While John waited, Steve relayed our request to Moussaoui for permission to bring his property to the INS office. He agreed. We understood that we did not have the ability to search these items, because earlier Moussaoui had unequivocally denied our request to do so, but at least the evidence would not be destroyed or lost. We wanted to prevent this at all costs because we could see plastic bags containing documents and notebooks, as well as the previously mentioned laptop. These represented a possible treasure trove of information about Moussaoui's history, associates, finances, and plans and we wanted to be sure we had all this stuff so we could obtain a search warrant which would allow us to examine it in detail. Moussaoui's agreement allowed us to hold the property until we could get a judge to sign a warrant.

The sun was beginning to set, and the shadows were growing long on that beautiful Minnesota evening as we finished loading Moussaoui's property in John's car. Al-Attas had worked willingly to assist us, both in determining which items were Moussaoui's and then in carrying them out to the car. It was a surprisingly large load of stuff and seemed as if Moussaoui might have all his things with him, rather than what he might just pack for a week-long excursion to Minnesota.

We left Al-Attas' stuff in the room, secure in the knowledge that he had already given us permission to search that. For that reason, we were confident Al-Attas would not claim any of Moussaoui's property as his own to protect his friend's secrets. We planned to search Al-Attas's property based on his consent, so either way we hoped to eventually go through everything in room 1414. As we shut the trunk on the last load, we looked at Al-Attas, sweating from the mild exertion of the repeated trips between the room, always accompanied by one of us, and the car.

It was time to talk.

CHAPTER 12

AL-ATTAS' STORY

We resumed our places at the kitchen counter. At my request, Al-Attas handed me his passport and Oklahoma driver's license. The license showed his address as being 209A Wadsack Drive, Norman, Oklahoma. I put it down on the counter and began looking through his passport, which, even before I opened its brown cover and began paging through it, showed a disconnect. Al-Attas told us he grew up in Saudi Arabia, but the cover proclaimed the passport I held was issued by Yemen. When asked about this, Al-Attas explained that he was not a Saudi citizen, despite having been born there, because his parents were Yemenis living in Riyadh for the last 30 years.

Unlike in the U.S., merely being born in Saudi Arabia did not confer citizenship. That came from the citizenship your father held. Therefore, despite never having been to the country, Al-Attas was a Yemeni citizen. Sure enough, a look at the photo page of the passport showed that Hussein Ali Hassan Al-Attas had been born in Riyadh, Saudi Arabia. A glance through the pages showed only a few entry stamps, most of which were to the U.S. That made sense since Al-Attas was here to attend school.

Al-Attas informed us that his father was employed at a furniture company in Riyadh. He had four brothers and two sisters, a large family by U.S. standards, but common in the Middle East. Al-Attas was the fifth oldest and all his older brothers were engineers. What Al-Attas said next was unusual, since he added it quietly, and volunteered the information without being asked: he said his family was not religious. This statement would become more important later, since we began to discover through our interview that Al-Attas *was* religious, extremely religious. It made that remark, delivered almost as a slight rebuke of his family, stand out.

When I asked Al-Attas about his plans, he replied that he intended to finish his Bachelor of Science degree in math at the University of Oklahoma and that he planned to go on to obtain a master's degree in the subject too.

I asked Al-Attas how he liked the U.S. He frowned before replying. When he answered, Al-Attas said he did not consider the U.S. his home and therefore traveled only between his apartment, his classes and the An Nur Mosque, located near where he lived. Al-Attas explained that he did so because he "did not want to mix in U.S. culture." I could attest to that. Even though he was wearing cargo pants and a T-shirt, Al-Attas looked about as American as Benito Mussolini. He was clearly uncomfortable even wearing Western style clothing and all three photos of him (his passport photo, the photo on his U.S. visa, and his Oklahoma driver's license showed him in a white thobe, the traditional ankle-length robe worn by men in the Arabian Peninsula.

That said something about him, too.

The photos also showed another change from the person sitting across from me. In each of them, he was sporting a full beard, a religious obligation among observant Muslims. The beard was scraggly and did not yet fully cover Al-Attas' face in any of the photos, but it was long and had clearly been the result of careful growth for years without shaving or trimming. Yet the young man sitting across from me was clean shaven except for a trendy goatee. I asked him about that, and Al-Attas replied that he shaved the beard quite some time before.

"And why is that Hussein?"

He hesitated, then replied, "Uh, because I was tired of it." That hardly rang true. Someone as religious as Al-Attas who just finished telling me he memorized the Koran as a kid and wanted to avoid mixing in U.S. culture was unlikely to have selected the current campus facial hair fad because he was tired of 1300 years of tradition. John, standing behind Al-Attas, shook his head at me. It seemed to us like he was starting to lie. We later learned nearly everything the guy told us was a lie, but this was one of the first we were able to detect.

To prevent Al-Attas from settling in on his own version of a coherent, but false, story, I changed gears and asked an open-ended question about Moussaoui, "So, how about Shaqil?"

Al-Attas informed us he first met Moussaoui six months before at the An Nur Mosque. Al-Attas stated he had always been drawn to religion and liked to spend time in nearby mosques wherever he was living. At An Nur in Norman, Al-Attas had become so involved that he became the assistant to the Imam there.

The distant relationship with Moussaoui changed when Al-Attas himself had a problem: his roommate had gotten married and asked him to move out. To find another place to live, Al-Attas then approached a friend, an Indian student named Mukaram Ali and asked to move in with him. Ali agreed, but informed Al-Attas that Moussaoui had also just come to him with a similar request. Therefore, the three of them would be living together. That was how Al-Attas and Moussaoui became roommates.

Because Al-Attas had been giving us some generalities, probably truthful ones, but generalities nonetheless, I amplified my question, "If we were to ask around, what would people at the mosque in Norman say about Shaqil?" We wanted Al-Attas to believe we had already done our homework in Norman, especially since they had been gone for almost a week and would probably not know we had not.

Al-Attas' reply to the question seemed truthful, and it concerned us. He described Moussaoui as an "extremely" religious Muslim who had gained a reputation for being far too hard line and outspoken in his beliefs. Coming from someone who seemed to be the most devout and religiously knowledgeable Muslim I ever met, Al-Attas' opinion carried some weight. He continued, explaining Moussaoui made himself very unpopular with the other attendees at the mosque by aggressively pointing out anything they did or said which he considered to be religiously impermissible, however minor.

And there was more. In response to a direct question about Moussaoui's stance on violence in support of religion, Al-Attas replied that he had personally heard him speak out against Israel and its actions towards the Palestinians, many times. He was angry that the Israelis were killing Muslims and pointed out that the American media always portrayed Israel positively.

Even though Moussaoui's dislike of Israel was not out of the ordinary, I asked some follow-ups on this topic. Under questioning, Al-Attas admitted Moussaoui had informed him that it is acceptable to kill civilians from a country that is harming Muslims. He went on to say Moussaoui also expressed approval of the actions of martyrs, which is a word extremists use to refer to people who carry out suicide attacks.

While the news after 9/11 became full of accounts of Islamic extremist suicide attackers wreaking havoc across the world, in 2001 suicide attacks, dubbed "martyrdom operations" by the terrorists, were less common. Suicide attacks at that time were the hallmark of only a few terrorist groups, Hamas, in the West Bank and Gaza, Hizballah, and Al Qaeda, being the most prolific users of the tactic.

We pushed on, asking Al-Attas whether he had ever heard Moussaoui discuss plans to kill those who harm Muslims, and in so doing, become a martyr himself. It was the pivotal question of the interview. Al-Attas had just laid the foundation by describing Moussaoui's ideology and beliefs as consistent with Al Qaeda. Now we were asking, directly for Al-Attas to admit his friend shared a belief common among terrorists. We decided to raise this question relatively early in the interview because we had some momentum. Al-Attas had already made some damning statements about Moussaoui in the last minute or so, and we felt this line of questioning might lead to a breakthrough.

Probably aware of what we wanted him to acknowledge, Al-Attas hesitated. We pressed, informing him we intended to interview others in Oklahoma. That did it, sort of. Lowering his voice, Al-Attas acknowledged he *"may have"* heard Moussaoui make plans to hurt those who harmed Muslims. When Al-Attas stopped talking, I silently held his gaze, waiting patiently for him to elaborate on what was unquestionably a significant answer. John clearly felt the gravity too, since he came back to the table and stood next to Al-Attas, expectantly awaiting his reply.

After a few seconds, Al-Attas lowered his gaze and sat there silently. When it became obvious he was not going to continue, I said, "Hussein, what were Shaqil's plans?" A pause, "You need to tell us now." No reply, so I asked again.

This time, Al-Attas looked at his watch and then looked to his right at the window, where the light of the day had faded to night. When he spoke, it was to answer my question with a question. "It is time to pray. May I?" Our answer was automatic, "Of course."

CHAPTER 13

THE PRAYER

Allowing Al-Attas to pray was a no-brainer. First, we had to be respectful of his religious beliefs in giving him time to pray. It was a consensual interview, and he could end it or take a break whenever he wanted anyway. Also, John and I thought we were at the point where Al-Attas was close to telling us about Moussaoui's plans. Maybe he needed to pray to reach the conclusion that the right thing to do was to give us the information we were seeking.

We stayed respectfully silent and out of his way during the Ablutions and the prayer. When he was finished, Al-Attas thanked us, and resumed his seat at the kitchen table. I asked again, "Now, what are Shaqil's plans? How is he going to hurt people who hurt Muslims?"

If John and I believed the prayer break was what Al-Attas needed to decide to do the right thing and tell the truth, we were bitterly disappointed. Al-Attas acknowledged, as he did ten minutes before, that he *had* heard Shaqil make some statements about hurting non-Muslims. He went on to explain, however, that because it is not in his own heart to do so, he "kept himself from hearing and understanding what Shaqil was saying."

I could feel myself getting annoyed. What Al-Attas was telling us was obviously a lie, but I kept my demeanor neutral. He refused to provide details, but it was an admission, nonetheless that Moussaoui was planning violence. No matter how we asked, Al-Attas would not admit to knowing any details, to include what role aircraft played in the plan or when Moussaoui's plan was supposed to happen. He also claimed to be unable to name anyone else who was involved and what role they would play.

In later years, John and I would discuss the moment when Al-Attas, having just made a key admission, asked for time to pray before continuing the interview. Although neither of us would have denied him the opportunity to practice his faith, we realized immediately after we resumed our discussion that Al-Attas' willingness to lie to us had hardened after prayer, not softened. Like the true Islamic extremist that he was, Al-Attas found religious justification to lie to protect the actions of someone he knew was embarked on a mission allowed by shared beliefs. Far from taking the time to search his conscience (which we now understand he does not have) and conclude he should speak up to protect other people, Al-Attas used his prayer interlude to double down on abetting murder.

We kept going.

We asked Al-Attas about Moussaoui's reading of Fatwas (religious rulings) because we knew Al Qaeda members studied and used them to guide their actions. He nodded and replied that he had heard Moussaoui referring to certain Fatwas in arguing his extreme beliefs. Al-Attas also had seen him reading Fatwas online. Reasoning that Moussaoui would almost certainly have talked about these rulings with one of the most religiously knowledgeable people he knew, we asked Al-Attas what they discussed. Al-Attas replied that they were just general Fatwas, discussing how people should live and treat one another. Hoping to try to identify some specific Fatwa which advocated violence, we asked for the names of some of the scholars who issued them. Al-Attas replied that he remembered one which was issued by Abdulaziz Bin Baz and indicated Bin Baz was someone in whom Moussaoui was interested. This was no help to us. I had not heard of Bin Baz and did not know where his opinions stood on violence.

We asked Al-Attas whether Moussaoui could read and write Arabic. With a smile and a headshake Al-Attas informed us Moussaoui's spoken Arabic was not good at all, let alone his written

Arabic. They communicated in English and all the Fatwas Al-Attas observed Moussaoui reading were written in English, too.

We needed more specifics from Al-Attas so our questions shifted to asking about things that would indicate preparations for violence. Nodding, Al-Attas acknowledged Moussaoui told him true Muslims must prepare themselves to fight. To that end, Moussaoui convinced Al-Attas to purchase a set of padded fighting gloves and shin guards when he purchased his own, and to begin physical exercise and martial arts training.

Al-Attas also informed us Moussaoui believed it was the highest-level duty for Muslims everywhere to know about and understand the suffering of their fellow Muslims in lands where they are being oppressed. Since this sounded like the statements of someone involved with the international jihad movement, I asked Al-Attas to name some places described by Moussaoui where this might be occurring. Without pausing to think, Al-Attas rattled off the Philippines, China, Kashmir, Kosovo, Macedonia, Palestine, and Bosnia. When he finished, I realized that was a nearly complete list of places where extremists were fighting or had recently fought jihad against various "enemies of Islam."

We also asked Al-Attas what he, himself thought about jihad. It was the first time we used that word in our interview, and its arrival caused Al-Attas to hesitate, "Jihad?"

"Yes, jihad'" I said. "It means, 'holy war.'"

For the second time that day, Al-Attas chuckled. Looking me straight in the eye, he said, "I know what it means." I believed him.

"Okay, then. What do you think about going on jihad? Is it something you are planning? Is it something you have considered?"

Al-Attas began an explanation we had heard before from other interview subjects. He explained the word "jihad" had two meanings in Arabic. The first, he said, was the "greater jihad," really a struggle against oneself to stay on the correct path and to avoid temptation. The second definition, that of the "lesser jihad," was about fighting. I explained to Al-Attas that since we were discussing how true Muslims needed to learn to fight and were required to understand the suffering of Muslims everywhere for the last several minutes, the jihad we were asking about was the one which involved fighting those harming Muslims. Al-Attas nodded.

Seeing that we were not going to be led off course into a philosophical discussion, Al-Attas replied that he might fight in a jihad himself someday if called. It was a frank admission, but not really that significant since we understood many mainstream Muslims also believed a true jihad in defense of Islam was a religious obligation. Al-Attas' statement was no smoking gun. What we wanted to hear was that he was embarking on jihad now, or at least very soon, in support of a group like Al Qaeda and at Moussaoui's urging.

That didn't happen. In fact, Al-Attas' next words pushed him father away from this. He went on to say that he was currently focused on his studies, but might be willing to fight in the future, if called to a legitimate jihad.

We then shifted our questions back to Moussaoui and his purpose for coming to Minnesota. Al-Attas informed us that he was accompanying Moussaoui on his trip to Minnesota "as a friend" and that he had no business of his own in Eagan. Al-Attas was aware Moussaoui was a flight student back in Norman and understood this trip was a continuation of his training. Al-Attas was not a flight student himself and knew nothing about aviation.

Al-Attas claimed to have no information about Moussaoui's source of income and did not believe he had a job. When asked where Moussaoui obtained his money, he shrugged. On hearing this, John, not happy with this lack of a response, turned and walked over to where we were sitting. As John approached, Al-Attas hunched over in his seat and cowered, clearly afraid he was about to be hit. Although John would obviously never have done anything to violate a subject's constitutional rights, for someone who grew up in Saudi Arabia, a beating from the police or security service was not out of the realm of possibility. After a few seconds of John standing there with no blows raining down on him, Al-Attas relaxed slightly, and straightened up in his seat.

When pressed for details, Al-Attas acknowledged that he knew Moussaoui had more than $10,000 in his possession and that this money came to him from overseas. That was at least consistent with Moussaoui's story to Clancy about having a business in the UK which he ran with his relatives. Maybe they were sending him money? If so, Al-Attas claimed to know nothing about it. At no time did Al-Attas indicate Moussaoui had a business or relatives in the UK and he stuck to his claim that he was unaware of where the funds originated.

I frowned. John and I both stopped talking to let Al-Attas fill the silence. We just looked expectantly at him, waiting for the truth to emerge. As always, the key to this technique was waiting. Waiting and hoping Al-Attas would fill the awkward silence, presumably because he realized his lies were not believed and that something needed to be done to fix the situation.

After a few seconds, Al-Attas did begin speaking, however what he did not do was tell the truth. Instead of providing detailed facts, Al-Attas began trying to explain why he did not know the answers to our questions. This is something people commonly do when they are lying. He explained Shaqil was extremely secretive, so secretive, in fact, that he only knew him by his nickname, Shaqil. Al-Attas told us that since he did not even know his companion's true name, it stood to reason that he would not know details about his income. I could feel myself frowning at At-Attas's lies, but I stayed silent.

What he said next made even less sense. With a quick glance at John, still standing nearby, Al-Attas said he himself planned to leave Minnesota on Sunday, August 19, 2001, to be back in Norman in time to register for class the next day. This would, he said, allow him to start classes at the University of Oklahoma the following week when they began. While that made sense from a getting-back-to-school-so-you-don't-lose-your-eligibility-for-your-student-visa perspective, it left Moussaoui stranded in Minnesota.

Pausing for effect, I asked, "So what happens to Shaqil then? You're leaving a day before he finishes training?"

Al-Attas blinked. He was clearly inventing an answer. "Shaqil told me we will be here longer. He needs more time to study on the equipment."

"So, you will be in Minnesota past the 20th? That is the last day Shaqil has scheduled."

Al-Attas nodded. "He needs two more weeks. Because of that, Shaqil wanted to move to a cheaper hotel. He found one on the internet."

That he just contradicted himself so badly made it apparent Al-Attas was lying. Despite having just told us of his own plans to head back to Norman on Sunday a few seconds before, Al-Attas was now speaking as if he planned to remain with Moussaoui for the long haul.

Inconsistency continued when he explained what came next. After the additional two weeks of simulator time, Moussaoui planned for them to travel to Denver, and then to New York City, before returning to Norman. Al-Attas said Moussaoui told him "They would see America."

"And how about after you saw America?"

A shrug. "I don't know."

I looked at John, mostly for the effect it would have on Al-Attas, but also because Al-Attas' story was unravelling. Al-Attas, who had begun to sweat, swallowed a few times, then mumbled that he may have told Moussaoui about his plans to return to school. He then fell silent again. We were getting nowhere. The lies were coming now, one after the other, but despite how obviously false his story was Al-Attas would not make any admissions, no matter how we pressed. We needed some facts to persuade him we knew more than we did, but we did not have them.

Switching topics, we asked Al-Attas to explain to us the purpose behind some of Moussaoui's more unusual possessions, things we noticed during our sweep of the room and while carrying the property out to John's car. For example, Moussaoui had a set of binoculars. Al-Attas claimed he did not know why this was and had never seen Moussaoui use them. When we asked again about the fighting gloves and shin guards, Al-Attas repeated that these were for training in martial arts. He stated that Moussaoui purchased a set of these items and persuaded him to do the same so they could train to protect themselves "against crime in America."

That was different from what Al-Attas told us earlier about it being a religious duty to know how to fight, so I asked, "Have you ever been a victim of crime in the U.S.?" A head shake. "Has Shaqil?"

He shook his head again, "No."

"Hussein, do you know anyone in the U.S. who has been a victim of a crime?"

"No."

These responses made Al-Attas' justification for the martial arts training ring hollow. Another lie.

"How about these," John asked, holding up a pair of heavy, tan colored waterproof work boots. From the clean condition and pristine soles, the boots looked new. We had observed an identical pair among Moussaoui's belongings, so it stood to reason the boots were purchased together, just like the martial arts gear.

Al-Attas replied that they purchased boots because they intended to hike and enjoy nature, and they needed boots to do so. Another ridiculous reply. For one thing, the boots were not made for hiking, they were made for working on a road crew or building a house. For another, Al-Attas did not look like someone who had ever hiked or intended to do so. His secretive friend Moussaoui also did not seem to be someone who would enjoy nature. For that matter, he did not seem to be the kind of person who enjoyed anything at all. John continued holding the boots up, hoping for a better answer, but Al-Attas stayed quiet.

CHAPTER 14

THE LAST WILL AND TESTAMENT

While John stood there holding the boots up, I noticed an 8 x 11 tan mailing envelope in front of me among the pile of documents on the kitchen table. Since we had gathered all the papers from there which Al-Attas said were Moussaoui's and put them in John' car, I asked Al-Attas, "Is this yours?" He swallowed and nodded.

The envelope looked new. It was unwrinkled and the paper was stiff and fresh, even the four corners. Looking inside, I saw two sheets of 8½ x 11 inch plain white printer paper. Looking at Al-Attas, I asked, "May I look at these?" He nodded again. I noticed he was sweating more than before and swallowed both before and after nodding.

Sliding the two sheets out of the envelope I saw they contained several lines of handwritten Arabic script, drafted in black ink. Like the envelope from which they emerged, the pages looked fresh and new. The writing on them filled up one whole page, and part of the second. Despite not being an Arabic speaker and being unable to read a single word, I looked at each sheet for a few seconds admiring the neat and precise strokes of the script and waiting for Al-Attas to possibly fill the silence by offering some explanation as to what I was holding.

When he did not explain, I asked "What is this?"

For the third time in 10 seconds, Al-Attas swallowed hard. When he spoke, it was a choked whisper. "It's my Will."

I exerted a serious effort to prevent any emotion from creeping into my voice or facial expression, and feigned nonchalance. What I wanted to say (scream actually) was, "Ahaaaaa!" What I said was, "Oh." Then after a pause, I asked, "Did you say this is your Will?"

Al-Attas nodded again and licked his lips. A dry mouth is a common and obvious sign of stress, and Al-Attas was showing it now with repeated swallowing and now the lip licking.

After waiting a few seconds to allow the tension to build, I asked the inevitable question: "Why do you have a Will?"

Al-Attas hesitated. He looked away. He adjusted his clothing and shifted his seat. He swallowed a few more times, ran his fingers through his hair and then mopped his now sweaty brow. In short, Hussein Al-Attas exhibited about as many signs of deception as it is possible for one person to display in such a short time. His reply was, predictably, a lie.

Al-Attas began to explain it was common for Muslims, particularly those who were traveling, to draft Wills in case they die unexpectedly.

Because I did not want him to become too entrenched or committed to what was an obvious falsehood, I countered by asking, "Even for someone in their early 20s who is completely healthy?"

"Yes. If a Muslim dies his last wishes must be known and his debts must be paid. If not, it's bad. I had to tell my family what to do."

Given our lack of knowledge of Yemeni customs regarding death and Will preparation, and because his family might have made him draft a Will for some reason, I was just starting to realize he had us there and that we would have to accept his answer. My hesitation allowed Al-Attas to fill the silence, and when he did, he went too far with his lie, adding, "I wrote it long ago."

Now, we knew *that* was not true. The envelope and the paper on which the document itself was written were new, even pristine. They were unwrinkled and unstained. There was *no way* Al-Attas had written that long ago, it was too perfect. There was also a plastic package with two other envelopes like the one containing the Will right on the same table. The envelopes had obviously been purchased very recently. There was nothing "long ago" about any part of that document.

Rather than confront him directly, we wanted more facts. "And the document we found in your car, the one providing instructions on how to write an Islamic Will...is that what you used to help with this?"

Al-Attas nodded and replied that he had used the pamphlet, copies of which were available at the An Nur Mosque. It was time to push on this. Holding up the pages of the Will, I pointed out to Al-Attas how obviously fresh and unwrinkled the paper was, just like the envelope. He blinked silently. I then asked how it was possible that he still had the instructions on writing the will, the pamphlet for which was also on new-looking and unwrinkled paper, since he had done so "long ago." No response. Just more swallowing.

Looking at the Will one more time, I sighed and began sliding it slowly back into the envelope. I did my best to show Al-Attas that I did not believe him, not one bit, but there was no real way to break the deadlock on that. What we did though was obtain his permission to take the Will with us that night, so we could copy it and return it to him the next day. We did so, and once back in the office, quickly requested that the Will be translated. At the time the Minneapolis Office did not have an Arabic translator on staff, meaning it was a few days before we would have the text in English. Once John and I read the English translation of Al-Attas' Will the following week, we understood why he had been so nervous. It was also clear to us that he had been particularly concerned because *he believed I had been reading the Will* and understood his secret.

By pausing as I looked at the words and the leafing through both pages, I had inadvertently persuaded Al-Attas I could read Arabic. The sweating and swallowing reflected his belief that I understood the words and instantly recognized what the Will really meant. If only that was true! We would have taken the interview in a different and much more direct path since this document was electrifying.

The translation we received the following week showed us Al-Attas's "Will" was really a farewell letter to his family. Far from a strictly precautionary document drafted just in case of an unlikely untimely demise, Al-Attas started off by declaring, "death has approached" with an inevitability few healthy men in their 20s would normally feel. He asked his parents to forgive him for his shortcomings and reminded them God shows favor to those who embark on "jihad." It is certain that in referring to jihad, Al-Attas meant combat against the enemies of Islam, not the inner struggle which he described to us. He expressed the hope that Allah will reward him with paradise and keep him with the prophets, martyrs and the pious. Al-Attas went on to tell his parents that he hoped they will all be together in paradise.

In wrapping up what were clearly intended to be his last ever words to his family, Al-Attas urges them not to ignore "the issue of the woman's veil, even for young girls." He advises his family to ensure women cover with "an Islamic attire" and cautions against letting them imitate the West, meaning they should make sure women and girls keep their heads and faces always covered in public.

In short, it was a classic example of the last words of an Islamic extremist who expects to die soon, obviously while fighting in a jihad. Sadly, we did not know any of that sitting in Room 1414 of the Residence Inn on the evening of August 16, 2001.

As Al-Attas spoke, I was leafing through the documents on the table between us. He had begun to lie consistently, and we wanted to move into a different avenue of questioning to prevent him from becoming too entrenched in any one story or too comfortable with telling one falsehood after another. As I had hoped, I found the next topic among the papers.

Holding a part of the pile of documents up with my right hand, I withdrew from the middle of the haphazard stack a partially completed application for a Pakistani tourist visa. Although most of the form had not been completed, the name of the applicant at the top was Hussein Al-Attas.

This was a significant find, and I held it up so John could see it. As he realized the importance of this discovery, we looked at each other. Here was Al-Attas, a Yemeni citizen who grew up in Saudi Arabia and was enrolled in college in Norman, Oklahoma, completing an application for a visa to enter there. Why? What legitimate business did he, could he, have in Pakistan?

Al-Attas again began to fidget nervously.

Although the obvious question was "why," I started off by asking, "*When* are you planning to go to Pakistan?"

Al-Attas hesitated, in a way we now understood he usually did before lying. He then responded that he was planning to go "soon." It was not a significant admission since the dates on the form told us that. Al-Attas indicated on the form that he planned to visit Pakistan in the next few weeks. This put him in a head-on collision with the answers he gave just a few minutes earlier about what he would be doing starting Monday. Now, it seemed he was going to Pakistan in the next few weeks, right smack in the middle of the semester, missing classes he claimed he would be attending.

Our next question should not have been unexpected: "Why, are you going to Pakistan?"

Probably because of its predictability Al-Attas seemed prepared for this question and his replies were somewhat more plausible. He explained he had an uncle in Saudi Arabia who was ill with cancer. Al-Attas took his uncle's test results to a physician in Norman to get recommendations. This physician happened to be from Pakistan and informed Al-Attas about the Inmol Cancer Institute, located in Lahore, Pakistan. He suggested Al-Attas' uncle might be treated there.

This sounded plausible, so far. However, under further questioning about the logistics of reaching Pakistan with his uncle, Al-Attas was able to provide few details. He had never been to Pakistan and did not know his way around the country. What he did say, however, was that the physician in Norman informed him his brother was also a physician, based in Lahore. When Al-Attas and his uncle arrived in

Lahore, they planned to call the brother, and he would arrange everything. That sounded thin.

Still suspicious of Moussaoui's involvement, particularly because Al-Attas told us minutes earlier regarding his violent beliefs, we asked what his role had been with the upcoming travel to Pakistan. Al-Attas swallowed again and paused, before admitting Moussaoui had been assisting him with completing the visa application by telling him how to answer the questions. He adamantly denied that Moussaoui encouraged him to travel to Pakistan for any reason. He also denied that Moussaoui would accompany him to Pakistan.

In asking Al-Attas about this travel, John and I remembered the Pakistani tourist visa we found in Moussaoui's French passport and wanted to find out whether the two of them might be planning to travel there together. Al-Attas shook his head again. He explained that Moussaoui had much more experience with foreign travel and was willing to assist, but he was not planning to accompany him and his uncle on the trip.

One discrepancy still stood out: How did Al-Attas intend to travel to Lahore, Pakistan while enrolled at in a full course load at the University of Oklahoma, scheduled to begin the following week? When we asked this question, Al-Attas, still relaxed, shrugged. He replied that he did not know either, but Arab morals dictated that he do something to help his family, so that was what he was planning to do.

We were out of topics and ready to wrap up the interview. I closed the folder I had been using to take notes and looked at John. John was done for the night too, but that shrewd and experienced investigator was not prepared to let things go entirely, particularly because Al-Attas had been lying to us so much. Appearing to look nonchalant, John thanked Al-Attas for his cooperation. Al-Attas nodded, obviously happy the questioning was at an end. It was then that John dropped this on him: "Oh, and since we will need some time to verify that you are enrolled as a student, please report to the immigration office tomorrow at 9 a.m."

As John spoke, concern crept back into Al-Attas' expression. Being firm, but nice, John made sure Al-Attas had the address of the immigration office and that he understood the summons was official and mandatory as part of an ongoing immigration investigation. Al-Attas looked unhappy, exactly like someone who had believed they were out of the woods, only to discover they were still under suspicion. Seeing this, John smiled broadly, and speaking in his most friendly Wisconsin manner, ended on a sincere sounding, "Have a great evening!"

As we drove back to the INS office, John and I discussed Al-Attas. Both of us were convinced he spent most of the last two hours lying. But even with the lies Al-Attas told us, we were still able to glimpse a picture of Moussaoui: secretive, knife-armed, inexplicably well-funded, angry at non-Muslims, extreme in his religious beliefs and engaged in training for physical confrontation. All those red flags were in addition to the reason he was under investigation in the first place: his highly unusual flight training.

CHAPTER 15

ENCOUNTER WITH THE MONSTER

When we met Steve and Dave at the INS Office, we asked, "How has Moussaoui been?"

Steve shrugged. "Pretty calm since we finished processing him. He asked whether we were going to let him go back to the flight school, but we told him that was up to you guys. We got him a veggie sub from Subway. He ate it and has been quiet."

I asked, "Did he ask for the veggie sub, or did you just get it for him?" Steve replied that Moussaoui had specifically asked for one, declaring that a veggie sub was all he would eat. Another sign Moussaoui was at least a very observant Muslim.

Dave handed me Moussaoui's large wallet, which contained several documents, including his French passport. They inventoried the cash in Moussaoui's money belt, and it was over $3,000. That was quite a bit of money to be carrying, although maybe not for a wealthy, globe-trotting French import-export guy.

John and I looked at all the documents, hoping for a clue as to what Moussaoui was doing in the U.S. There was a lot of information contained there, and we took our time reading over them. The background knowledge would help us determine where we should be going with the interview. The Al-Attas interview already gave us reason for concern, so now we would have to see whether Moussaoui's replies would alleviate our suspicions or deepen them.

Once we confirmed after 9/11 that Moussaoui was in the U.S. as an Al Qaeda operative, we realized he had been careless with how he distributed his documents. The large wallet on his person at the time of his arrest, and therefore subject to our search, contained French passport #00AE2716. As I looked at the photograph on page 2, I was surprised. While it was clearly Moussaoui's face looking back at the camera, the man in the picture was thinner and much less muscular than the person we arrested. One other thing struck us immediately. In the photo, Moussaoui was smiling, projecting a picture of cheerful happiness. In the short time I had known Moussaoui, his demeanor had been so dour that I could not imagine him ever being happy.

While the contrast with the photograph was interesting, what we found upon further review of the passport was cause for considerable suspicion. On page 9 of the passport was Pakistani visa #VB086976. The visa was a page-sized white sticker with green lettering, issued by the Pakistani High Commission in London on December 4, 2000. The visa was good for multiple entries to Pakistan until December 3, 2001.

Conveniently located on page 8 of the passport, just to the left of the page bearing the visa, was one entry stamp (in green ink) and one exit stamp (in red ink) for Quaid-e-Azam International Airport, in Karachi, Pakistan. The green entry stamp reflected that Moussaoui entered Pakistan at Karachi on December 9, 2000. The red stamp showed that he departed Pakistan via the same airport on February 7, 2001. With that, we now knew that Moussaoui spent two months in Pakistan recently, and his departure date from there was two weeks before he arrived in the U.S.

Extremely suspicious.

Also in the wallet was a UK driving license which indicated Moussaoui was licensed to drive cars and small trucks in the UK. Other than giving us his address, there was nothing more useful in the driver's license, so we moved on.

The next document was highly significant: a Deposit Agreement from Arvest Bank, located at 200 East Main Street, Norman,

Oklahoma, in Moussaoui's name. The document was dated February 26, 2001, three days after he entered the U.S. and showed he used his French passport as identification when he opened an account and deposited $32,000. That was a lot of money, and we wanted to know how Moussaoui came to have it.

We were ready to go.

John and I went with Dave and Steve back to the detention area and stopped outside the cell where Moussaoui was waiting. Because the facility was designed only for short-term detention, his cell was sparsely furnished with only a bed, a sink, and a toilet. We could observe through the large glass window that Moussaoui was lying on the bed with his feet up on the white-painted wall. He looked relaxed.

When he saw the four of us standing outside his cell, Moussaoui swung his feet over the edge of the bed and sat up, looking at us expectantly. When Steve unlocked the door, Moussaoui realized we were not just there to check on him and he stood and walked over. John addressed him, "Mr. Moussaoui, we'd like to speak to you a bit. Maybe we can clear this up."

Moussaoui nodded and replied, "Of course."

We then led him out of the detention area, to a nearby office, which was vacant. While we were walking and talking, I was able to observe Moussaoui closely. He was approximately five feet six, and stocky, with a shaved head and goatee. He still looked African American, continuing the impression I formed when I first saw him walking to Al-Attas' car. The "normal" impression was enhanced by his clothes: khaki cargo pants, a blue t-shirt and sandals, a leather jacket, and a Nike ball cap. This illusion was only dispelled when Moussaoui spoke, his heavily French-accented English with a distinctive lisp marking him clearly as someone from overseas.

My efforts at rapport building did not get far. Almost immediately, Moussaoui raised the question of when he would be able to resume his flight training and wanted to discuss little else. I also noted Moussaoui had a very decisive, even forceful way of speaking, not at all the apologetic tone someone in his spot should have taken.

It revealed an underlying anger that was certainly not typical of people in his position and by the time we reached the interview room it was obvious he was intensely hostile towards us.

John and I agreed Steve and Dave would watch the interview from a nearby office for as long as they wanted. When they were tired, they would go home, as it was getting close to 9 p.m. John and I told them we would transport Moussaoui to Carver County jail when we were finished.

When we entered the office, we directed Moussaoui to a chair in front of the desk, while John and I sat behind it. Both of us stayed standing until Moussaoui was seated, a technique calculated to subtly convey that we were in charge. Moussaoui seemed to take no notice of his surroundings. He was looking intently at us. We observed when we first arrested him that Moussaoui had quickly gone from mildly annoyed to extremely upset in seconds and were on guard for that now.

John and I intended to forestall or prevent such an emotional escalation today, at least until we thought it might assist us, so we stayed calm and clinical in our manner. We had already previously agreed we would not push Moussaoui too hard on this first interview so we would leave open the possibility there would be a second one the following day.

We wanted a second interview to give us time to check out the information Moussaoui provided during the first one. Even if those checks came up empty, we could try to bluff and persuade him otherwise. Any guilty knowledge Moussaoui had might make him more likely to reveal additional details on the second day if he believed our checks overnight developed new information about him. Also, we wanted to ask Moussaoui similar questions two days in a row to compare how consistent his answers were. The truth is easy to remember but fiction made up on the spot is much harder, so if Moussaoui did lie there was a good chance the answers would differ from one day to the next.

Therefore, John and I decided in advance not to push or confront Moussaoui too strongly on anything yet. We would certainly challenge him and be constantly probing for facts. We would just do so without direct confrontation or accusations which might cause him to end the interview. The hard accusations would come later.

As we explained the purpose of our interview, Moussaoui listened carefully. He seemed impatient to start telling his story, and I took this as a good sign that we would at least be getting something from him. After his freak-out in the car, I was concerned that he would just continue to act as if he were too sick or upset to continue, stalemating our ability to speak with him. I was happy we seemed to be moving on from that.

First, however, we needed to safeguard his rights. Because Moussaoui was in custody, John slid an INS Miranda warning form in front of him. In plain language it informed the person about to be interviewed by law enforcement that they had the right to remain silent, and that anything they did choose to say could be used against them in court.

After reading the document, Moussaoui nodded and said, "Yes. I will sign." We handed him a pen and he added his distinctive signature, along with the date and time. He slid the form back to us, along with the pen.

The interview began.

CHAPTER 16

THE TALE

John and I observed that Moussaoui's manner in the more formal setting of the office was now controlled. This was not a surprise because he had plenty of time to calm down. Upon closer observation, however, there were little signs that although Moussaoui was trying to appear cooperative and calm, underlying a veneer of agreeability was anger. Moussaoui started off by informing us that he was highly suspicious of all immigration officials in general because of a problem he had in the UK in 1993. When we asked what happened, Moussaoui explained he was traveling on a French identity card issued by the French Consulate in London when he was stopped and questioned by British immigration officials who believed he was Algerian. Moussaoui informed us they persisted in this belief, even though he had valid French documents, and this made him angry. He claimed the deadlock was only broken when he was able to contact a friend who knew a French senator, who was able to come to his assistance. Moussaoui was unable to recall the name of the senator. He was likewise unable to recall the name of his friend. Although we did not know it yet, this was the beginning of a two-day trend where Moussaoui claimed to be unable to recall the names of nearly anyone with whom he had contact in the last decade.

We assured him we believed he was a French citizen and that he would be treated fairly in the U.S. Moussaoui did not respond to this reassurance but began raising what became a common theme of our interviews: his desperation to continue his flight training. Moussaoui first raised this while being arrested a few hours before, mentioned it again to Steve and Dave during the transport and then went on to ask about it many times during the interview. At one point, he even offered to return to immigration custody when finished, if only he were permitted to complete instruction at Pan Am. This request was even the last thing we would discuss with Moussaoui later that night as John and I drove him to Carver County Jail.

Moussaoui went on to explain that he believed submitting his request to extend his visa waiver meant he was legally in the U.S. He informed us that if he had known it was not, he would have left the U.S. for the UK and applied for a visa at the embassy in London which would allow him to continue his training.

John nodded, "That would have been the legal thing to do."

Moussaoui looked at him, "But I came here to become a pilot, and my training was not complete."

Like almost everything having to do with Moussaoui's interest in flying, this struck me as odd. He had no pilot's license and minimal aviation experience, yet Moussaoui paid more than $8000 to receive training in a high-fidelity 747–400 simulator, money he was now likely to lose because of his immigration mistake.

Another thing that struck us was that Moussaoui's priorities seemed out of whack. In custody and facing deportation from the U.S., his overriding concern was to return to this training? Moussaoui did not ask whether he would ever be able to come back to the U.S. or if he might be in legal trouble and he brushed aside my suggestion that we would ask Pan Am for a partial refund for him. Instead, he persistently focused on getting into that simulator.

When I pointed all of this out, Moussaoui informed us that he had long dreamed of becoming a pilot. He claimed that he chose the United States for flight school because the cost of obtaining a license in the UK was several times higher. That made sense. I knew several people who traveled from Europe to the U.S. or Canada for private flight training. In addition to lower costs, there are many more schools in North America and much more unrestricted airspace for flight training. The weather is also usually better.

What Moussaoui did not explain is why he abandoned his private lessons to leapfrog over several levels of training to get into a 747 simulator. When we pointed this out, Moussaoui avoided answering this question and just continued discussing the high cost of training in Europe. He said flight training in Europe was so expensive because the student is required to hire an additional airplane and pilot to always follow him. Moussaoui followed by explaining Airman Flying School in Norman, Oklahoma is full of foreign students.

In addition to avoiding answering, Moussaoui's statements about learning to fly in the UK were lies. Preposterous ones. I had never heard of having to hire another aircraft to follow you, anywhere, in any country. When I looked it up later in the UK private pilot guide just to be sure, there was no mention of another aircraft. In fact, the requirements for a UK PPL (private pilot's license) were remarkably like those for a private pilot rating in the U.S.

Moussaoui informed us he had been a flight student at Airman since he arrived in the U.S. in February 2001. He admitted that he had not been progressing in his training there.

"Why is that Mr. Moussaoui?"

Moussaoui's eyes darted over to me. Shaking his head, he replied, "The instructors were too young. They did not know how to teach me to fly."

Moussaoui claimed that after he had approximately 50 hours of flight time in the Cessna 152 aircraft, he stopped making progress.[2] When I asked him specifically what maneuvers or what aspect of flying had given him trouble, Moussaoui shrugged, "All of it." Moussaoui had also taken the FAA written exam but failed it. For this reason, he did not want to take the practical exam. The "practical" is the actual flight test in which he would fly with an FAA examiner to demonstrate his ability to perform maneuvers safely and to the standards set by the government. This statement did not make sense either. It

2 Moussaoui's logbook showed that he had 56 hours in the Cessna 152 when he arrived in Minnesota.

was not his choice whether to take the flight test, FAA regulations did not permit him to do so until he passed the written exam. He also needed a flight instructor to certify he was ready. It sounded like he was not even close.

Once his progress stalled, Moussaoui claimed he had been told by his instructors that he was not cut out to be a pilot. That also sounded odd to me. For one thing, flying an airplane is not that hard. There are some basic concepts to understand, a few skills to master, and lots of rules to learn. Involved, yes, but hard, no. Sixteen-year-old kids get their pilot's licenses all over the world every day.

Also, these schools made their money training people to fly and were paid (handsomely) by the hour for flight instruction. When I was a student pilot, I listened to the often quite young instructors complain to one another about students who were not progressing, but never did I hear them tell anyone to quit. On the contrary, they remained encouraging and got all but the most dangerous of student pilots through the program, especially since the remedy for poor performance was more flight training, and thus more income for the school.

Moussaoui went on to explain that because his progress had been so slow, he decided to "follow his dream of flying a big airplane." That was why he came to Pan Am for the 747–400 simulator training. Moussaoui told us that after the simulator training, he intended to resume flying real airplanes. Obvious by its omission was the lack of a convincing explanation as to how the simulator would assist him with getting his flight training on track. If he could not handle a Cessna, the solution for that was more flight time...in a Cessna, not a 747–400 simulator.

Listening to Moussaoui, I understood it made no sense for someone not progressing in his training in a Cessna 152, which at that time cost around $40 per hour of flight instruction to fork over $8,300 for training in a 747 simulator. This would in no way assist Moussaoui in his goal of becoming a pilot, nor would any serious flight instructor ever recommend such a course of action. When I pointed this out, Moussaoui replied he was doing so "purely for enjoyment," a statement which was inconsistent with his desperation to return to Pan Am. If Moussaoui had $8,300 in extra money laying around, the way to "follow his dream" was to pay for more flight time in a Cessna 152 so he could improve his skills.

On one final, but intangible note, as a pilot, I found Moussaoui's discussion of aviation and airplanes very odd. Most pilots discuss flying with great enthusiasm. We love airplanes and revel in the challenge of mastering a skill most people do not understand amid the exhilaration of escaping the earth. When Moussaoui discussed airplanes, he did so flatly and clinically without any joy. There was no passion and no detail in his narrative, making his claim that he dreamed of flying a big airplane, or any airplane, decidedly out of place. He was no pilot and clearly had no serious interest in becoming one.

As for his background, Moussaoui informed us that he was born in the city of Saint-Jean-de-Luz to Moroccan parents. He stated that he was educated through secondary school in France before moving to the UK to attend university. Following graduation with his master's degree, Moussaoui remained in the UK, where he claimed he worked various jobs. This gave us an avenue to explore, so we asked about employers. That $32,000 deposited in Arvest Bank had to have come from somewhere.

There were problems with Moussaoui's replies right away. When we asked about jobs he held in the UK, his responses were vague. He would only say he worked in a variety of places over the years. When asked to name some of his employers, Moussaoui indicated that he had worked for a short time as a freelance telemarketing researcher. The problem was Moussaoui could not recall the *name* of that company. After some continued questioning, he remembered that the company was called "NOP." He did not know what the initials stood for, or the address of the company. When pressed, Moussaoui remembered the "N" was for "National," but that was it.

That was also suspicious. I can remember the names of all my employers, starting with when I had a paper route for the Philadelphia Bulletin in junior high.

When I pointed this out, Moussaoui gave me a sideways look. He claimed he started a business initiative which involved phone cards issued by a company in Indonesia, but followed up by adding that this did not work out, so he never actually worked for the company. For this reason, he could not remember the name of his employer in Indonesia or the names of anyone who worked there. In addition to going 0 for 2 in naming the first two employers he described, Moussaoui did not mention owning an import-export business in his initial reply. This stood out to us since this is what he told Clancy he did for a living! He also used that at Pan Am to justify why he had enough cash to joyride in an expensive simulator.

Seeing we were unconvinced, Moussaoui added that he also earned some income from "relations in Saudi Arabia." We asked who he was related to in Saudi Arabia, and where they lived. Moussaoui answered that he had an aunt in the city of Khobar. In reply to what should have been a completely predictable follow-up question seeking details about the nature of his aunt's business, Moussaoui choked. After a too-long delay, he answered that it was "absolutely legal, but private."

Controlling my rising exasperation at the absurdity of his constant lies, I calmly asked, "Mr. Moussaoui, how can a business be private?"

After a few minutes' back and forth on this, Moussaoui claimed he had been trying for a short time to establish a business to import "some product" from France to Saudi Arabia, but stated that this had not worked out, either. "Some product" was not descriptive enough, so we kept at it. Finally, Moussaoui indicated the product was grape leaves, but none were exported because the business was never started. He offered no explanation for the failure, so again, we asked. He finally answered that there was not enough of a demand for grape leaves in Saudi Arabia. Moussaoui could not recall any other jobs he held, indicating only that he worked "here and there." He was likewise unable to name a single coworker or supervisor.

This made the $32,000 Moussaoui had deposited upon arrival in Oklahoma suspicious, to say the least. For a person who was unable to name even one job he held, this was a significant amount of money.

We pointed this out.

Moussaoui's reaction was pronounced. He became extremely angry, declaring that he had been working his whole life and saving money and the cash he brought to the U.S. was the result. This was a lengthy rant, with Moussaoui sputtering angrily. John then asked once more for the names of his employers, a question that seemed to make Moussaoui angrier. He began to speak in a choppy, halting manner, telling us that he had been working from the age of sixteen at a variety of jobs, all the while saving his pay. Moussaoui claimed that this was not unusual or suspicious. Even after repeated prodding, he still proved unable to name any previous employer or coworker who might verify his story. He was also unable to tell us when he received the funds he brought to the U.S. or to name his annual salary. Moussaoui did add that he did not pay income tax in the UK in 2000, so he was unsure of how much he earned the previous year. Not enough income to pay taxes, yet he had $32,000 on arrival in Norman?

During this rant, Moussaoui worked in a description of his academic qualifications, to include an undergraduate degree in international business from Southbank University and a master's degree in commerce and technology from the "Institute of Export," both located in the UK. This seemed to ring true. Moussaoui spoke English like someone who had been educated, even if it was not his first language. However, without being able to name an employer all the academic qualifications in the world still did not justify his possession of a large sum of money.

Although Moussaoui grew agitated at these questions, John and I kept our cool and stayed clinical in our manner. We did not accuse him of lying and merely pointed out where his answers were inconsistent. This did nothing to lower what we both could feel was hostility towards us. Despite his best attempts to conceal it, Moussaoui hated us, and we could tell.

Because Moussaoui mentioned the UK, we took the opportunity to discuss his life there. He informed us he liked the British people and for this reason he decided to stay when he finished school. We asked about his residence, which, according to his driver's license, was located at 23A Lambert Road, London. Moussaoui was able to tell us his address, which helped his credibility slightly. Believe it or not some criminals and terrorists were not sharp enough to remember the addresses on their own fake IDs, but Moussaoui rattled his off without difficulty.[3]

However, knowing your address is one thing, being able to name some roommates or neighbors who can verify your story is another. When we asked about that, Moussaoui replied that he lived in this apartment with an unspecified number of other Moroccans who were "mostly restaurant employees." While he was in the U.S., "the flat in London" was being sublet to friends. As with his employment history, Moussaoui was unable to name any of the people he just described: roommates or sublet tenants.

We were getting nowhere asking Moussaoui about friends, colleagues or even acquaintances. He apparently wished us to believe he had none, so we moved on to family. Surely, he would remember his relatives' names. Moussaoui told his family still resided in France, including his mother, older brother, two sisters, and his father.

As we discussed each of them in turn Moussaoui claimed he was estranged from his father, brother, and one sister. He would not tell us why, but as was becoming the norm, Moussaoui said it was for personal reasons. John and I wanted more details, but Moussaoui tried to close out the line of questioning by indicating he had not been in contact with his father for years. The estrangement from one parent and siblings was important to us. Both John and I had encountered terrorism subjects in the past who dropped contact with family and

3 Despite the ease with which Moussaoui remembered the address, it *was* fake. We would later learn that prior to coming to Norman, Oklahoma, Moussaoui most often lived in al Qaeda guest houses in the Afghan city of Kandahar, the group's main base during the late 1990s. During his brief visits to London, Moussaoui slept in mosques or at the residences of other members or sympathizers of the group.

friends when their religious beliefs became too extreme. We silently wondered if this was the case here.

For the first time, when Moussaoui replied that he was not answering for personal reasons, it rang true. A person can become estranged from parents and siblings for any one of a variety of reasons. And, unlike the names of their past employers or co-workers, some people do prefer to keep these reasons confidential. Pushing further on Moussaoui's family right now was pointless. If the falling out really was over religion, he was unlikely to tell us. We would revisit that later.

Besides, we had another topic to discuss and were extremely interested to hear his answers to this question:

"How about foreign travel? Please tell us the countries you've visited."

In a measured tone, Moussaoui replied that he traveled to Morocco and "all over Europe." That made sense. His parents were from Morocco, and he was born and raised in France so those were logical destinations. He stopped, without providing any additional details, as usual.

We waited. Still nothing, so after a few seconds we asked, "Anywhere else?"

Continuing to speak slowly and deliberately, Moussaoui answered that he visited Indonesia, as part of the telephone card business he tried to start. Moussaoui informed us he spent about a month in Indonesia attempting to get the business up and running. Hoping he might now disclose the actual name of the company, we asked again, and again met with a shrug.

Since we knew from an examination of Moussaoui's passport that there was at least one other country he visited, I asked, "Where else?"

Continuing controlled cadence, Moussaoui said he also visited Malaysia for about three weeks, "for business."

"And what was that business?"

"The phone card business."

So, now the Indonesian phone card business had a component in Malaysia as well. As we questioned him Moussaoui revealed he spent seven weeks between these two countries working with a company whose name he was unable to remember. More lies. How do you not remember the name of a company *you* start?

"And where else?" We asked this question with certainty because we knew there was another country. The Pakistani visa and entry and exit stamps in the passport showed Moussaoui spent two months there shortly before coming to the U.S. for flight training.

"Pakistan."

"When were you in Pakistan?"

Moussaoui, his effect very flat, replied that he visited Pakistan approximately six months ago.

I asked, "Why? What were you doing in Pakistan?"

Moussaoui replied that the visit to Pakistan was also in connection with the Indonesian telephone card venture. "So, this start-up also took you to Pakistan?"

"Yes"

We pointed out to Moussaoui that an examination of his passport showed he spent two months in Pakistan in late 2000. This was double the amount of time he spent in Indonesia, where the unnamed parent company was based. When asked why the Malaysian and Indonesian visits were so much shorter than his trip to Pakistan, he explained that his reasons for visiting Pakistan were both connected to the business venture as well as "personal."

"And what was the personal part, Mr. Moussaoui?"

Moussaoui's eyes narrowed. Still the anger. "I went there to get married."

"And did you?" John asked him, smiling brightly.

"No."

None of this made any sense at all, so we had plenty of additional questions. Before we asked them, however, I tried an additional tactic to try to shake something loose. I was getting annoyed at Moussaoui's evasiveness, especially because some of his claims were outright silly, like not being able to name a single friend, coworker, or employer. I wanted to push him a little.

CHAPTER 17

THE FBI

Up until this point, Moussaoui believed he was of interest solely to the Immigration and Naturalization Service (INS) because he overstayed his visa waiver. Since we were now talking about his being in Pakistan, the gateway to Afghanistan which was the current base for Al Qaeda, and since he was providing answers ranging from vague to nonsensical, I felt like it was time to increase the tension. Reaching into the left cargo pocket of my pants, I withdrew my credentials and showed them to Moussaoui, the light blue lettering "FBI" clearly visible to him. Dropping his air of nonchalance, Moussaoui rotated towards me in his chair. He looked at the credentials and then back at me with a gleam of understanding in his eyes.

"Mr. Moussaoui, you may think that this is just an immigration issue, however I think it is important that you understand I work for the FBI."

Moussaoui nodded.

"We are working together with INS to help determine whether it is a good idea to let you continue your training here in the U.S. So far, you have not given us nearly enough detail in your replies to our questions to allow us to verify *anything* you've said. No verification will likely result in a decision to deport you."

We asked again about Pakistan. Eventually, Moussaoui said he traveled to Karachi, where he stayed in hotels the entire time. We asked who he knew in Pakistan, to which he replied, "No one." Obviously, the FBI reveal had not worked. Worse, Moussaoui's answer was false because it was completely inconsistent with the culture. If

Moussaoui was truly in the country to meet a prospective wife, then he was most likely working through a male family member of the prospective bride. Pakistani families, particularly religious and traditional ones did not allow their daughters to just marry foreigners off the street, sight unseen. Moussaoui would certainly have needed an introduction to the woman's family and the most likely route to this was a male relative who could vouch for him. Even if this was not the case, he presumably at one time knew the name of his intended betrothed. When we asked for her name, he claimed to be unable to remember it. Really?

We pointed out that his story had some inconsistencies and asked again who he contacted in Pakistan. Looking annoyed, Moussaoui replied that he was in touch with the brother of a close friend of Pakistani origin who resided in London. We asked for the brother's name, which Moussaoui could not recall. "How about your 'close friend' in London, what's his name?"

To our surprise, Moussaoui replied that his friend's nickname was Talil. Our excitement was short-lived. When asked for something more descriptive, particularly since they were close, Moussaoui replied that he could not recall his friend's last name. As we had done many times already, we called him on that, pointing out that most people knew the names of their close friends. Moussaoui not only claimed to be unable to recall Talil's real name, but, for good measure he asked us why we needed to know that information. Sighing, I explained again to Moussaoui that his behavior in paying cash for flight simulator time was suspicious, suspicious enough that the flight school had called the FBI. I informed him that the more details he gave us, the quicker we could resolve our concerns and get him back to what he wanted to do. I added that he was not helping himself this way.

On hearing this, Moussaoui told us he could not remember Talil's last name, but his first was Ahmed. In response to the what should have been unnecessary follow-up questions which Moussaoui forced us to ask, he informed us Ahmed did not reside with him, or even near him in the UK. In fact, it came as no surprise to John or me that Moussaoui could not remember where Talil/Ahmed lived or what his phone number was.

"Is there anyone else in Pakistan who can verify for us why you were there? It would preferably be someone we can contact."

As expected, Moussaoui replied, "No. There is no one"

Because John and I understood Pakistan was the gateway into Afghanistan for members of various Islamic extremist terrorist groups, the next question, though subtle and open-ended, was aimed at getting Moussaoui to admit he traveled there: "While you were in Pakistan, did you visit any other cities? Did you travel to any neighboring countries?"

A simple "No" would have sufficed—and Moussaoui had not been shy about saying that word all evening. But that is not what he said in response. Instead, he seemed to instantly become angrier, almost shouting, "No! No!" These denials were accompanied by vigorous shaking of his head and waving of his hands in front of him.

Such an emotional outburst told us something. In fact, it was unmistakable. John and I, resisting the urge to allow our own emotions to rise to match Moussaoui's sat calmly until his denials seemed to exhaust themselves. When he finished, one of us asked Moussaoui why that question upset him. Still clearly agitated, Moussaoui claimed that he was aware of our accusations and what we were trying to do. He said, "I watch television," and petulantly refused to discuss the matter further, looking a little like a spoiled child as he sat there, arms folded, shaking his head, and looking back and forth at each of us.

Moussaoui's response clearly indicated we were onto something. The mere suggestion he traveled to Afghanistan freaked him out. My instincts were telling me to push on this, as were John's. This was clearly a hot-button issue for Moussaoui, and we were starting to think we knew why. However, because we were careful not to cause Moussaoui to end the interview, we moved on. Both of us recognized that the Pakistan travel was highly interesting, and we knew we would circle back on this during the next interview. I even wrote a short note on my pad, "Pakistan," and underlined it twice.

In another slip up on his part, Moussaoui must have forgotten that there were no entry or exit stamps for Indonesia or Malaysia in his passport when he admitted traveling there. When asked why these did not appear, he indicated that his current passport was a recently issued replacement for one that had gone through the washing machine. The washing machine story was another sign. John and I knew terrorist operatives who traveled to suspicious locales routinely destroyed or reported their passports stolen so they could obtain new documents without tell-tale entry and exit stamps. Unexplained visits to too many countries added up to questions from law enforcement each time the passport was shown, and Moussaoui clearly was bad at answering these. He would have been wiser to not tell us about his travel to Indonesia and Malaysia, but he obviously forgot these stamps were in his old passport, not the one he had now. Without his admission, it would have been difficult for us to have discovered this travel on our own.

Now we knew Moussaoui "accidently" destroyed his old passport, a highly suspicious occurrence. Given the weight of information piling up, the washed passport story was another significant data point. It was a definite example of what was looking increasingly like terrorist trade craft.

As regards his foreign travel, Moussaoui also later told us that he had been to Saudi Arabia once, in 1996, for the Umrah religious pilgrimage. Since we were on the topic of religion, John moved smoothly into discussing Moussaoui's involvement with mosques. We knew from our interview of Al-Attas that Moussaoui was an attendee and active participant at the mosque in Norman, so we asked about his attendance there. Moussaoui replied that he attended the small mosque near the University of Oklahoma in Norman, which was where he met Al-Attas. Moussaoui described Al-Attas as "the second Imam" at this mosque. He also informed us that he considered himself a religious Muslim, and stated that Al-Attas was, too.

Like the skilled and experienced investigator that he was, John seized on this line of questioning. Without changing his tone or intensity level to avoid alerting Moussaoui to the importance of his next few questions, he asked a little more about Al-Attas' participation at the mosque. Casually, John wondered aloud about Al-Attas' duties there. Clearly not understanding where John was going and seeing no harm in replying, Moussaoui told us that Al-Attas led prayers at the mosque almost daily. In addition, he frequently delivered the khutba, or sermon, at Friday prayers. John continued, "With his knowledge of the Koran, does he teach any classes?" Moussaoui replied that he did.

And now, Moussaoui was conditioned to reply freely on this topic when John asked the critical question: "Does he receive any money from the mosque for doing this stuff?"

Moussaoui replied, "Yes." Bingo. Clear evidence Al-Attas might be in violation of his student visa.

Moussaoui's replies to this series of questions were so important because they had a bearing on Al-Attas' immigration status in the U.S. Al-Attas proved to John earlier that evening that he was in the U.S. on a *student* visa. If he received compensation for working, then he might be in violation of that status. Whether he was in violation was dependent on two things: first, whether we could prove Al-Attas received any money for what he did and, whether he had ever applied for and received permission to work. It was possible to obtain work authorization if in the U.S. on a student visa, but the application had to be made, it was not automatic. Even though this was not conclusive, and nothing involving immigration law ever was, it was a good lead for us to follow. Maybe we would be able to arrest Al-Attas yet?

CHAPTER 18

MORE LIES

We also asked Moussaoui about the mosque he attended in the UK, where he lived before coming to Oklahoma. He replied that he attended the Brixton and Finsbury Park mosques for worship. As usual, he claimed not to know the names of any fellow worshippers. He also added that he occasionally visited the Regent's Park Mosque but had no details about that place. I knew all three of these mosques were in London, having heard of them. Despite claiming he prayed at each mosque, Moussaoui predictably was unable to name any of the Imams or anyone with whom he socialized there.

We also asked Moussaoui whether there were any religious leaders or Islamic scholars he followed. He shook his head. As we were prodding him more on this response, Moussaoui became angry again. It was not the kind of arm-waving, shouting anger the questioning about Pakistan had provoked. It was silent rage which we could sense from his manner and body language. Moussaoui claimed he did not need to follow any scholars because "things are very clear" for him. Because he was able to think for himself, Moussaoui indicated he did not need anyone's guidance. He stated that he particularly followed the law governing prayer five times per day and was careful to always help his Muslim brothers.

"How about fatwas? Which do you follow?"

Moussaoui looked at me, his anger seeming to subside. "I don't read them. They are only in Arabic, and I don't read Arabic. I don't understand what they say." He smiled slightly.

We knew that was a lie. Fatwas are translated into English and someone as observant as he admitted to being would certainly have gotten his hands on those. Plus, Al-Attas told us he read them. We then took the discussion right into another hot-button issue for Muslims, the Arab Israeli conflict. "What do you think about what is going on in the Middle East, between the Arabs in the Israelis? How does the Israeli treatment of the Palestinians make you feel?"

He shrugged.

"Mr. Moussaoui, how does that make you feel?"

Moussaoui replied in a somewhat flat voice, "The situation makes me sad."

I thought, "How does that not make him angry?" Even moderate Muslims and many non-Muslims for that matter were moved to anger at what was regarded as Israeli heavy-handedness. Besides, Al-Attas informed us a few hours before about Moussaoui's rage at the way Israel was treading Muslims yet receiving favorable coverage in the U.S. media. Surely Moussaoui was angry at Israel?

"No" was his reply to our repeated questions about this.

"Then, how does that situation make you feel?"

"Sad. It makes me feel sad," he repeated.

"Really? Sad? I'd say more than a few Americans and many Muslims worldwide would say they are angry about what is happening there."

On hearing that, Moussaoui gave a more complete answer than usual, "Yes. Seeing a six-year-old child shot in the head by a soldier makes me *sad*. Seeing the Israelis taking Arab land, that makes me *sad*." That did the trick. Although the word he was using was "sad," Moussaoui's rage was palpable.

"Well, have you ever been so 'sad' about how Muslims are being treated, that you spoke openly about hurting people in retaliation?" More info from the Al-Attas interview. We knew Moussaoui had done so.

It seems Moussaoui, realizing his emotions had led him to go too far, seemed to visibly gain control of himself. He smiled slightly and said he would have to think about whether he had ever said anything like that. His reply was accompanied by a wave of his hand, as if trying to dismiss his anger. In contrast to some of the other questions which seemed to shock or throw him off balance, Moussaoui was able to regain his composure quickly. He never gave us an answer, though. It did not matter. By now we knew.

Since we learned from Al-Attas that Moussaoui believed all Muslims needed to know how to fight, we asked him about any military training he received. We knew about Al Qaeda's terrorist training camps inside Afghanistan and that many jihadis from the West attended them. We also understood that as a French citizen, Moussaoui was required to serve in the French military. It therefore seemed likely that he was trained somewhere. Moussaoui replied flatly that he never had any military training, another obvious lie.

I pointed out that seemed unlikely because we knew of his requirement to serve in the French military. Moussaoui replied that he had avoided being drafted into the French army because of "family problems" and the fact that he was studying for a degree at the time he reached military age. He reiterated that he had no weapons training of any kind but admitted he had shot handguns once or twice in France with friends. We were not surprised when he was unable to name any of these gun-owning friends.

And then, Moussaoui did what several other terrorist subjects would later do when I interviewed them during other cases in the future. Because this was the first time I saw it, it seemed incredible to me and probably resulted from some psychological phenomenon where the subject wants his interviewers to know something about his achievements but is obviously unwilling to make any direct admissions. What John and I observed was some odd form of hypothetical statement which subtly communicated to us that he *had*, in fact, been trained in the use of weapons.

As John and I were pausing to allow Moussaoui to fill the silence following the absurdity of not remembering the names of yet another group of friends, he smiled slightly. Looking at us with his body turned away and his head cocked over his left shoulder, Moussaoui began speaking in a friendly, conversational tone so different from his clipped and annoyed answers. With a slight smile, he said, "You know, I would like to learn to use weapons someday, as he I am curious about them..."

"Well, Mr. Moussaoui, we are pretty sure you have been trained to use them."

Instead of getting angry, he shook his head and simply repeated that he had never previously been taught to use weapons. The smile never left his face, and his closed body language and the fact he was turned away from us clearly showed us he intended to avoid telling the truth. When subjects lie, one of the things they may do is to turn their body or their feet away from the interviewer. It is a subconscious self-defense or pre-flight mechanism, and Moussaoui was sure demonstrating it now.

When we discussed this later, John and I shared the same opinion: Moussaoui was clearly lying when he claimed he had never been trained in the use of weapons. So strongly did I feel this was the case that I wrote the following in my report: "Minneapolis opines that Moussaoui was being deceptive in stating that he has never been trained in the use of weapons, based on his reaction to the question." Later we would learn that not only was Moussaoui trained in the use of weapons during his time in Chechnya and Afghanistan, but during 2000 in Al Qaeda-controlled sections of the Afghan city of Kandahar he was someone whose status in the group allowed him to be armed with an AK-47 while walking around town, even when rank-and-file members were supposed to leave their weapons behind at the training camps or front lines.

In response to our questions about his immediate plans in the U.S., Moussaoui informed us that upon completion of his flight training in Minnesota, he and Al-Attas planned to travel to New York City to "see sites," including the Statue of Liberty, the "Empire State," and the "White House." He also informed us he planned to travel to Denver to do some unspecified business with United Airlines.

Moussaoui never could tell us what he planned to do at United Airlines Headquarters and, of course, he was unable to name anyone at that company with whom he had been dealing or had an appointment. Moussaoui indicated that when this travel was complete, he planned to return to Oklahoma and fly back to the UK. Nowhere in there did Moussaoui explain how his expensive simulator instruction in Minnesota would help him become a pilot. In fact, he never once said when and where he intended to continue flight training. As with all his answers, Moussaoui's responses were completely inconsistent with the way normal people led their lives. Also, these fabrications were completely unverifiable because he never named a single person who could corroborate any aspect of his story.

By now we had run through questions on all the topics we planned to cover with Moussaoui, and he had done a remarkably poor job of answering them. John and I were both tired, so by previous agreement we informed Moussaoui we were finished speaking for the evening. We explained that even though he gave us little to go on, we were willing to look into some of the facts he had just provided us to see whether it might be possible to resume his simulator training.

We told him that he would have to spend the night in custody, but that we would like to bring him back the next day to resume our discussion. Moussaoui agreed to meet again the next day. Though he was obviously disappointed, he claimed he understood. The underlying anger was still present.

We returned Moussaoui to his cell in the detention area for a short time while John confirmed a bed for was reserved for Moussaoui at the Carver County Jail, approximately 30 minutes south of the Twin Cities. Because it was around 11 p.m., the detention supervisor apologetically informed us we would have to transport Moussaoui ourselves. That was fine with us. We wanted to continue to try to build rapport with him and to ensure nothing would happen to further antagonize him. If John and I drove him to Carver County, we could do our best to keep him happy.

When all was ready, John and I walked into the secure garage, with Moussaoui between us, and slightly ahead. With my left hand, I was holding his belly chain in the back, just to keep control of him. John had Moussaoui's INS paperwork, including a detainer signed by an immigration official. This would be provided to the jail as proof of the U.S. Government's legal authority to hold him in custody.

Once we reached the garage, John darted ahead to bring the car to us. I asked Moussaoui to stop walking, and we waited for the car. I could see from the glint on top of his bald head that he was sweating heavily and could smell his body odor. It was time to try rapport building. Edging out to his right side so he could see me, I opened with: "I noticed from your birthdate that I am two months older than you, so we grew up at the same time. How was growing up in France?"

He chuckled, "It was okay. Better than this," jingling his chain and cuffs.

"Yeah...sorry about that. We'll work to get this cleared up as soon as we can." I made Moussaoui no promises, and we *were* working hard to clear this case up.

The night was now cool, and Highway 169 was all but empty as we headed south towards the Carver County Jail, located in Chaska, Minnesota. There really was not much more to talk about, but I wanted to keep building bonds, if possible. "Did you enjoy flying the 152?"

"Yes. But it was very hard. I wasn't getting more skilled as time went by." That sounded odd to me. The Cessna 152 was the airplane I trained in. It had simple systems, which allowed the student pilot to focus on flying. It was light, adequately powered, and responsive on the controls. Most people progressed rapidly flying that airplane. But, as with most of his answers tonight, Moussaoui's commentary on flying indicated he saw the world through a different lens than the rest of us.

After a few minutes of silence, Moussaoui asked from the darkness in the back seat, "Do you think I will be able to return to the simulator?"

We were amazed he was still worried about that, even after the completely evasive interview he just gave and as he was being taken to jail by the FBI and INS. However, because we were determined to speak with Moussaoui the next day, I replied that there was a chance, provided he could give us some information to verify. We asked him to get some rest that night and to try to remember details which might give us a chance to confirm his source of income and his past travel. "Okay," he replied, simply, but unconvincingly. The rest of the ride passed in silence.

CHAPTER 19

A SECOND ARREST

Friday, 08/17/2001

I was in the office a little after 7 a.m. and ran the incomplete names Moussaoui had provided the day before through the FBI database. I was not shocked when those came up empty. I then went into Greg's office to update him. He was pleased with the aggressive attention we were giving the case and I promised him I would keep him updated on our results.

I arrived at John's office in Bloomington a little before 9:00 am so we would have time to discuss our strategy before Al-Attas arrived. John and I were now completely convinced Moussaoui's reasons for seeking flight training were nefarious and involved a terrorist plot of some kind. The trick was getting him to admit it and reveal details and identify associates to allow us to stop the plot.

Our go-for-broke strategy dictated that we would push both Al-Attas and Moussaoui aggressively for answers, confronting them with their lies and making direct accusations where appropriate. We decided to do so even at the risk of getting them to end the interviews. Our reasoning was that more of the same from the previous night was unproductive. Keeping them talking might eventually be beneficial but allowing them to become entrenched in fairy tales was unhelpful, especially if this stretched out over several days. Today was the day we needed answers. Lies would no longer be okay.

In Al-Attas' case, John also planned to try to confirm the evidence needed to arrest him. Instead of levelling with us, he spent the previous evening trying to protect Moussaoui and whatever he was planning. And ironically, the key to his arrest originated with Moussaoui since we understood from him that Al-Attas had been paid for his work as "the second Imam" at An Nur. An arrest of Al-Attas would serve two purposes. First, it would get him off the street and prevent him from carrying out the plot in Moussaoui's absence. Second, it might pressure him to come clean. We tried it the easy way the evening before, maybe the hard way was what Al-Attas needed now.

As we were wrapping up our discussion, John learned from the receptionist that Al-Attas was waiting in the lobby. We went out together to get him. In the bright sunlight shining through the glass doors, Al-Attas looked as tiny and forlorn as he had the night before. He was still dressed in an ill-fitting and entirely incongruous tee shirt and cargo pants and looked uncomfortable in them.

John and I began the interview trying to persuade Al-Attas, whose cooperation the day before had been poor at best, that Moussaoui revealed the details of a terrorist plot to us when interviewed later. We hoped this would pressure Al-Attas to reveal any details that he knew about the plot and about Moussaoui's other associates.

It did not work.

During his second interview, Al-Attas reiterated much of the same information he provided previously. Our more aggressive strategy did keep Al-Attas on track, because when he began to hesitate or denied knowing something obvious, we reminded him that he or Moussaoui had admitted that the night before. We were therefore able to move along more quickly, keeping Al-Attas making admissions as we went.

Following up from our line of questioning of Moussaoui the night before, I asked Al-Attas whether there were any Islamic scholars Moussaoui followed. Al-Attas nodded. There was a sheikh whose teachings Moussaoui followed, but he never revealed this man's identity to Al-Attas. When asked why Moussaoui kept the sheikh's identity a secret, Al-Attas replied that Moussaoui told him he did so because he was sure Al-Attas would not approve of the sheikh, both because of his beliefs and because of his national origin. Apparently, despite their shared interest in Islam and in practicing it in its strictest form, Al-Attas had been unable to find out the identity of the religious scholar his enigmatic friend admired.

Skeptically, one of us asked Al-Attas whether this mysterious sheikh was Usama Bin Laden. Al-Attas shook his head, claiming he did not think Moussaoui's sheikh was Bin Laden. We asked if Bin Laden's name ever came up in conversation. Al-Attas replied that it had, one time. Al-Attas explained that he and Moussaoui had been watching CNN when Bin Laden's photo flashed on the screen during a story about Al Qaeda. Upon seeing Bin Laden's photo, Moussaoui called Al-Attas' attention to it, but did not comment further. Al-Attas claimed to remember no additional details about this incident.

When asked whether there were other Islamic teachers who shaped Moussaoui's beliefs, Al-Attas nodded. He named Omar Ibn Khattab as one such scholar. In response to our question about which of Khattab's teachings Moussaoui followed, Al-Attas said Moussaoui often quoted his saying, "Teach your children how to swim, how to ride a horse, and to know how to fight." Al-Attas acknowledged this is the justification Moussaoui cited for engaging in martial arts training and preparing himself for combat. Al-Attas indicated Khattab was one of the companions of the Prophet Mohamed, and as such, his words carried significant authority.

Looking at the still nervous young man in front of us, John asked why Moussaoui hated living in the U.S. and why Moussaoui had urged him to leave as soon as possible. Al-Attas replied that Moussaoui disliked living anywhere where Sharia was not strictly followed. He went on to say that Moussaoui also quoted the Prophet Mohamed when he said, "If he does something good in Islam, love him that much. If he does something bad in Islam, hate him that much."

"So, where is Sharia followed? I mean a version of Sharia that would make Shaqil happy."

Al-Attas shrugged.

Questions aimed at identifying Moussaoui's source of income, reasons for being in the U.S., foreign travel, or any additional associates met with repeated declarations of ignorance from Al-Attas. John and I realized we had reached the stage of our interview where we seemed unlikely to obtain new information because Al-Attas had finished providing any. It was time for John to try to obtain confirmation Al-Attas worked in the U.S.

Casually working it in in the context of a seemingly innocuous question, John asked, "You're pretty knowledgeable about most people at the mosque?" Smiling slightly, Al-Attas nodded.

"Do you have a position there, or do you just attend? Your friend Shaqil told us last night that you were the second Imam."

Al-Attas acknowledged that he assisted the Imam on occasion, and that he "did other work" around the mosque too.

"Like what? What other work?"

"I teach classes on Islam to the children."

John asked, "Really? Doesn't that take time away from your studies? Hopefully, you get something in return."

Not sensing the danger, Al-Attas smiled, and informed us that although he really enjoyed teaching about Islam, the mosque did pay him $200 per week for teaching there. John had very skillfully gotten a key admission from Al-Attas. Unless Al-Attas had applied for and obtained authorization to hold a job, he was now subject to arrest.

Without alerting him that anything might be wrong John told Al-Attas we would be taking a short break and called Steve in to keep an eye on him. John and I walked back to his office to double-check Al-Attas' immigration file to ensure there was no work authorization. As we did so, we chatted about where to go from here. John informed me that it would help the immigration case against Al-Attas if he executed a signed, sworn statement acknowledging he worked at the mosque. That way, it would be hard later for him to recant his statements in front of an immigration judge. I thought about this. Because we would have Al-Attas in the mode of signing documents, I asked John whether he minded if I asked him to do a second signed sworn statement about Moussaoui, specifically documenting the most alarming behaviors, including his training for physical combat and his religiously motivated hatred of the U.S. Of course, John agreed.

I never used a signed, sworn statement before, but John and I were already convinced we needed one. Most importantly, Moussaoui's denial of our request to search his belongings meant we needed a search warrant. I figured having a signed sworn statement from the one person Moussaoui invited to accompany him to Minnesota declaring him an Islamic extremist might help persuade a judge to sign that warrant. I was also thinking of FBI Headquarters. I was all too familiar with how skeptical they could be when we asked them for help and having it in writing from a co-conspirator that Moussaoui supported violence *might* be what was needed to convince them of the seriousness of the case.

A quick glance at Al-Attas' immigration file confirmed what John wanted to see. There was no work authorization, meaning Al-Attas was in violation of his status as a student. As we later learned, working at the mosque for a couple hundred bucks a week was the tip of the iceberg for Al-Attas' immigration issues, but on August 17, 2001 it was all we had. Fortunately, it was enough to take him into custody.

When we returned, Al-Attas was sitting comfortably enough, obviously not realizing what was coming. John asked him to do a couple of signed, sworn statements to help prove what he said was true. Al-Attas agreed. John swore him in, and Al-Attas proceeded to repeat what he said in response to our questions about working at the mosque. Once John finished writing that down, he had Al-Attas read the form and then sign that everything he said was true.

Then I took over, asking the questions about Moussaoui and documenting Al-Attas' responses on a separate form. Al-Attas repeated his statements that Moussaoui was training to fight and planned to hurt non-Muslims who he perceived were harming Muslims. Despite repeated questions to obtain more details Al-Attas remained adamant that he did not know the specifics of any plot. Once I finished asking the questions and had written down Al-Attas's replies, I asked him to read and sign the form, if it was accurate. Al-Attas did so, his eyes moving over the page as he read each of the facts, which I wrote down in short sentences using plain English. Even though Al-Attas was a college student in the U.S., I wanted to be sure he understood everything clearly. When he was finished, he looked up and reached for the pen. We watched him sign.

"Now, Mr. Al-Attas," John said, "Is there anything else you'd like to add?"

Al-Attas shook his head, "No."

John stood up, "Well then, sir, I am sorry to tell you that you are being placed under arrest."

Al-Attas' face fell. He barely choked out, "Why?"

As John placed him in handcuffs, he explained that Al-Attas had been working in the U.S. illegally, since his immigration file contained nothing which showed he obtained prior employment authorization. Al-Attas nodded, seeming to understand. He asked what would happen to him now, clearly fearing he was facing treatment like he would receive in Saudi Arabia. John spoke reassuringly, "You'll be okay. You will be processed here and held in jail until you see an immigration judge. You will have the opportunity to bond out of custody if you or someone you know has the money."

On hearing this, Al-Attas looked plaintively at John. "It would be much easier for me if I were back in Norman. I have friends there."

"Sorry," John replied. "This is where you'll see the judge." And with that, the discussion was over and two officers from the cell block gently led Al-Attas away to be fingerprinted and photographed.

As I watched him go, I remarked on what a sad little man Al-Attas was, and how I felt a little sorry for him.

John frowned and shook his head. "No, that guy knows more than he's telling. Having him in jail keeps him out of play. It may also help him decide to talk." John was right, of course.

CHAPTER 20

MORE LIES

At around 1 pm Moussaoui was brought in after his night in jail by two green-uniformed detention officers. We stood and smilingly directed him to the chair in front of the desk. Moussaoui was now wearing blue prison scrubs instead of his own clothing from the night before. His handcuffs had been removed, and he looked comfortable and relaxed. As soon as I saw him, I began eagerly observing Moussaoui's body language for any clues as to how today's interview might go. Moussaoui sat there impassively, looking blankly at us.

We started by reminding Moussaoui that he was still under no obligation to speak to us, and that all the Miranda warnings from the day before still applied. He nodded.

Before John or I could ask any questions, Moussaoui began speaking. From his very neutral demeanor and unusually cohesive speech, it seemed as if he was running through a rehearsed monologue. He certainly had time overnight in jail to come up with something. Moussaoui informed us that he had never been arrested before and that his "file is clear." He explained he had never been in jail and never been questioned by the police. For this reason, he was nervous and had been unable to remember many things the day before.

John and I nodded, trying to convey an understanding and sympathy we did not feel.

Moussaoui indicated his father had been in trouble with the law, but not him. Seeing this as an opening, we asked why. He replied that his father had been a "builder" who undercut projects and built buildings which were not to standard. Because he was a criminal, his father was estranged from the rest of the family.

It was obvious to us from the way he replied to our questions that Moussaoui was attempting to maintain a subdued manner and appear cooperative during this interview. So far, so good.

The mention of his family led us to, "How many brothers and sisters do you have?" Moussaoui replied that he has one brother. We asked his name. He replied, Abdsamed." As he did so, we saw a flicker of yesterday's annoyance return.

"Where does Abdsamed live and what does he do for a living?"

More annoyance on Moussaoui's face, "He is an engineering professor in Montpelier, France."

"Wow!" I replied. "That's quite an achievement. Your family must be proud of him!"

On hearing this, Moussaoui glared at me, "I have no idea what my family thinks!" The anger was back.

I cheerfully ignored it. "Why is that?"

"I don't speak to my family."

"Why don't you speak to your family, Mr. Moussaoui?" No reply, just another glare. We stayed quiet to allow him to fill the silence.

When Moussaoui began again, he stated that his reasons for not speaking to his family were private. Although we asked questions about this, Moussaoui refused to reply as to what caused him to be estranged from his family. Now the anger was back to stay, there was no more pretense of being a nice guy. We could see it in Moussaoui's body language, and we could hear it in his voice.

We would later discover why Moussaoui was estranged from his family and his brother Abdsamed in particular. We learned this because after the 9/11 attacks and Moussaoui's indictment, Abdsamed wrote a book entitled "Zacarias, My Brother: The Making of a Terrorist," originally published in France. In his book, Abdsamed detailed Moussaoui's radicalization while a student in the UK and his own unsuccessful efforts to dissuade him from pursuing a life of jihad and violence as he watched his younger brother slip into a murderous lifestyle.

Despite his initial efforts to persuade us he was being cooperative, Moussaoui, as he had the day before, proved unwilling to answer what were straightforward questions about his family, friends, finances, and his reasons for coming to Minnesota. After a series of "I don't know" replies John and I decided to ratchet up the intensity. There did not seem to be a downside to this, as Moussaoui clearly was not responding to our rapport-building efforts, and the added pressure might lead to admissions.

We pushed him on finances. "How is it possible that you do not know where you obtained the $32,000 you deposited in the bank in February? Anyone would know where they acquired that amount of money and would be able to speak about it in detail. That is, if it's not illegal."

Moussaoui snarled in reply, "It's not illegal! I received it from a friend!" This contradicted the statements of yesterday when Moussaoui claimed the money came from his employment.

"What's your friend's name. You must remember the name of someone who gave you that much money." We explained to Moussaoui that we were looking for names and phone numbers of people who could verify his story regarding employment, residence in the UK, travel history, and interest in flight. We made it clear that we could not and would not release him to continue flight training unless we could confirm what he was saying.

Moussaoui considered this for a second and then indicated that he had a friend in the UK named Talil who supplied the funds. He informed us he had not been able to recall Talil's name the day before.

"What's Talil's last name"

Moussaoui smiled slightly and shrugged.

"Really? Talil gives you $32,000 and you don't know his last name?" Silence. "Why did he give you the money?"

"For business." Again, Moussaoui made a deadpan delivery of a generic answer which conveyed no meaning.

After a pause, John leaned back in his chair and shook his head. "Mr. Moussaoui, we're getting nowhere. You're not explaining anything."

I added, "It's not looking good for you to return to flight training."

In response, Moussaoui elevated his voice and waved his hands, "What do you expect from me?"

"We expect that you would know your friend's last name, especially when that friend gives you more than $30,000 in cash! We would expect that you would be able to supply a reason for the transfer of such a large sum of money which sounds better than just 'business.' You know, that is more than many people make per year in the U.S., or France, for that matter. You are not telling us anything."

"Ahmed Atif. Talil's real name is Ahmed Atif."

I blinked, trying not to look surprised. After probably three hours of fruitless interviews over two days, Moussaoui had just given us a first and last name. This success would, unfortunately, not last. "Where did Mr. Atif get this money?"

The old Moussaoui was back. "I don't know. Work, maybe?"

"And where does Mr. Atif work? What does he do?"

"He is an executive for a Dutch company. I don't know what he does."

Despite follow up questions on Atif, Moussaoui was unable to name this Dutch company, indicate where Atif's office or residence were located, or provide a phone number for him. Moussaoui also indicated he had not been in touch with Atif since coming to the U.S. According to Moussaoui, Atif had not stayed in touch with him to see whether the funds he supplied to Moussaoui were being put to good use.

No one would do that, and we pointed that out to the angry man across the desk.

Again, an eruption. "You ask me all these questions and then don't accept my answers!"

"That's because your answers don't make sense. They are lies. Mr. Moussaoui, right now if you asked me to name a few friends of mine,

I could. I could tell you their first names and last names. I could tell you where they work and where they went to school. I could tell you where they live and what their phone numbers are. You named one friend in two days. A guy who gave you $32,000 no less, and you apparently know nothing about him!"

"He did not give me the whole $32,000. Someone else gave me some of that money."

"Who"

If we were hoping for a detail-rich narrative (and we were) we were disappointed. "Habib."

We knew "Habib" was not a real name. It is a nickname meaning "beloved one." That is why one of us asked, "What is 'Habib's' true name?"

A shrug.

"Where does he live and work?"

"Germany."

And that was all on Habib. No matter how we asked, Moussaoui claimed not to know what city in Germany, could not tell us where Habib worked, or what he did that would allow him to supply part of the money. He was also unable or unwilling to tell us how, when or where he met Habib. Naturally, Moussaoui did not have a phone number for Habib and had not been in touch with him since arriving in the U.S.

Sighing, I reiterated to him that normal people with legitimate jobs could name their bosses and colleagues and provide phone numbers, especially if this meant the difference between their being deported from the United States or allowed to continue some "very expensive" flight training.

Without addressing this issue directly, Moussaoui began what seemed to us to be another rehearsed reply about how his interest in learning to fly was genuine and that this was his reason for coming to the U.S. It was a little out of place and did not address our concerns. Nonetheless, Moussaoui explained that he had researched numerous flight schools in the United States with this goal in mind. He named Flight Safety International and the flight training program at the University of Minnesota as two of these. Moussaoui claimed he finally decided on Airman in Oklahoma because their advertisements said they trained many foreign students.

Once this training did not work out, Moussaoui settled on Pan Am International Flight Academy in Minnesota. At Pan Am he began dealing with a salesperson he named in their Miami headquarters. The salesperson, he said, informed him such training was open to him. That is why he did not understand what the problem was.

The way Moussaoui pulled out the salesperson's name so quickly was intriguing. Clancy gave us the same name the day before, so we knew the name Moussaoui just provided was the Pan Am salesperson. "Who were some of the other people at Pan Am?"

Without skipping a beat, Moussaoui replied that he dealt with "Alan" and that "Clancy" had been his instructor, but that he was supposed to work with a "Rich" in the future. The answers to those questions proved Moussaoui was NOT bad with remembering names. He just recalled perfectly the name of a guy he emailed and spoke to on the phone only once or twice (the salesperson), as well as the name of a guy with whom he only had incidental contact (Alan) and a guy he had not met yet (Rich). I was willing to spot him Clancy since they spent some time together recently, but his recall of the other three names was perfect, too. Surely, then he should have been able to remember the names of friends and coworkers.

If Moussaoui realized the purpose behind this question, he did not show it but instead continued his description of how he came to the U.S. for flight training. He informed us he researched flight schools on the internet, and this is how he learned about Airman and Pan Am. Moussaoui then offered to show us the schools' websites if we would allow him to get on a computer. Uncharacteristically helpful...

Ignoring this offer, we asked Moussaoui if it might not be more useful for us to check the history of the internet searches on his own laptop computer. We informed him we brought the laptop to the INS office with us after he was arrested and could go get it so he could show us the searches on that computer.

Moussaoui, who had his head down and to the right when asked this question, quickly snapped upright in his chair, and looked directly at us. He replied forcefully that there was nothing on his computer and again denied us permission to view the contents. Although we tried to persuade him that using the original computer on which he conducted the searches for flight schools (along with the date and time in the browser history) would be the best way to prove what he said was true, Moussaoui refused to consider this and shut down this line of discussion quickly.

We then transitioned to asking why he chose to come to Minnesota. Moussaoui replied that this is where Pan Am told him to come and that when he initially contacted them, he believed he would be going to Miami for the training. When he learned Pan Am International Flight Academy's simulators were in Minnesota, he came to Eagan.

"And your friend drove you here because you don't have a car?"

"No," Moussaoui shook his head. "I have a car. It's in Oklahoma."

Moussaoui indicated he owned a beige Ford Taurus which he left parked in front of his apartment building. "Then why did your friend drive you here? Why didn't you drive your own car?"

As with so many seemingly simple and straightforward questions, Moussaoui proved unable to provide a convincing answer. "He came as a friend. That's all...as a friend!"

Since we had been going for an hour or so and had gotten little information, John and I were a little talked out. We told Moussaoui we would take a short break. Two deportation officers came in to take Moussaoui to the restroom and to watch him while we were gone. He stood and left the room with them, staring straight ahead and showing no emotion. Watching him walk out, it occurred to me that through two days of interviews, we had built exactly zero rapport with Moussaoui.

John and I agreed now would be the time for direct accusations. After two days of this we were pretty sure that what Moussaoui was working hard to conceal was his membership in a terrorist organization. The fact that he had $32,000 unexplained dollars in cash on arrival in the U.S. meant that his group was probably global in scale. Because Moussaoui and Al-Attas were Sunni Muslims, that ruled out Hizballah, which was a Shia group. Therefore, we understood we had a member of a well-funded Sunni Islamic extremist group with connections to Pakistan. There were only a very few organizations that fit this description.

John and I stayed out of the room for longer than was necessary, just to get a break from Moussaoui. Conversation with him was tiring since he was such an argumentative, quarrelsome person whose hostility towards us was palpable. We needed the few extra minutes away from him just to regroup emotionally. Despite what is depicted on TV and in movies, a real law enforcement interview is not a short and snappy series of clever exchanges between investigators and suspect which inevitably leads to a tearful confession. Instead, it is a repetitive, probing conversation in which the same questions must often be asked several times in different ways. Along with the accusations, denials, and counterclaims come emotions, often strong ones. It is draining on both sides of the desk.

The delay was also worthwhile from an investigative perspective. We wanted to give Moussaoui the impression we obtained some additional incriminating information while we were out of the room, another classic interview tactic. If Moussaoui believed we had been able to learn something about him by some other means, he might make an admission. Keeping him waiting could help our claim, which we planned to make in the next few minutes, that our checks had resulted in some information linking him to terrorism. We intended to try to sell this convincingly since we were doing our best to ensure we had every advantage for what we understood would probably be the final round of interviews of Zacarias Moussaoui. If he thought we knew about his terrorist connections for sure, maybe he would admit it.

CHAPTER 21

GO FOR BROKE

Moussaoui looked up at us expectantly when we entered. John and I began this round not with questions, as previously, but by making statements to Moussaoui that much of what he had told us over the past two days had not checked out or had been too vague to verify. We informed Moussaoui that it was obvious he had not been telling us the truth about his business connections, his past employment, his associates, his reasons for being in the United States, and his true purpose for flight training. As he listened, his facial expression progressed from neutral, to wary, to angry, with a set jaw and narrowed eyes.

When he spoke, Moussaoui, as expected, responded angrily, and began shouting at us that he had been telling us the truth. He started repeating that he was a legitimate businessman who was simply in the United States to learn to fly.

Because this was an early instance where we directly accused Moussaoui of lying, it was a key point in the interviews.

Moussaoui's response said it all.

It is an axiom taught to new investigators in "Law Enforcement Interviewing 101" that any person who is telling the truth reacts angrily at being accused of lying. While individual responses vary widely based on the person's temperament, mood, and relationship with their accuser, no one likes being called a liar when they are really being truthful, and this shows in their emotional response. Even if the person does not lose control, the signs of anger are there.

As a survival instinct, humans are very adept at sensing the emotions of others, especially when that mood is anger. This is especially true in the case of law enforcement interviewers engaging in behavior which should elicit an angry response, like accusing someone of lying. When a person who is directly accused of lying does not become angry, it is an obvious flag.

This is because someone who really *is* lying generally does not become resentful at being accused of this but instead changes their approach and tries to persuade their accuser that they are telling the truth. They feel a strong need to convince the person of their truthfulness. One thing they seldom do is react with anger because they know that what they said *is a lie*, and therefore that the accuser is correct. In the case of someone who has not been trained in deception or who is not an accomplished liar, there is no anger, only persistent attempts to convince their accuser they are telling the truth. Put another way, being called a liar is deeply offensive—unless of course you really are lying.

Because Moussaoui's baseline demeanor throughout the two days of interviews had been emotionally charged already, he should have been enraged at being told by us that nothing he said over the previous two days was true. When we began itemizing his lies to him, he responded quickly and in a raised voice as you might expect of a truthful person. He glared at us and began loudly repeating the same vague and unverifiable explanations which had prevailed over the last two days. Despite the volume of his voice and his gestures and facial expressions, careful observation of his verbal and non-verbal communications showed he was not actually angry.

Posturing and histrionics aside, we could see Moussaoui was in full control of himself. He did not stand up abruptly, his muscles were not tense, his jaw not clenched, and his eyes were alert and continually searching ours to see whether we were being persuaded by his vehement denials and explanations. In short, Moussaoui was not truly angry. ***He was lying.***

John then smoothly transitioned to direct accusations. He informed Moussaoui that we were aware that he was participating in flight training to conduct a terrorist attack and then stopped to let him fill the silence. Moussaoui did. He began denying this, claiming all his answers were true. He was responding vehemently and forcefully, but now plainly looked extremely concerned at what John said. We listened impassively, faces neutral at his continued explanations. As Moussaoui received no reaction from us, his denials slowed and then stopped.

When it became clear he was not going to make any admissions, I spoke up again and informed Moussaoui that his suspicious behavior and obviously false story made it clear that he was a terrorist. I hinted that our checks on his name, (which, in truth had not yielded anything at that point), showed his ties to terrorism. Moussaoui now looked alarmed, and made only a few denials, shaking his head and gesturing, but watching me the entire time. I kept my face expressionless, as did John.

I continued, explaining to Moussaoui that we were aware others were involved in his plans. "You know, Mr. Moussaoui, they're free, but you're in custody. If they go ahead with whatever all of you are planning and people are hurt or killed, you will be the one the American people hold responsible. Why would you want to be the one to take all the blame?" I thought this might work.

It did not.

Moussaoui had been looking back and forth between John and me as each of us spoke in turn. He had stopped yelling at us in response to our accusations and was clearly listening...and thinking. Moussaoui was obviously worried because first John and then I had accused him of being a terrorist. We explained information in the possession of the U.S. Government had confirmed this and we informed him that he better come clean before getting into more trouble. Instead of reacting the way 99% of the innocent population would at being accused of being a terrorist, Moussaoui, continued responding abnormally, trying to *persuade us* that we were wrong instead of flatly denying it.

Now think of how any innocent person would react to being accused of this or any serious crime. Most people would deny it vehemently. In addition to making strong and genuinely angry denials I am certain I would ask to see the evidence against me and want an explanation of who was accusing me. While I might respond politely at first, continued insistence that I was a liar and a terrorist would likely make me angry quickly.

While Al-Attas might have grown up in Saudi Arabia, where staying polite in the face of law enforcement accusations was necessary to avoid being beaten, or worse, Moussaoui was born and raised in France and educated in the UK, both democracies with limits on police powers, just like the U.S. Moussaoui knew we were not going to beat him up. Besides, he had been anything but cordial from the second we met him and certainly was not being cooperative or accommodating because he was afraid of us. Given this already hostile demeanor towards us, being called a terrorist should have provoked enraged responses and a severe challenge to his self-control.

But Moussaoui showed no signs of this. He was clearly trying to figure out how much we really might know about his true past and his actual mission. It was practically written on his face. We could see his mind racing as he considered his options. Far from losing control, Moussaoui was thinking fast and rationally.

Understanding this, John continued to press. He stood up and leaned towards Moussaoui without speaking and paused for effect. Moussaoui looked at him almost eagerly, as if unable to look away. Calmly, but with certainty, John said, "Mr. Moussaoui, we know you are a member of a group planning to carry out an attack in the United States using airplanes." He paused. Seeing the alarm on Moussaoui's face, he continued, "Please tell us about the plot. Tell us who else is involved. Tell us which Islamic scholars or leaders you are following."

It was a great line of questioning and was delivered masterfully. John's words were calculated to show Moussaoui that we knew everything and to present him with the inescapable conclusion he should be telling us the truth. Although we did not yet have any confirmation of this beyond circumstantial evidence, telling Moussaoui we did was a worthwhile gamble. John was basing this question on our knowledge of how terrorist groups (especially al Qaeda) operated because we knew this had a good chance of ringing true to Moussaoui. We were both hoping that this would persuade Moussaoui to begin telling the truth.

At the mention of the word "group" Moussaoui became panicked. I could see new beads of sweat form on his forehead and watched as his eyes widened, at first fixed on John's face, then looking away. Even though John continued talking for thirty seconds or more after telling Moussaoui we knew he was a member of a group, Moussaoui was clearly no longer listening. The word "group," which produced the surge of emotion, now shut Moussaoui down.

What Moussaoui did do when John paused was open and close his mouth a few times without speaking, his eyes still wide with fear. When he finally said something, Moussaoui swallowed and then spoke much more quietly than usual. Looking at neither of us directly, Moussaoui stated in his distinctive French accent that since we believed he was a member of a group, he thought it would be best for him to speak to an immigration lawyer. In making this statement, Moussaoui did not yell or gesture. His effect had gone flat.

John and I looked at one another. No sweeping admissions. No confession. And even the "facts" which Moussaoui had given us and which we still needed to check out, would prove to be lies. We both understood we were done interviewing Moussaoui. This is because all questioning must stop once a person who is in custody asks for an attorney or refuses to speak further. It is the law.

Moussaoui would now be transported to Sherburne County Jail which would be his home until he was removed from the U.S. We watched him walk out, his body odor swirling after him and filling the room. Both of us understood that unless Moussaoui agreed to talk again and waived his right to an attorney for a second time, we were finished speaking with him.

Because we were concerned that Moussaoui might attempt to contact associates from jail to warn them of his arrest or provide them other instructions, John asked the detention officers transporting Moussaoui to ask the deputies at Sherburne County not to allow him to make phone calls to anyone but an attorney. The officers agreed to relay this request to the staff when they booked him in. John followed this up the next day with a call to the Sherburne County Jail to request this himself. The jail agreed to limit Moussaoui's telephone use and to contact John should he attempt to use the phone.

CHAPTER 22

NEXT STEPS

By now, it was after 7 p.m. and we were beat. We had done four intense subject interviews and spoken to five witnesses in two days. Our efforts resulted in two arrests and mounting evidence of a terrorist plot involving airliners. As we talked it out, it became clear what we needed to do next.

Despite Moussaoui's refusal to cooperate, we were optimistic we could still bring the case to a successful conclusion. Because of deft thinking on John's part the day before, much of the evidence we thought we needed in the form of Moussaoui's possessions in Room 1414 of the Residence Inn in Eagan was preserved.

From what I could see as I helped to carry his property to the car that first evening, Moussaoui was a prolific notetaker. We also had Moussaoui's all-important laptop computer which he had proven so anxious to protect. As I looked inside the case to see whether there was anything dangerous, I saw there were a few floppy disks in addition to the laptop itself. All these belongings now resided safely in the INS evidence room. Much like the proverbial buried wooden chests of pirate days, John and I felt strongly these materials would yield treasure in the form of clues as to what Moussaoui was planning and who his associates were. We just had to get the information.

The problem, which we hoped would prove temporary, is that Moussaoui had twice denied us permission to look through these items. And in the absence of facts which told us there was an imminent threat to life, we needed a search warrant. To obtain one, the government must demonstrate that probable cause exists to believe a crime has been committed. The standard for "probable cause" is that you should be able to swear in front of a judge that based on the facts, you are at least 51% sure a crime has happened. The second requirement was for Agents to be willing to swear that to the best of their knowledge evidence of the crime could be found in the location they wanted to search. With those two pieces in place, Agents go to an Assistant United States Attorney (AUSA)—a federal prosecutor, to draft an affidavit. Once the affidavit is complete, the Agent appears before a magistrate judge with that document in hand.

The magistrate then reads the affidavit while the Agent waits. If something is not clear, the judge can ask clarifying questions. Once he or she is satisfied that probable cause exists, the magistrate places the Agent under oath and has them swear to all the facts in the affidavit. When this has been done, the magistrate then signs a second document the Agent has with them: the search warrant itself. The warrant describes the location to be searched, as well as any items to be seized as evidence, if they are present. The directions in the warrant must be rigidly adhered to in the execution of the search.

Given the facts which we had gathered in the two and a half days since the Moussaoui case was opened, John and I were sure first an AUSA and then a judge would agree we had what was needed to permit a search warrant. We just needed to get those facts down on paper in an affidavit. However, before we could even begin doing so, and this was a critical point, we needed to obtain permission from the Department of Justice, Office of Intelligence Policy Review (OIPR) to communicate these facts to the U.S. Attorney's Office in Minneapolis.

Unfortunately, no one in the Minneapolis FBI Office could communicate directly with OIPR. We had to go through Martin at FBI Headquarters. Convoluted, but that is the process that was in place in August 2001.

To get that chain of events started quickly, I was in the office early the next morning, Saturday, August 18, 2001. Once in front of my computer, I made some strategic choices. First, I did something I had never done before: the Electronic Communication (EC), which was the document I sent to FBIHQ was marked "Immediate" precedence. Immediate ECs were supposed to be responded to within 24 hours. We were told at Quantico that leads with immediate precedence were usually only set in kidnapping cases or some other event which could involve an imminent loss of life. Based on what we learned so far, this counted.

Also, instead of sending the EC to Martin in RFU, I addressed the communication to Jeb in the Iran Unit. I wanted to give the requests the best chance of being considered fairly and I considered it unlikely Martin or anyone in RFU would even give the EC a look before saying "No."

I included our Legal Attaches in London and Paris with a full explanation of our investigation to date. The EC requested that they ask their British and French counterparts whether they had ever heard of Moussaoui or Al-Attas. Although I already sent a quick email to Jay in Paris about Moussaoui earlier, the document I was drafting now was far more detailed. In addition to passing all the information we learned from our interviews, it also included a formal request for assistance from the Government of France. Finally, I copied the terrorism squad in Oklahoma City on this communication because I wanted Agents in Oklahoma City to understand what we found and to do some investigation on Moussaoui's and Al-Attas' associates who were still in Oklahoma.

Once we had permission from OIPR, I planned to ask the U.S. Attorney's Office for search warrants for the items we brought out of Room 1414, for Moussaoui's apartment in Norman, and for Moussaoui's car in Norman. I also planned to ask them to send subpoenas to Arvest Bank for Moussaoui's financial records and subpoenas to his telephone provider so I could obtain his call records. These checks would give us our best shot at learning the names of Moussaoui's associates, something he had been most reluctant to disclose.

After laying out all the facts, I ventured some opinions. One of the most important was that our investigation led us to believe that Moussaoui, Al-Attas, and others whose identities we did not yet know about were involved in a terrorist conspiracy. Furthermore, I wrote we had reason to believe this conspiracy involved a commercial aircraft. I think it is worthwhile to quote some of this EC:

> *"On the basis of investigation to date, Minneapolis has reason to believe that Moussaoui, Al-Attas and others yet unknown are conspiring to commit violations of federal criminal code as set forth in Title 18 Section 2332b, entitled Acts of terrorism transcending national boundaries, in that they are 'attempting or conspiring to destroy or damage any structures, conveyance or other real or personal property within the United States.' Further, statements made by both Moussaoui and Al-Attas demonstrate that they have used interstate and foreign commerce in furtherance of that offence.*
>
> *In addition, information developed relating to Moussaoui's training on the Boeing 747–400 aircraft gives reason to believe that he is also conspiring to commit violations as specified under Title 18 Section 32, entitled Destruction of aircraft or aircraft facilities, in that, on the basis of his possession of weapons and his preparation through physical training for violent confrontation, his plan is believed to involve the performance of violence or incapacitation of individuals on aircraft in the special aircraft jurisdiction of the United States or on any civil aircraft employed in foreign air commerce, for the purpose of seizing control of the aircraft for his own ends. Investigation has not yet shown what these ends are, but information pertaining to this is expected to be developed through future investigation."*[4]

As a finishing touch on the documents, I deviated once more from the norm, and listed Ray, our acting SAC as the approver. The

4 These paragraphs are quoted from the third document in the Zacarias Moussaoui case file, 199M-MP-60130 Serial 3. This document was introduced in the Moussaoui trial by his attorneys as Defendant's Exhibit 472 and can be found and read on the EDVA website.

usual procedure was to have the squad supervisor sign them, but I felt we needed the extra emphasis that came from the approval of the head of the office. I hoped doing so would make our requests in the EC harder to ignore. I worked on the documents that whole weekend, only stopping Sunday evening when the lengthening shadows told me night was coming.

CHAPTER 23

IN JAIL

That Monday we learned that Al-Attas was set to bond out of INS custody later in the day. A friend of his from Oklahoma City had flown up to provide the funds. This person was an African American convert to Islam with an extensive and violent criminal history who had hastened up to Minnesota to return Al-Attas to Oklahoma. Suspicious, to say the least. An interview of the friend in the lobby of the INS office yielded little, since he told one lie after another about himself, Al-Attas, and their associates in Oklahoma City.

Given the circumstances, John and I thought it made sense to speak with Al-Attas once more before he was released. So far, the only two of that little guy's associates we encountered were both demonstrably violent men. Al-Attas himself told us about Moussaoui's views on hurting non-Muslims and the friend from Oklahoma City possessed a criminal history dating back to the 1960s that spoke eloquently of a person who had no problem engaging in violence. And both had connections to Pakistan, where Al-Attas was planning to travel, and which was the gateway to Afghanistan and Al Qaeda.

We headed down to the cell block to talk to Al-Attas. He had not invoked his right to an attorney and was thus still fair game for an interview, provided he agreed to waive his Miranda rights.

When we entered his cell, I observed that Al-Attas looked even smaller and more scared than usual in his prison scrubs and molded one-piece plastic sandals. He looked up at us from the chair in which he was sitting, recognition spreading over his face. I looked for signs of anger, particularly since we were the ones responsible for his arrest. There was no sign of that, only concern.

"Hi, Hussein!" John's tone was cheerful and friendly. "How're ya holding up?"

"Okay," he replied. "I don't want to talk with you!" His face flushed red.

Anger. Plus, our little friend probably also received "legal" advice from someone in jail.

"Ok, then," I said, "Just listen." Pausing for what I hoped had the effect of conveying the seriousness of the situation, I began, "We just finished speaking with your friend, Mujahid. He flew up here today from Oklahoma to bail you out."

Al-Attas was looking at me and listening carefully.

"Doesn't it seem strange to you that a guy like him would hop on a plane with $5000 to bail you out, along with an airline ticket to fly you back the same day?" Because it was a rhetorical question, I continued, "It seems strange to me. Maybe strange isn't the right word. I'd say it's pretty scary."

Al-Attas' eyes widened slightly, almost imperceptibly. While not taking his eyes off my face, Al-Attas, probably without realizing it, slid both of his feet out of his sandals and placed them on top of them.

I continued, "Between Shaqil and Mujahid, you're hanging out with some pretty dangerous guys. You already told us about Shaqil and what he wants to do to people who don't agree with him. Then, you add Mujahid to the mix...that guy is even more violent. He's been killing people since before you were born." Killing may have been a stretch on my part, but the guy *was* an armed career criminal.

Without taking my eyes off Al-Attas's face as I spoke, I could see his feet begin nervously drumming on the tops of his sandals.

John began speaking, and Al-Attas shifted his gaze to him. "Those guys know that you know their plan. They also know you spoke to us. What do you think they're going to do about that?"

Al-Attas' eyes widened more, and the foot drumming quickened.

"If they were really just trying to help you out, they would simply bail you out of jail and let you drive back on your own." John continued, "No, Hussein, they're here to find out what we know about the plan, and you're the only guy who can tell them."

"And you signed a sworn statement for us." We paused.

Al-Attas' feet positively pounded the tops of his sandals, accompanying a tune only he could hear, his face and neck were flushed and blotchy and his forehead was now covered with sweat. I thought he might finally tell us what he knew. However, when he spoke, he chuckled slightly and seemed to get control of himself with an effort. He smiled and said, "No, they're my friends. They won't hurt me." Al-Attas spoke like someone trying to persuade himself, kind of like a kid psyching himself up to ride on the big roller coaster. He really did not sound all that convinced.

I tried to look concerned. "I sure hope you're right."

Al-Attas nodded and swallowed several times.

As we left his cell, John called over his shoulder, "Good luck."

When we were back in John's office, Steve handed us a call log and a tape of a telephone call from the Carver County Jail where Al-Attas spent the weekend. The INS transportation team had picked these up at Steve's request when they brought Al-Attas in for his hearing. That was excellent forethought on Steve's part since that phone call was almost certainly how the guy from Oklahoma City found out Al-Attas and Moussaoui were in jail in Minnesota. Although it took him awhile, Al-Attas eventually reached a male with whom he engaged in a heated conversation in a foreign language which the Sergeant presumed was Arabic. As I took the tape from Steve, I realized getting a translation of that conversation would be a priority.

CHAPTER 24

REQUESTS

The next morning, Tuesday, 08/21/2018, I completed the detailed paperwork on the initial steps of the investigation and had them signed out. Ray's initials made the documents official, including the requests. After a few hours, I followed up with a phone call to Jeb at headquarters, figuring he would have had time to get a start on reading the EC. Because things like this can fall through the cracks or otherwise go astray, I dialed Jeb's desk number to make sure he saw our request and knew what we needed, namely, quick permission from OIPR to talk to the U.S. Attorney's Office.

Jeb answered. I informed him I just e-mailed him some documents which had just been signed out by my SAC. He acknowledged that he saw them. Great. Continuing, I started to explain that we needed him to quickly get us permission to apply for a search warrant. Jeb stopped me. "Uh, Harry...It's pretty obvious this guy you have is not connected to Iran."

Uh oh. I did not like where this was heading. Jeb continued, "For that reason, we're handing this off to another unit here in CTD."

My heart began to race. I knew what he was about to say. "Martin from RFU was just here. I gave him the rundown on your case and forwarded him the documents. I will be re-assigning the leads to him so he can help you." Jeb sounded cheerful and upbeat, though why that was I had no idea. He was passing the buck and walking away from a chance to help on a worthy case.

Resisting the urge to scream at him or slam down the phone, I asked Jeb why he had not considered working on our requests while we tried to determine Moussaoui's exact affiliation. I pointed out that the reassignment seemed premature. Jeb hesitated but quickly regained his composure. "He's not linked to Iran, so the case belongs to RFU."

I could see this was going nowhere, so I quickly got off the phone with Jeb. He was obviously happy to pass the case off as quickly as possible.

Now, things were going to get bad.

Literally everything about my experience with Martin told me he would be working hard to prevent this case from getting the attention it deserved. Although I tried to avoid having him touch this investigation, circumstances pushed the Moussaoui matter right back into his lap. For better or worse, the fate of the case was now under his control. And it would be worse, much worse.

Therefore, after taking 30 seconds to get my emotions under control, I called Martin. Just hearing his voice when he answered caused my pulse to quicken, but I consciously worked hard to remain calm and professional. I explained Jeb had just informed me the new investigation on Moussaoui had been transferred to RFU. "Yes. SSA Jeb explained some facts about your new case." Officious, as always.

Despite my perception that his tone did not sound encouraging, I persisted, "Okay, well, what we would like to do is for you to go to DOJ/OIPR to get us authorization to go to the U.S. Attorney's Office. We want to speak to an AUSA so we can obtain a search warrant for..."

Martin's hasty interruption, while not unexpected, was still annoying, "Whoa! Give me some time to read your documents and speak with my Unit Chief. Then *we'll* decide what to do."

"Right," I thought. "A person 1200 miles away prefers to read what I wrote rather than listening to what I am trying to tell him! Then, once he is sure he has the picture based on what we learned, he and his boss will decide what to do."

"Okay, Martin. But there is a time crunch here. We do not have all the subject's associates identified and we urgently need to view what is on his laptop and among his personal items. A search warrant is our best bet."

Martin's replies continued to be irritating, "Well, did you ask for consent from him to search that stuff?"

"Yes, several times. He emphatically denied it. He grew up in France and was educated in the UK so he knew he could deny us permission, and did..."

Another interruption, this time with a little snicker, "When I was in the field, we had ways of getting around that."

Despite every fiber of my being wanting to scream at the absurdity of what Martin had just said, I remained silent, no small feat for me in any circumstance. Once a person denies a law enforcement officer consent to search his property, there are no legal options left for that officer to do so, absent a threat to life or a search warrant. I was not aware of any "ways to get around that" that were constitutional. Martin's suggestion that he was somehow wise and experienced enough to get around the knotty problem of the Bill of Rights was stupid. And it implied we missed an opportunity.

Trying my hardest to sound reasonable, I continued, "Well, he denied consent. So, we need a search warrant from the U.S. Attorney's Office to see what he was planning and who else is involved. I don't see another option."

"That's not true. There is another option. You could apply for a FISA warrant."

Martin's suggestion caught me off guard. Several of us had been down the FISA application route with him before, and along with making it abundantly clear he did not like going to the FISA court, he also made the application process slow and extremely painful for us in the past. Clearly under some imaginary stress and in fear of being sanctioned by higher FBI or DOJ authority, Martin had been short-tempered and quarrelsome throughout the time it took to prod, cajole, and beg him to move the FISA application along last time. Now he was suggesting we might apply for a FISA?

"Why a FISA, Martin? We have significant probable cause to believe a crime is being committed. What we do not have is a compelling nexus to a foreign power."

"I am just telling you there are other options." His tone indicated he was weary of this back-and-forth. "My Unit Chief and I will discuss this and get back to you, but I am not sure you have enough..."

Now I interrupted, "Not sure we have enough? How can you say that? Our office just spent the last five days investigating this and compiling compelling evidence Moussaoui intends to do something involving an airliner."

Clearly irritated, Martin retorted, "I am just saying it's a high standard to get OIPR to approve going criminal. FISA may be our best option. Have you spoken to your CDC?"

That question threw me. CDC stands for Chief Division Council. Every office has one. CDCs and their assistants are Special Agents, usually experienced ones, who are also licensed and Bar certified attorneys. They are usually heavily involved in policy matters and often assist with legal issues pertaining to criminal cases. In the pre-9/11 era, I never heard of any CDC being involved in the FISA process. It certainly had not happened in Minneapolis on the FISAs we already obtained. I suspected Martin was trying to find things for me to do to slow the process down.

"Martin, we have never gone to our CDC before on any of our other FISAs. Why now?"

"Because we now have a question as to whether criminal or FISA is the appropriate route to take. Check with your CDC to see whether one of these will be appropriate. Based on what he says, we may decide which to use."

I began, "Well, I hope so. If the permission to go criminal is not approved and we are unable to apply for a FISA search warrant, I shudder to think..."

I was about to say, "I shudder to think of the threat we will be leaving unaddressed" when Martin cut me off, hard. Shouting now, he responded, "Don't you dare question my Unit Chief! He's been through a lot, and he knows these cases! We will get back to you." He hung up.

I was frustrated, but hardly surprised at Martin's reaction. It was so typical of him based on his past track record. The question was, how to keep this case moving along despite opposition from him? My first thought was to expand the scope of the investigation beyond what Martin could control. I wondered how to do that, finally hitting on an idea: It was highly conceivable that Moussaoui and his co-conspirators might be seeking to use a 747 to attack the White House and threaten the president. While no evidence of that had yet been found, Moussaoui was clearly up to no good with his flight training *and* had mentioned to us that he planned to visit the White House when we interviewed him. It was enough that I thought it might be a sensible precaution to notify the Secret Service, which was the Agency responsible for protecting the president. If the Secret Service took the threat seriously, they might pressure the FBI into a more aggressive investigative posture than Martin seemed to be prepared to take.

Spinning my chair to the left, I began typing an email to Martin. In it, I pointed out the potential threat to the president and asked that the Secret Service be informed of our case and the findings so far. I explained that any airplane which could reach New York from the UK could also reach Washington, D.C., making this a credible threat. My message was as much intended to prod Martin to action as to convey a message to the Secret Service, but I considered both goals worthwhile.

If I thought that my conversation with Martin or the follow-up Secret Service email would provoke a quick response, I was disappointed. By lunchtime, my impatience overcame my desire to appear professional, much less patient, and I called Martin again.

"So, Martin...any chance we'll get permission to go to the U.S. Attorney's Office today?"

His reply was a flat, "No." After a pause, he continued, "I spoke with Devin, my Unit Chief. He wants you apply for a FISA instead of applying for a criminal search warrant."

I started to argue, and Martin cut me off, again, "He said you can call him if you want, and he will explain the reasons for his decision."

Because Martin had been nothing but an obstructionist on this and other cases, I jumped at the chance to bring the issue to his boss.

"Ok, thanks. I'll call him now." I hung up. It would be impossible to overstate the emotional toll it took on someone with my personality to continue to be cordial to Martin, someone who was so obviously working to undermine what our team in Minneapolis was doing. But because I cared about the case, I had to continue doing so to avoid giving him an excuse to stop working altogether.

CHAPTER 25

DENIED

As I dialed Unit Chief Devin's number, my pulse quickened. Devin answered his own phone and when I explained who I was, he responded as if he was expecting my call. He sounded pleasant enough. This continued as he seemed to listen to what I had to say. After I finished explaining our need for a criminal search warrant, Devin replied that he understood, but that his concern was that our evidence linking Moussaoui to criminal activity was weak. Although I disagreed, I did not say so directly but noted that there was a great deal of suspicious activity, none of which had been explained by the subjects in our interviews.

"I agree." I was shocked to hear someone at headquarters saying that. Devin continued, "But the problem is that a judge may not. If we go to a judge for a criminal search warrant and the request is denied, we will have to disclose the fact of a denial to a FISA Court judge when we apply for a FISA search warrant. It will make it much harder to get a FISA search approved then."

That made sense. I did not want to be in an even deeper hole by having to tell a FISA court judge that a magistrate in Minnesota had turned us down. However, I knew that at least one magistrate judge in Minnesota was pro-government when it came to FBI terrorism cases. The Honorable J. Earl Cudd was a tall, thin elderly jurist who ran his courtroom with dignity and decorum. I'd participated in a few hearings in his courtroom before and knew Judge Cudd ruled favorably for the government when we had solid facts on our side. I told Devin about him and about an aggressive AUSA in the office who would help.

"You can't take that chance" Devin replied. "You will have to apply for a FISA warrant. Martin will help."

While I was not exactly happy with this decision, it was not yet a disaster. We needed access to Moussaoui's possessions, and I was not picky how we obtained this, provided it was legal. Both the criminal search warrant and the one obtained in FISA court were signed by federal judges, so they were equally effective. My only real objection to the FISA technique was that Martin needed to be involved. Now his boss had taken the time to hear me out and to explain his rationale for wanting to pick one technique over the other. Finally, Devin pledged Martin's assistance in pushing the FISA application through. Not my Plan A, but a solid Plan B.

"Okay. We are also preparing to open a parallel criminal case." As I said this, I glanced down at the form I had already filled out requesting the opening of a 265 matter, a criminal investigation of terrorism. However, before doing so, we needed headquarters' permission to open the case. I thought I was being clever by sneaking this verbal request in while speaking with Devin, rather than passing it via Martin. I figured that if I could get Devin to approve it while we were on the phone, Martin would have a much harder time stopping it later.

That hope was dashed when Devin responded, "No. Don't open a parallel case. Since we're going FISA, you won't need it. Everything you have will be classified under FISA."

Sighing inaudibly, I began to get a sense Devin was just a smoother and more experienced obstructionist than Martin. For every fact I raised, he politely but firmly presented an objection. Despite the softer tone, he was still saying "No" to every one of my requests and completely ignoring the underlying facts, and the danger. Because of this, as soon as I hung up, I wrote on the now useless opening form, "Criminal case not opened on 08/21/2001 per the instructions of Devin."

Sitting back in my chair I thought, "Now what?" After deliberating for a minute, I decided to call for a quick meeting of the team to discuss what we should do next. Once we were assembled Joe reiterated what we all understood: to obtain a FISA, we now needed to prove Moussaoui was an Agent of a Foreign Power. As I learned from Harold's training session at Quantico months before, a Foreign Power is defined as a government or terrorist group not substantially composed of United States persons. Under the law, we needed to link Moussaoui to one of those.

Running through the facts acquired so far, I realized we were not there yet. The most logical Foreign Power for this case under the standard definition was "a group engaged in international terrorism or activities in preparation therefor," but other than Al-Attas' statements about Moussaoui's interest in hurting non-Muslims and his one reference to Usama Bin Laden, we had no factual basis to connect him to a terrorist group. We needed more.

Because Moussaoui had been so evasive in answering questions about his life before arriving in the U.S., we had little to go on as far as linking him to any overseas organization. A look at the reference guide I kept on my desk showed there were more than a dozen Sunni Islamic extremist groups which had been identified and designated by the U.S. State Department as foreign terrorist organizations (FTOs). There were even more groups which had been identified and were known to be operational, but which, for a variety of reasons, did not yet carry a State Department designation as an FTO.

A quick word on the importance to our story of a group being designated a Foreign Terrorist Organization. Once a group has been designated as an FTO, it makes charging members under federal criminal terrorism statutes much more straightforward. What it does not do, is change the equation under FISA. It does not matter under FISA whether the Foreign Power is a designated FTO or not. If the group is engaged in "international terrorism or activities in preparation therefor," *it is a Foreign Power under FISA law*. We therefore just needed a terrorist group, any terrorist group. The meeting broke up with no clear resolution to break the deadlock, but at least we had a goal.

Because I wanted to be seen to be following headquarters' instructions to the letter, I made the trek up two flights of stairs to the 11th floor to see our Chief Division Counsel. Martin had instructed me to consult with our CDC, and I was going to do so, however absurd the request. I did not want to leave him any excuse to delay or refuse our requests for a search warrant.

Despite Martin's use of the "he" pronoun, our CDC was a Special Agent we will call Celia, a female veteran of more than 20 years in the FBI. Because she had not been involved in *any* terrorism cases in Minneapolis since I arrived, I had no professional interactions with her. My only encounters with Celia were at firearms and other group settings where she came across as mildly eccentric with her large glasses and rapid and earnest way of speaking. She was a slender, petite woman of around 50, with silver hair, usually pulled back. When she addressed other Agents, it was always as "Mr. Samit," or "Ms. Heiser," like a very formal high school English teacher. I never heard her use another employee's first name. Celia seemed nice enough, but I knew nothing of her legal acumen or background working cases.

As I approached her office, I could hear Celia was on the phone. While I should have turned around and come back later, I was impatient (I usually am) and wanted to obtain her verdict on whether we should go FISA or criminal. I stepped into view of her desk, which faced the door.

Celia looked up, still in mid-sentence. I was hoping she would either cut the call short while I waited, or at least know I needed her help, so she could call me at my desk when she was done on the phone. She did neither of these. Celia told the caller on the other end to hold on and held the handset against her chest. Looking at me, she said, "Yes?"

"I have a new terrorism case and headquarters asked me to come get your opinion on whether we should go to the U.S. Attorney's Office or seek a FISA for a physical search of the subject's effects. The subject paid big bucks for some highly unusual flight training in a way that suggests a possible hijacking. He already denied us consent to search. I think we have enough to go to criminal, but headquarters is concerned that if we do that, and come up short, we will have to disclose that to the FISA court when we apply for a FISA warrant. Our headquarters unit has been somewhat less than eager to advance FISA requests in the past, and I know AUSA Peg would be interested in helping get this pushed through to a magistrate." I wanted to explain more, but Celia had not invited me into her office and was still holding the phone as she looked at me through her too-large glasses.

"Maybe, but the guys on the criminal squads have been having trouble over there (at the U.S. Attorney's Office) lately. Stuff has been getting kicked back on the thinnest of pretexts." With that, Celia looked at me. I disagreed with her. Despite her pessimism, my experience with Peg had been good, a fact Celia did not consider. When I did not begin speaking again immediately, Celia flipped the phone back up to her ear and resumed the call. Our legal consultation over, Celia and I would not discuss this case, or anything else again until the morning of September 11.

Much to my disappointment, Celia's hastily considered opinion had not given me any ammunition with which to refute the Devin-Martin theory that FISA was the way to go. Still, I had done what Martin asked me to, and I was hopeful that would shut down any suggestion that I was not following headquarters' instructions or that I was not sufficiently energized on the case to run down all possible angles which might help us gain additional insight.

At the end of the day, I went home to my still-empty house and ate dinner. The case was obviously on my mind, making it hard to concentrate on working to replace the stairs on my deck, which was my major project for the time Terri and the boys were away. I needed to talk to someone with insight and Chris was that guy. Since moving up to ASAC, Chris had been staying clear of JTTF cases because these were under Ray's branch. Chris was assigned to the criminal branch and was careful not to be seen to intrude on investigations overseen by the other ASAC. I needed some intrusion now. As he had when he was my supervisor, Chris answered his cell phone immediately, even though it was 8:30 p.m.

As usual, Chris had an answer to my problems: he suggested I call Chuck at CIA.

That made sense. Chuck was an FBI supervisor at the Unit Chief level. Instead of being assigned to work at FBIHQ, he was detailed to CIA Headquarters in Langley, Virginia. In his assignment, Chuck handled important exchanges of information between our two agencies. He could harness CIA's considerable resources to help with our investigation.

CHAPTER 26

FRANCE TO THE RESCUE

The morning of August 22 dawned as the proceeding ones had, with my house empty of the sounds of my wife and kids. The one good thing was that I was busy, my days spent with the Moussaoui case and my nights working on projects around the house. Terri and the boys were due home in a few days, and I was glad about that. Time was passing quickly, the more so because I was haunted by the nagging feeling we were in a race with an unseen group of terrorists who might be moving forward to continue with plans for the attack.

When I arrived at the office early, as had become a recent habit, I logged into my computer and was excited to see an e-mail from Jay in Paris. Attached was an EC, drafted earlier that day by Jay, which relayed some information from the French authorities. As I read, my pulse quickened with excitement and by the time I was finished reading the short EC I was convinced the investigation was saved. The French were aware of Moussaoui. Moreover, I could see they sent their response very quickly, almost immediately in fact. And Jay was quick too! Not only had he sent off my request to the French immediately, but he also had to translate their response into English before emailing it to us in Minneapolis. A varsity investigative performance!

The French explained that their investigators became aware of Moussaoui because of his association with a fighter in Chechnya, whose alias was Masood Al-Benin. I knew Islamic extremists had been fighting the Russians in Chechnya since the 1990s, and that made anyone who fought there a concern. Al-Benin had a father from the African country of Benin and a French mother. The French informed us Al-Benin died in Chechnya on April 12, 2000, *fighting with the mujahideen.* Their document went on to say that Al-Benin was a computer expert and worked for Emir Al-Khattab Ibn, aka Al Soualiem Samer, a Saudi known as the Black Arabian and a leader in Chechnya. Jay saved the best for last. Following Al-Benin's death, French authorities interviewed an associate of Al-Benin, who informed them *he was recruited to go to Chechnya by Zacarias Moussaoui.* The interviewee also stated that Moussaoui was "the dangerous one."

By the time I got to the end of the EC, I was reaching for the phone to dial Jay's number. Even though it was 7 a.m. in Minneapolis, Paris was 7 hours ahead of us, so it was early afternoon there. Jay answered right away. "Apparently the French know all about your boy," he began. "That guy Al-Benin who died in Chechnya was of interest to them. They follow up and investigate all French citizens who are killed fighting overseas for the mujahideen. There was a big write up on Al-Benin on a jihadi website. I'll send it to you. What's your fax number?"

I quickly passed it to Jay and thanked him profusely for his assistance. I explained to Jay that headquarters was leaning towards making us go the FISA route, despite our strong preference for a criminal search warrant. "Well then, the info from the French should help," he said.

Jay was so right. I spent the previous evening on the phone with Chris lamenting the fact that Devin and Martin were forcing us to apply for a FISA search warrant for Moussaoui, even though we had no information linking him to a Foreign Power. This one document, arriving as it did in such a timely fashion, provided compelling intelligence which proved that link. If Moussaoui recruited a person who was later killed fighting for the Chechen Mujahideen, that was proof he had worked on their behalf. It was the very definition of "Agent of a Foreign Power." I did not know a lot about the Chechens, but I was pretty sure they were "a group or organization not comprised primarily of U.S. persons" as defined in the FISA law and explained to me in training by Harold.

Jay signed off, promising to fax the internet information on Al-Benin.

Now alone with my thoughts, I was so elated after I reread the EC, I stood excitedly and looked around my still-empty squad area for someone with whom to share the news. No one was there yet. Even still, I was sure we would soon be viewing the contents of Moussaoui's belongings which he had been so eager to conceal.

I snapped out of it when I heard the fax machine beep and whirr to life. It was the fax from Jay. The contents were a printout of several pages of the "Jihad in Chechnya" website from Qoqaz.net. These contained an article entitled, Story: Qoqaz.net Correspondent Shaheed Masood Al-Benin, martyred 12 April 2000. A quick glance showed this was an article memorializing the service in Chechnya of Masood Al-Benin. More accurately, the article referred to Al-Benin as *Shaheed* Masood Al-Benin. "Shaheed" is a title bestowed on a Muslim who dies as a martyr fighting in a jihad.

The article was a well-written English language propaganda piece describing the life and death of Al-Benin. According to the article, Al-Benin was born to a "blue eyed native French woman" with his father being described as a "tall African man from Benin." Apparently, Al-Benin was not raised as a Muslim. The article detailed how Al-Benin went from France to the UK to continue his studies. It was while he was pursuing his master's degree in business studies that Al-Benin became a Muslim, in the words of the article, "Allah opened his heart to Islam." Following this, Al-Benin learned about the importance to his new religion of jihad and met some ex-mujihadeen. As the article explained, Al-Benin "had become surprisingly alarmed of how Muslims had neglected the duty of Jihad, during a period whereby Muslims were being slaughtered in large numbers across the globe."

This was solid information. As I was to learn during many subsequent investigations, terrorists feel very free discuss the activities of colleagues who are deceased. Because Al-Benin was dead, whoever wrote the article discussed his thoughts and actions in detail, with the goal of inspiring others to fight. It was a big departure from the extreme secrecy usually practiced by terrorists, for whom security is paramount. Secrecy was so important because it preserved their ability to move between the West and conflict zones like Afghanistan and Chechnya. They understood that if the governments of the West were aware of their participation in a jihad, they would be viewed as a threat. Because Al-Benin was dead, this was not a concern and the author shared freely, hoping others would be eager to emulate him.

The article described the journey of a man from France to the UK for business studies and a master's degree. Once in the UK, Al-Benin became a Muslim, learned about jihad, met some former fighters, and resolved to travel to fight. The article explained that although Al-Benin originally wanted to fight in Afghanistan, one of his associates, Abu Azzam, was able to plan travel to Chechnya during 1994–1996, and Al-Benin and a third associate, Mu'adh, decided to go there. The article went on to explain that Al-Benin remained in Chechnya for several years, contributing greatly to the jihad, and rising in esteem and responsibility among his colleagues. In particular, the article noted his knowledge of computers was an asset to the Chechen Mujihadeen, both for setting up networks for their court system, and for editing propaganda videos produced by them. Inevitably, the article concludes by describing the wounded Al-Benin's heroic death at the hands of the Russians, noting he "preferred to die rather than to fall into the hands of the cowards." In doing so, he was killed on April 12, 2000. The article appeared to have been written by someone close to Al-Benin less than two weeks later, on April 25, 2000.

I noticed right away that like Moussaoui, Al-Benin was raised in France and traveled to the UK for master's degree studies in business. Also, like Moussaoui, Al-Benin developed a strong, and in his case fatal interest in jihad.

Obviously, the French information was of great relevance to our investigation. With two documents, our allies neatly solved our foreign power problem. Although I still planned to call Chuck at CIA that morning, this was less of an immediate concern now that we had our FISA question answered.

I was optimistic as I dialed Martin's number. I was hopeful that I would have some good will in the bank with him since I had not fought too hard against his suggestion that the FISA warrant was the way to go as opposed to my idea of a criminal warrant. Also, within a day of his suggestion, the investigation had provided compelling links to the Chechen Mujihadeen, meaning we had our foreign power. Things were looking good!

No.

To my disbelief and growing anger as I listened, Martin snorted as I informed him of the French information and summarized what I had read over the phone. "Send me that stuff, and we'll see."

Suppressing yet again my urge to scream at Martin, I provided him with the Serial number of Jay's EC so he could pull it off the system. I then faxed him the pages sent to me by Jay.

When Martin called me back later that day, he provided his answer with a question, "How do we know the Moussaoui guy that INS arrested is the same person as the guy mentioned by the French?"

Martin's entire question was preposterous. First, Moussaoui was arrested by the FBI and INS, working as part of the JTTF. While the arrest was on INS authority, it was a terrorism case and there were two FBI Agents present and involved. I ignored Martin's reference to INS, believing it was merely a barb, trying to needle me. What I was to discover later was that this was the opening shot of a multi-front campaign, one aspect of which was to claim that the Moussaoui was strictly an INS problem.

"Well, Martin," I said with rising anger, "we passed the French Moussaoui's passport, complete with photograph. You read their response. The French are sure we have the same guy. Also, the background of the Moussaoui I arrested and interviewed closely matches Al-Benin's. It's the same guy."

"No. The FISA court won't accept that. We'll need more."

"What more could you possibly need?"

"How many Moussaouis are there in France?"

"What?"

Martin spoke as if he was explaining a complex subject to a three-year-old, "We need to persuade the FISA court there is no mistake. One way of doing that is telling the court how many people named Moussaoui there are in France."

I exploded, "And how would we do that?"

Martin responded just as angrily, "Have the LEGAT go through phone books!"

It was obvious what Martin was doing: he was trying to delay our request, and I was not having it. "We're not doing that! How would you find out how many Moussaouis there are? It's not possible."

"Well, that's what you're going to have to do. Have the LEGAT check phone books in France to see how many Moussaouis there are in there. Then we'll know."

"Martin, that's ridiculous, and you know it. How would the LEGAT even do that?"

"We'll need to provide an answer to the question of how many people with that name live in France." Without waiting for my response, Martin ended the argument by hanging up.

It was time to call Chuck at CIA Headquarters.

CHAPTER 27

THE INTELLIGENCE ANGLE

In August 2001, Chuck was the senior FBI Agent assigned as a liaison to CIA. He was the conduit of information between our agencies' headquarters. If I could persuade Chuck to take an interest in our case, then he should be able to bring the whole of CIA's capabilities to bear. This was particularly important in Moussaoui's case since he was born and raised overseas and, until February of 2001 had never been to the U.S. Therefore, it stood to reason there was a good chance CIA would have something on him.

Chuck answered his own phone. He seemed a little gruff, but pleasant enough. I explained I was on the JTTF in Minneapolis and that my ASAC was Chris, who he knew, so dropping the name helped. I went on to say that we had a *highly* unusual investigation. As I began to explain the facts of our case, I could tell Chuck was growing interested and listened patiently, occasionally jumping in to ask a question or make a comment. When I got to the end, he asked, "So what do you need from here?"

I explained that our original plan had been to obtain a criminal search warrant for Moussaoui's belongings, but that RFU thought FISA was the more appropriate route. Because intelligence was the fuel that drove FISA requests we were hoping to obtain information from CIA which would bolster our argument. In my first contact with Chuck, I refrained from describing Martin's obstructionist efforts, mostly because I did not know where he stood.

Chuck seemed to get it right away. "What can you send me?"

"I'll shoot you the opening EC on e-mail as soon as we hang up."

Reassuringly, Chuck responded, "Do it! I'll see what these guys have for you."

Within one minute of hanging up, I did just that. Most significantly, I added a paragraph summarizing the information we just received from the French, including Moussaoui's role in recruiting Al-Benin to fight for the Chechan Mujihadeen. That was all the information we had so I hoped there was enough in what I sent to give CIA a start.

With that sent, I felt better. Chuck sounded reassuring and it was nice to have someone in authority outside of the Minneapolis Office who agreed with us that Moussaoui and his associates were up to no good.

Around this time, I remembered Cathy. Like Chuck, Cathy was an FBI Agent detailed to another partner agency, in her case, [Redacted by the FBI]. More importantly for my current needs, [Redacted by the FBI] also uses its considerable capabilities to spy on the communications of unfriendly countries, as well as terrorist groups. They are therefore privy to some of the most sensitive and helpful information about the bad guys, mostly because they overhear them speaking in their own words.

I met Cathy the year before at the same in-service training where I learned about the intricacies of the FISA Act from Harold. Cathy came to speak to my class about her role at [Redacted by the FBI], and to sell the capabilities of the Agency. She came across as polished and competent, and most importantly like the highly experienced 20+ year Agent that she was. Now, months later, I was glad I had a way to contact her.

I dashed off a quick e-mail to Cathy, explaining my case and attaching some documents which summarized our findings. I asked whether her colleagues at [Redacted by the FBI] would check to see whether Moussaoui had ever come up in their collection. Cathy responded quickly to my email acknowledging she had what she needed and would ask the right people at [Redacted by the FBI] to see whether they heard of Moussaoui.

The next day, August 23, 2001, marked a week since Moussaoui's arrest. That afternoon, I received a call from Scott in Oklahoma City. In response to my request for investigation sent the day before, the JTTF there had been busy. He spent the day conducting interviews in Norman on our case. Scott explained he visited Airmen Flight School and spoke to Moussaoui's instructors and some administrative staff there who dealt with Moussaoui. Although they provided some background on him, no one at the school admitted to knowing anything about Moussaoui being an extremist or having violent ideas.

He had more. After leaving the school, he headed to 209A Wadsack Drive, the residence Al-Attas claimed he shared with Moussaoui. "Gee, thanks, Scott," I began, "I am curious to know what you found there!"

"Yeah, well...that's the thing. While we were on the way over, this supervisor from headquarters called and told us not to make a big deal over this. He asked that we not stir things up."

I felt my face get hot as I stammered, "Was the SSA named Martin?"

"Yes. He said he has this case at headquarters and they're trying to keep it from getting out of control."

I kept calm, but barely. "So, did you turn around?"

"No, we went to Al-Attas' apartment, but we kept it pretty low-key." Scott filled me in on some details he got from speaking with Al-Attas. It was obvious Al-Attas was doubling down on his story and trying to distance himself from Moussaoui.

Still trying to control my temper, I thanked Scott. He promised to get the EC detailing the information to us right away.

After I hung up, I sat there, stunned. In my time in the FBI, I had sent plenty of leads to other offices and covered many leads in Minneapolis for other offices too. But never had I heard of a supervisor from headquarters calling another field office to dumb down an investigative request. I realized then and there that Martin was no longer passively letting time slip away on the Moussaoui case. He was now actively interfering.

I relayed the news of Martin's meddling in Oklahoma City. Greg was the one who signed that EC out requesting investigation, so I was hoping he would be as indignant as I was. As I described what Scott said about Martin's call preventing in-depth investigation, Greg frowned. "I'll call him," he said.

I was encouraged and headed back to my desk.

CHAPTER 28

SUPPORT FROM LANGLEY

I was reading through e-mails a few minutes later when I noticed Greg at my desk, notepad in hand. Greg frowned, "That guy is a piece of work!"

"Uh oh. What now?"

"So, Mike told me we do not have enough for a criminal search warrant."

"Right. He told me that, too. So did his unit chief."

"Yes, but now he's saying we don't have enough for a FISA, either."

"What? How is that possible? We have information from the French linking him to the jihad in Chechnya!" Joe came over from his desk to listen to Greg.

Greg went on to explain that the jihadists fighting in Chechnya, collectively referred to at the time by the U.S. Intelligence Community as the "Chechen Mujihadeen," were not a "named group." Greg, who had less experience in international terrorism investigations than Joe and I then asked, "What is the legal definition of a 'named group?'"

Joe snorted angrily, "There isn't one. It's made up." He laughed bitterly.

Pulling the binder out of my desk which contained printouts of the PowerPoint presentation from Harold's FISA class, I began flipping through the slides, looking for something which referred to a "named group." I reached the end without finding anything. As usual,

Joe was right. "Named group" was a term Martin invented to impose ever higher, but completely false standards on us.

Looking down at the end of the PowerPoint, I saw Harold's last slide included his phone number. Remembering his briefing concluded with a description of how it was his job to help us get the FISA we needed, I decided to call him. Who better than the FBI's self-proclaimed FISA expert to set Martin straight?

When I spoke to Harold, I did not receive the promised-for assistance. In fact, in stark contrast to his manner in the briefing at Quantico, Harold sounded cold and unhelpful on the phone. I explained what we had learned so far in our case, to include being in receipt, in writing, of intelligence from a friendly foreign service that linked Moussaoui to the jihad in Chechnya. I explained our position that the Chechen Mujihadeen was the foreign power. Harold was lukewarm to this, responding that it was not a sure thing.

Growing more concerned, I began reading his own slides to him from the still-open binder on my desk. I particularly emphasized the information which described Foreign Powers as any group not substantially comprised of U.S. persons. I concluded by saying, "Martin from RFU is misinterpreting the law. There is no such thing as a 'named group' under the FISA. We have our foreign power."

Unfortunately, Harold backtracked hard on his earlier bombastic claims. Sounding like a completely different person, he informed me that the FISA court might not agree with that, and that Martin was "a good man." Harold assured me that his judgement was sound.

Likely because I was pretty much at my limit on stonewalling by headquarters, but also in part because Harold had sold a bill of goods which he was not clearly delivering, I was much less diplomatic than previously. "No, Harold, he's not. Our experience with him in Minneapolis has not been positive. Martin has already explained to me how he has no intention of going to the FISA court because of the possibility of mistakes. We have our foreign power. Our application should go to the court."

Harold listened, so that was something. Ultimately, however, he pronounced himself unconvinced. In the end he advised me to put the application in writing and they would see what could be done. Frustratingly noncommittal, Harold was like so many bad lawyers who promised much but delivered nothing.

Only after the 9/11 tragedy would I learn Harold had already been consulted on this case, almost certainly by Martin himself. While being interviewed by one of the numerous government bodies investigating the intelligence failures which led to the attack, I was handed a printout of an e-mail from Harold to Celia, Minneapolis' CDC. The e-mail was sent at 10:57 a.m. on 08/22/2001 and asked Celia whether she had been consulted on the Moussaoui case. Celia replied in an e-mail to him at just after 5:00 p.m. that same day that I had spoken to her about the case and that she believed that a judge would likely sign a criminal search warrant. However, because our U.S. Attorney's Office sometimes had a higher standard, she advised me to go the "other" (FISA) route.

This e-mail was clearly sent by Harold after being told by Martin that he directed me to consult with the CDC. While Harold *may* have been connecting with Celia to get her legal opinion of the merits of the case, what he was also certainly doing was checking to see whether I was doing as headquarters asked. Either way, what he was not doing was listening dispassionately to the facts. Harold was working to support RFU's conclusions, not to advance the case.

We had hit another dead end.

I decided to call Chuck at CIAHQ. It had been a day since we first spoke, and I wanted to pass him the latest news that RFU was stonewalling us on the FISA application. I explained Martin decided the Chechen Mujihadeen were not a "named group," and thus did not meet the Foreign Power requirement. Chuck sounded gratifyingly surprised and disgusted at this. That was good for my morale.

More important than lending us sympathy, however, Chuck, like the experienced operator he was, had taken some concrete steps to help advance the case. He had spoken with Mary, a counterterrorism expert at CIA Headquarters. Chuck explained Mary was familiar with the jihad in Chechnya and its connections to Usama Bin Laden. Then, thrusting aside all formality, Chuck then said, "Here, talk to Mary" and handed her the phone.

The voice on the other end of the phone was that of a young woman who sounded like she was about my age. Mary came across as earnest and intense, and over the next few days she would display a great sense of humor and would prove to be tremendously reassuring that we were right in pushing this case as hard as we did.

What I would not learn until long after 9/11 is that Chuck and Mary had done way more than offer sympathy and brainstorm some ideas of how to break the deadlock with Martin. In sad contrast to the obstructionist way in which my own headquarters was handling the Moussaoui case, CIA, which admittedly had little at stake by doing so, was at least moving the information on to senior decision makers. The day before (08/23/2001) CIA briefed the Director of Central Intelligence (DCI) using a one-page PowerPoint slide carrying the very descriptive title, "Islamic Extremist Learns to Fly." This short briefing was obviously taken from the information I provided Chuck on 08/22/2001 and listed all the information we knew at that time, minus the intelligence we received from the French. The fact that CIA officials deemed this information important enough to pass the highest levels of their agency reflected Chuck and Mary's efforts, and I am grateful to them, even now, for believing in this case.

I did not have long to wait for a response from Mary. Within a few minutes, she replied using Chuck's FBI email account since we did not have a way to e-mail between agencies at the time. As I read Mary's words, my morale rose, again, another "up" on the rollercoaster of emotions which marked this case. Mary's email is worth quoting here: "French info also was highly interesting—am not sure why this is not enough to firmly link Moussaoui to a terrorist group—Ibn al Khattab is well known to be the leader of the Chechen Mujahidin movement and *to be a close buddy with Bin Ladin from their earlier fighting days* (my italics). From a read of the [Redacted by the FBI]

French info, Moussaoui is a recruiter for Khattab. I can confirm from our own info that in fact the dead guy [Redacted by the FBI] in fact was a fighter for Khattab who perished in Chechnya in April 2000."

Mary's information was significant for two reasons. First, she made a solid link between Ibn Al Khattab and Usama Bin Laden. If Khattab was linked to Bin Laden, and Moussaoui was linked to Khattab, then Moussaoui was linked to Bin Laden. Inherent in this relationship was the fact that Bin Laden's terrorist group, Al Qaeda, was a designated Foreign Terrorist Organization. Although the Chechen Mujihadeen were certainly enough of a Foreign Power under the FISA law, this argument had not prevailed with Martin. I certainly hoped the introduction into the mix of Al Qaeda would be enough to meet Martin's fictional "named group" standard. It would be hard for him to deny that someone working for Al Qaeda met the standard for FISA.

With the intelligence Mary supplied demonstrating a link to Bin Laden and Al Qaeda, combined with that Pakistani visa in Moussaoui's passport and Al-Attas' intention to apply for one as well, I figured we finally might have what we needed.

I asked Greg to call Martin.

CHAPTER 29

FINALLY, FISA

When Greg came out of his office after the call he was exasperated, as all of us were anytime we spoke to Martin. Greg, who was an acting supervisor and closer to Martin's rank than the rest of us, reported that he was able to get Martin to acknowledge that the intelligence linking Moussaoui to a terrorist group was mounting. After some serious arm-twisting, Martin reluctantly agreed to allow us to submit a request to the FISA court to search Moussaoui's belongings. He was careful to warn Greg that this was no guarantee the application would move forward, just that RFU and the lawyers in NSLU would consider the facts.

Hearing that, I planned to write a FISA request that was so compelling it would be impossible to ignore, even by the cowardly and risk-averse managers at RFU. First, though, I called Chuck and asked to speak with Mary. I needed her permission to use what she told me about the Ibn Khattab connection to Bin Laden. It was one thing for her to helpfully suggest this in an email, it was another to include it in a declaration which would be submitted under oath before a District Court Judge sitting on the FISA Court. Chuck listened and handed the phone to Mary.

She gave me permission to use the info right away.[5]

5 Per Defense Exhibit #938 on the EDVA website, "Mary" later backed this assertion up with a sworn document noting that if she were called to testify, she would say under oath that the connection between Khattab and Bin Laden had been known by CIA for years. CIA employees, because of their covert status, were not called to testify in the criminal trial, but instead were permitted to submit sworn statements as substitution for testimony.

I now had all I needed to begin writing my FISA request. Once drafted, Martin and an attorney from OIPR would go before a FISA Court judge and swear to those facts under oath. If the judge was persuaded Moussaoui was acting as an agent of a foreign power, he or she would sign an order giving us authority to search.

Once I started writing, I realized there was plenty of background material already written on Moussaoui, so I was able to cut and paste from previous documents. I was sure to add the most impactful and crucial element to this document, including the French information linking Moussaoui to the Chechen Mujihadeen, and then the CIA information linking the leader of that group, Ibn Al-Khattab to Usama Bin Laden. I felt certain the document established a connection to a foreign power. When all the facts were spelled out, I requested emergency authority from the FISA court to search Moussaoui's property seized at the time of his arrest in Minnesota, as well as a search of his residence back in Norman, Oklahoma. Because I was requesting authorization for an emergency FISA (something I had never done before), I added a couple of sentences explaining why we considered the request urgent, namely that we did not know how far advanced the plot was.

This request was marked "Immediate" precedence, meaning it was supposed to be completed within 24 hours. Specifically, I asked RFU (Martin) to go to the FISA Court to get us a FISA Search Warrant. And I asked him to do it right away.

When that was finished and sent off, I began reviewing e-mails and other communications flagged for me in the ACS system. I saw an EC from Oklahoma City and opened the document. It was the write-up of Scott's investigation in Norman, Oklahoma, which he did two days before. As I read the document, I was grateful for the investigation Scott did, as well as the quick turnaround in getting it all written up. His interviews at Airman Flight School, where Moussaoui received his initial aviation training confirmed what we knew of his strange and unsociable habits, as well as his lack of progress in mastering pilot skills.

Scott also obtained a significant piece of information we did not know at that point: he learned the e-mail address Moussaoui used to communicate with Airman Flight School. From his interview of the admissions director for the school, Scott learned Moussaoui used the address pilotz123@hotmail.com with the screen name "zulu-man tangotango." Scott also included copies of the e-mails between Moussaoui and Airman as Moussaoui worked through the process of gaining admission and paying for the training. These would come later as attachments to the hard copy of the EC, but at least we had an e-mail address for Moussaoui now.

And even as I left the office that evening, I was aware the next day was likely to bring a renewed battle with RFU. I was certainly right about that. What I was not to learn until well after the 9/11 attacks, is that even as Martin appeared to concede in his phone call with Greg that we could submit a FISA request, he was working behind the scenes to sabotage our chances. Emailing a senior official at FBIHQ to answer that person's question about Moussaoui, Martin's response is so utterly and egregiously false, that I have chosen to quote it here in its entirety:

> "[Redacted by the FBI], Legats London and Paris were furnished photos and bio info on Moussaoui earlier this week. These were shared w [Redacted by the FBI] and both were asked to attempt to i.d. and determine background on the guy.
>
> [Redacted by the FBI] pocket litter of Moussasoui and al-Attas were sent to Chuck today w/req to pass to [Redacted by the FBI]. Photos of these two were also forwarded to Chuck this afternoon. We'll pass along add'l info when/if we obtain it.
>
> *Please bear in mind that there is no indication that either of these two had plans for nefarious activity, as was apparently indicated in an earlier communication.*" (My italics)

Although Martin annoyingly claimed credit for work we in Minneapolis were doing, the real damage was done by the last sentence, in which Martin lies so blatantly in writing to a senior official about what the investigation revealed, nine days after its opening. By the time Martin wrote that lie on the afternoon of Friday, 08/24/2001, we had ample indication of Moussaoui and Al-Attas' nefarious activity, which we had been sending to him as quickly as we obtained it. The reason he undercut our investigation then, as he would continue to do until long after the smoke and horror of 9/11 subsided for most of America, is known only to him.

CHAPTER 30

PLAN C

When I awoke on Monday, 08/27/2001, I was energized because Terri and the boys were due home that day. But as happy as I was about that, I knew this was also likely to be a day of confrontation with Martin, since the immediate lead to obtain a FISA search warrant would be waiting for him in his e-mail when he arrived at work. Strangely, when I arrived at the office, it was quiet on the Moussaoui front. Since neither I nor Greg had received anything from Martin in the way of shutting our FISA request down, I assumed all was well and progressing. Still no word by the time I left the office to head to the airport. That was fine with me because I was anxious to welcome my family home without distractions.

When I returned to my desk at around 1:30 p.m. after dropping Terri and the boys at home, the voicemail light on my phone was lit. As I retrieved the message, I heard Martin's by-now familiar voice. It was not good news. Martin informed me that we did not have enough for a FISA search warrant of Moussaoui's property, either the items we seized in Minnesota or those at his residence in Norman, Oklahoma. Insultingly, he repeated his earlier inane statements that when he was in the field, he obtained consent from people to search their property and wondered aloud why we had not. He also implied that for some reason he believed we had not included all the information in our possession in our communications with him. I responded to his voicemail with an e-mail. I did so because I wanted my response to be in writing. I pointed out to Martin once again that we *had* asked Moussaoui for consent to search his belongings, and that he had unequivocally denied this. I also informed him that we also asked Al-Attas for consent to search his property, and that this had been granted. I made sure to summarize all that had been done to run down all the information we did get from Al-Attas and again reminded Martin that we expected to find a great deal more once we received our FISA search warrant.

I then went and discussed this latest gut punch with the team. In summary, after telling us they would not seek authorization for us to apply to the U.S. Attorney's Office for a criminal search warrant because they wanted to preserve the FISA option, RFU was now telling us we did not have enough for a FISA. It was obvious to us what was happening and the immature, aggressive child in me wanted to lash out, but this would obviously not help the case.

It was then that we began seriously considering a third option, one that had been suggested by Jay in Paris earlier. Jay had been staying up to speed on the roadblocks from headquarters and like all Agents assigned to LEGAT Offices, he was serving two masters: the FBI and the French.

I don't know how Jay came up with "Plan C," but he communicated to us in phone calls and later e-mails that French law permitted a full search to be conducted of personal property when a person entered France. That made sense. The same was true in the U.S. under border search authority. Further, the French were interested in finding out all they could about Moussaoui, particularly since he was a French citizen with connections to terrorism. For this reason, they informed Jay that they were willing to receive Moussaoui and his belongings should he be deported to France. On his arrival, they would conduct a complete search of his property, including the all-important laptop.

When Jay first raised this as a possibility a few days earlier, I was still pinning my hopes on the FISA and getting into Moussaoui's belongings myself. Since that chance was receding, the French offer began looking increasingly attractive.

Because we wanted to be sure we would receive immediate access to the results of a search by the French Government, we decided that if we had to exercise the option of removing Moussaoui to France, John and I would accompany him. That way we would be present in Paris during the search to make copies to take home with us. Jay also confirmed the French wanted the FBI case Agent to come to France, in part for the reasons specified above. In addition, they wanted an in-person briefing from those most knowledgeable of the FBI investigation. We tabled the French idea for now. We were still intent on fighting for the FISA and it was time for Greg to call Martin, again.

As with so many previous calls between Minneapolis and RFU, this chat did not advance our cause. Greg forcefully informed Martin we did not agree with his conclusion that we lacked the intelligence needed to obtain a FISA. Using an argument Joe and I formulated during our strategy session, Greg suggested that it might be best to let the FISA application process play out as it was supposed to, with RFU taking the facts submitted by the field (us) and drawing on headquarters' greater resources and visibility of the national and international threat picture to *add intelligence* to what we had. Not only was RFU in a position to draw on the experiences of other FBI Divisions to add facts, but they could also call on representatives from the whole U.S. Intelligence Community as well as allied nations.

Martin quickly deflected this suggestion and brought up two spurious arguments. First, he returned to his earlier assertion that the Zacarias Moussaoui we arrested might not be the same one as referred to by the French as being connected to the Chechen Mujihadeen. It was preposterous, and Greg pointed this out, but Martin remained unmoved. He again asked whether the LEGAT Office in Paris was able to do a search of phone books in France to determine just how many Zacarias Moussaouis there were in the country, claiming the FISA court would want to know. Greg promised to follow up on this. Second, Martin suggested to Greg that Minneapolis may not have provided everything we had in our possession. Greg reiterated what I said to Martin earlier: everything we learned from interviews and from partner Agencies was passed to him immediately. Greg then reiterated his request that Martin do what was asked of him in the lead sent to him, namely: advance our FISA application. Martin remained noncommittal and continued to bring up peripheral issues.

Finally, in desperation, Greg informed Martin that the French were willing to assist with a search of Moussaoui's property if deported there. My guess is that Greg was hoping to show Martin that if an allied nation was willing to do the search, we should be, too. Although the implication appeared to have no effect on Martin's willingness to help with the FISA, the idea of deportation did seem to interest him. He asked Greg how soon until INS would be deporting Moussaoui. Greg did not know but felt confident the process would take some time. Greg informed Martin that our plan was to have me and John escort Moussaoui to France, there to resume our investigation using French legal authority to search his possessions. Martin appeared uninterested in this idea and the call ended in an impasse.

After being handed yet another defeat by Martin it was time to go home, and I, for one, was anxious to get there before bedtime for the boys. After clearing it with the team, I planned to take a day off the next day to take my family to the Minnesota State Fair, a much-beloved event at the end of every summer. I left the office that evening with no sense of dread at the impending battle that would occur the next day.

CHAPTER 31

SQUASHED

My family and I arrived at the State Fair in bright sunshine on the morning of 08/28/2001. At around 10 a.m. as I was riding in the whirling teacups with the boys, laughing as we were thrown around, I felt the Nextel on my belt vibrate and heard the distinctive chirp of someone trying to contact me. As the cups spun slowly to a stop, I pulled the phone out of its clip and saw it was Greg.

After making sure Terri had the kids, I replied, informing Greg I was free to chat. Greg was grim. "Sorry to bother you at the fair, but Martin sent me a draft of the LHM he intends to submit to DOJ and it's got some problems." The importance of Greg's word hit right away "A draft of the LHM he intends to submit," meaning a document *he* wrote?

Quickly replaying all my other FISA applications in my head, I realized this was the first time anyone at headquarters had *rewritten* an LHM I submitted. Normal practice was to carry the document from the field forward precisely, so there were no factual errors of the kind which Martin feared would get him into trouble. It seemed to be the opposite of what made sense. I asked Greg why Martin had done this now. He did not know. What Greg did observe is that in drafting his version of a summary of the facts, Martin *removed* all references to Ibn Khattab and Khattab's connections to Usama Bin Laden.

Naturally, I was beyond angry. This was behavior consistent with Martin's obstructionism from the beginning. Now, however, he had deliberately removed the one set of facts needed to persuade a FISA judge to sign a search warrant. Greg agreed and noted that a side-by-side comparison of the two LHMs showed Martin had softened other statements too, including removing direct quotes from Moussaoui himself, Al-Attas and the document from the French Government. It was clear Martin was attempting to fatally sabotage the request. He was able to do so since we did not have a direct channel to OIPR at DOJ. The application *had* to go through his unit, and he had not so subtly weakened the request by removing the precise set of facts needed for approval.

I asked Greg, "Do you need me to come in?"

"No. I will write a response to him. Is it okay if I call you again if I have any questions?"

"Absolutely," I replied. It made sense for Greg to do that anyway, since he was the acting supervisor, and his email should theoretically carry more weight than mine.

Greg and I spoke a few more times that day as he sought to clarify some issues. He then sent an e-mail to Martin with six bullets in which he attempted to have all the pertinent facts put back into the FISA request. Greg's e-mail was a masterpiece of persuasion and perfectly pointed out all the issues with Martin's intentionally flawed rewrite. His first bullet really cut to the heart of the matter, and is worth quoting here, "I'm curious as to why the Khattab/UBL info will be added later *if it is what is required to make the foreign power connection and therefore make the LHM fit the foreign power requirement*. It seems that we are setting this up for failure if we don't have the foreign power connection firmly established for the initial review." Exactly.

A few hours later, Martin responded with an e-mail of his own. He attempted to address all Greg's points, none adequately in my opinion. Martin's first bullet also referred to the absent foreign power connection, "Rosa is pulling together the foreign power stuff. If we get to the point where we can send this to OIPR, we will add it to this LHM. Don't worry about this part." The Rosa to whom Martin was referring was his analyst in RFU. What Rosa was doing to "pull together" anything to help us, then or at any time in this case remains a mystery to me. No word was ever received in Minneapolis about that.

The importance of the foreign power part, about which Martin suggested we not worry, was on display in Martin's last e-mail of 08/28/2001, which he sent at 1:56 p.m. Perhaps to emphasize his point, but more likely to avoid me, Martin committed a serious etiquette violation in addressing his e-mail not to the case Agent (me), but to Ray, our acting SAC. The e-mail is quoted in its entirety here:

> *"Ray, Greg:*
>
> *We just left a meeting Malcolm, with #1 in NSLU. He says that we have even less than we thought. Apparently, even if we could show that the ZM that recruited [Redacted by the FBI] in France is the one you have locked up in INS detention, we still don't have a connection to a foreign power. We would need intel to indicate the guy was actually a part of the group, an integral part of the movement or organization, and not just an individual that told a brother how he could serve Allah.*
>
> *Greg: Give me a call and we will talk about what to do next. As I said yesterday, you all did a great job to i.d., interview and neutralize this guy. There are a couple more things we can still do—w/the assistance of our LEGATs.*
>
> *Martin"*

We will meet Malcolm, the hopelessly incompetent, flagrantly dishonest, yet forceful and aggressive head of the National Security Law Unit (NSLU) again later, along with a cast of misfits in his unit who were more careerist and tragic-comically inept than any Hollywood could ever invent. Unfortunately, by the time Malcolm, a non-Agent attorney who simply never should have been in a decision-making position anywhere in this country's national security apparatus could be persuaded to read the facts submitted by the Minneapolis Office, the 9/11 attacks had already happened.

This incident showed us for the first time Martin was willing to lie in writing. Although FISA was not dead yet, it was certainly fading. The next day would see renewed efforts by our office to think creatively.

CHAPTER 32

CIA AGAIN

On 08/29/2001, we had a visit from James, my friend from CIA Headquarters. James was tall, thin, and distinguished with a neatly trimmed mustache and glasses. He was always well dressed and infallibly courteous. Born to parents who emigrated from the Middle East to Detroit, he was a native Arabic speaker who could also read the language a little. Before joining the Agency, James had been a police officer, so he was law enforcement savvy.

James was impressed with our case and concurred with our assessment that Moussaoui was up to something and that he was motivated by Islamic extremist ideology. I updated him that we had started the ball rolling with his headquarters and that Chuck seemed willing to connect us with the right people to get us some answers. James confirmed Chuck was well thought of at Langley. That was positive.

We also showed James the few documents from Al-Attas we copied. When he got to Al-Attas' Will, he paused and looked intently at the paper. "Right," I thought, "James can read Arabic!" Since we had not received the official translation back yet, this would be an opportunity to see what the document said. "James, Al-Attas told us that was his Will. We sent it out for translation, but it's not back yet."

James rubbed his chin, his eyes scanning the paper. He smiled. "Well, I can't get most of this stuff, but he does say something about death being near. He also says he believes those who participate in jihad will be favored by God. He signs off by talking about the hijab. He says either that people either should or shouldn't ignore wearing the hijab. I can't tell which." Even though his ability to read Arabic was rusty, James pulled out some important points for us. He also confirmed our suspicions that it was unusual for young, healthy 22-year-old, Muslim or not, to draft and carry a Will with him, despite Al-Attas' claims to the contrary.

Although James's ability to read Arabic was not great, he certainly spoke it well enough. For this reason, we played the audio recording of Al-Attas' call to El Hadj Ndiaye, the Imam at the mosque in Norman, from jail on 08/17/2001. We received the official translation about a week after James' visit, but for now, he was as close to an Arabic linguist as we had. James listened to the tape, occasionally stopping the recording and backing it up. When he was done, he smiled again, "Those are some bad guys."

"Why do you say that?" I picked up my note pad to take some notes as he spoke. "Well, for one thing, the sheikh your guy called got extremely upset when he heard Moussaoui is being deported. The caller actually had to calm him down, and the caller is the one in jail!"

We laughed.

James continued, "Here's the kicker: the sheikh told your subject, 'I heard you wanted to go on jihad.' As soon as the sheikh said that the subject replied, 'Don't talk about that now.'"

Jihad. So, Al-Attas *was* planning to go on jihad. This was no surprise given how religious he was and the company he was keeping. Although we discussed this excitedly for a few minutes and all agreed this new information was significant, it did not get us any closer to a foreign power. While we would certainly pass this new information on to Martin as we had done all along, no one was optimistic James' informal translation was going to move him any more than the multitude of facts we already provided.

"Anything else you can see here? Anything else we can be doing?"

James thought for a second. "You guys seem to have done quite a bit. I can't think of anything else." A pause, "I guess you can't put a source next to him in jail?"

Now, that was an idea. Thinking out loud, I started slowly, "Well, that might work. We'd need to be sure the source doesn't ask him any questions since Moussaoui already invoked." The idea behind this is that the source is acting as an agent of the government. Once the subject asks for a lawyer, it does not matter whether I am asking the questions, or my source is. It all constitutes questioning by the government. For that reason, no questions were permitted.

Joe added, "Yeah, but if Moussaoui volunteers information, that's fair game. Just so our source doesn't question him, and only listens, we're good."

We discussed this plan for a while, even exploring the idea of putting James in jail next to Moussaoui. This idea really wasn't feasible in the end since CIA is an intelligence gathering agency, not one set up to conduct criminal investigations and the Agency was not willing to risk James' cover. This idea, though creative, was not workable.

While the drama with FBI Headquarters was raging, we also sought an expert able to give an opinion on Moussaoui's behavior. As the many televisions shows and movies on the topic will attest, the FBI invests a significant amount of talent and effort in the celebrated Behavioral Assessment Unit, or BAU. BAU is an elite unit of experienced Agents with expertise in analyzing various criminal behaviors. Their most publicized cases are those on mass murderers or serial killers, but BAU also has experts on national security subjects.

Special Agent Joe Navarro of the Tampa Division was one such expert.[6] I first encountered Joe when I was back at Quantico for in-service training. He came and delivered a lecture to my class on various aspects of human behavior, and how we as investigators could, with enhanced understanding, use these to advance our cases. Joe spoke about indicators of deception, ways to subtly establish dominance in

6 Retired Supervisory Special Agent Joe Navarro is now the author of numerous books on behavioral assessment and is a world-renowned expert on body language and nonverbal communications.

an interview, and techniques to lead subjects and reluctant witnesses to the inescapable conclusion they should talk.

Joe's lecture was fascinating, to say the least, especially given my limited exposure to advanced interviewing at that stage. I took detailed notes on his tips and techniques, making sure I noted his phone number for future reference. I found his discussion on behavioral analysis so compelling, in fact, that contacting Joe was one of my first ideas as I was writing the initial communication to headquarters. In the years since, I have had many dealings with Special Agents from both BAU itself and from profilers located in field offices. They were uniformly knowledgeable and helpful to our understanding of subjects and sources.

When I called Joe Navarro, he listened to the Moussaoui story with interest. When I finished and he began giving me his opinion, I noticed he was keying on certain behaviors or phrases John and I also noticed. For example, Joe placed significant importance on the fact that Moussaoui seemed to have a single-minded interest in flight training, and that this thought seemed to preoccupy him, even as he was being arrested. Joe pointed out that most people in that situation would be concerned with regaining their liberty and would be much less concerned about the flight training, particularly when it did nothing to enhance their professional standing or employment opportunities. Joe was also interested in Al-Attas' description of Moussaoui's violent ideas on religion and felt Moussaoui's statement to us about how things were "very clear to him" was a confirmation of uncommonly strong beliefs. Joe felt these were the kind of convictions, in fact, which might motivate someone to commit acts of religiously or politically inspired violence.

Thankfully, Joe also concurred with our assessment that Moussaoui was an extremist engaged in a plot. He and I spoke several times between Moussaoui's arrest and the 9/11 attacks. During each call, Joe would analyze new information as I relayed it to him and then provide reassurance we were on the right track. As it became obvious to all of us what headquarters was doing, Joe became increasingly concerned. I appreciated his perspective both as a member of BAU and as an experienced Agent. I was so impressed with Joe's analysis that after weeks listening to RFU dismiss the threat, I asked him to call Martin. Joe was a very senior Agent, and I felt that, plus his status as a profiler, might sway headquarters. Sadly, it did not and his call with Martin came to nought.

CHAPTER 33

MORE TERRORIST CONNECTIONS

The next day, August 30, 2001, brought new information from Jay in Paris. Our French allies had not been idle and sent new details to us in their attempts to help our investigation. That itself was a sign of the importance of Moussaoui. Again, Jay hurriedly had translated the document they provided and sent it to us in an email. In his e-mail, Jay informed us the French were interested in further exploring the option of deporting Moussaoui to France. He also copied the still-reluctant ALAT in London on the e-mail, and notified him that he was authorized by the French to share the information with the British.

As always, Jay's timing was excellent, and I include the relevant paragraphs because they show just how concerned the French were about Moussaoui:

- "MOUSSAOUI is an individual of superior intelligence who has a Master's degree from Cambridge University. It was while residing in London that captioned subject was 'taken in hand and initiated by the fundamentalists of Backstreet and Finsbury Park mosques.'

- MOUSSAOU was a close associate of [Redacted by the FBI], a Mujihadeen who was killed in Chechnya in April 2000. [Redacted by the FBI], like captioned subject, was recruited and indoctrinated by the 'Backstreet' and 'Finsbury Park' group.

- He was further described as an individual who is extremely cynical, completely devoted to the Wahhabist cause, and concerned with progressing that cause. He was depicted as a cold, stubborn man, capable of nurturing a plan over several months, or even years and of committing himself to this task in all elements of his life and is potentially very dangerous.

- Moussaoui was arrested by the Moroccan police upon his arrival in Morocco in 1997.

- That same year, Moussaoui went to Narbonne, France. His ardent and emotional preaching in favor of jihad agitated a large number of his childhood friends who he had not seen since his departure to Great Britain.

- In France, the local Muslim community representatives were advised of the moral danger that MOUSSAOUI could represent for a number of young Muslims losing their religious bearings and social placement. As a result, the subject was driven from at risk urban areas by his coreligionists for propagating his message of intolerance and hatred.

- MOUSSAOUI is believed to have traveled to Kuwait, Turkey and Afghanistan.[7]"

The facts in this report from the French were very compelling to anyone with knowledge of terrorism. Surely, this additional information was enough to push our FISA request over the line? The descriptions of Moussaoui's extremist beliefs, to include actually preaching jihad in France were certainly interesting, but of greater

7 I am not sure why the French believed Moussaoui received a degree from Cambridge in the UK. We later learned his master's degree was from Southbank University in London. The other statements in their message proved to be true.

significance was the very last bullet, indicating the French believed Moussaoui had *traveled to Afghanistan*. I let my hopes rise again that we might prevail with our FISA request with this new and compelling intelligence.

Because we were once again hopeful the FISA would be approved, our plan was to invite the French to send a team to Minneapolis participate in our search, so they could immediately access the information we found. The thinking behind this was twofold. First, the French had been outstanding in responding to our requests and that partnership should be recognized by bringing them in, particularly since it was their intelligence which gave us the key portions of the FISA request. Second, and more selfishly, Moussaoui was French, and I was hopeful they could use the results of the search to further the investigation there in a way that would continue to help the FBI.

Greg lost no time updating Martin on the new information from the French as well as James' informal, but probably accurate translation of the telephone call where the Imam of Moussaoui and Al-Attas' mosque informed Al-Attas he heard about his plans for jihad. By now it was a familiar story, but none of the new information obtained on the 29th and 30th of August swayed Martin in the least. He remained adamant that we lacked enough to even apply to the FISA court. Nothing we learned made any impact on him.

It was sometime during this period that I also called Rosa, Martin's intelligence analyst to try to sway her to our side. I had some dealings with her in the past, and I was aware she had been around for a long time. Before 9/11 analysts were support employees who generally were rewarded for their longevity by being assigned to operational units at headquarters. Few had formal intelligence training, and most had reached their ceiling for advancement. That, plus the fact that they were often the long-term continuity in their units meant that they could generally be counted upon to be less careerist and more knowledgeable than their bosses, the SSAs. Even if I was unable to sway Rosa to my side, I hoped to get some information on what was being done in RFU to try to add weight to our request, as Martin had claimed. If RFU really was doing anything to help us, which I doubted, they would be trying to take our information and add some additional reporting to it as Mary from CIA did.

Rosa proved to be a disappointment. She was clearly irritated that I called, prompting me to ask her what the problem was. In an exasperated voice, Rosa sputtered, "You're trying to get everyone spun up on your case!"

"Yes, Rosa, I am. These guys represent a threat!"

"Well," she continued, obviously angry, "What we're doing here is trying to keep people from getting spun up!" So much for the value added described by Martin.

"I got that, Rosa. Your unit has done nothing to support this case." I was angry now and understood the call was clearly not going to be a success. We agreed to disagree and hung up.[8]

It was also during this period that Greg, during an increasingly acrimonious call with Martin, uttered the subsequently much quoted: "Martin, we're trying to keep this guy from getting control of an airplane and flying it into the World Trade Center!" The statement, which I heard Greg make, happened during a call sometime after the August 30 receipt of the new French information. Greg was

8 Well after 9/11 I was to confirm my suspicions Rosa had done absolutely nothing to support our case, particularly in assisting our FISA request. Defense Exhibit #951 on the EDVA website is a substitute for the testimony of Rosa, and an FBI NSLU attorney, Shari. Although Rosa claims she "conducted research to try and bolster Moussaoui's connection to a recognized for power," the facts do not bear this out. Defense Exhibit #951 notes that FBI records reveal that on 08/22/2001, Rosa printed an 08/10/2001 EC from SA Ken Williams of the Phoenix Division. In his EC, later dubbed the "Phoenix Memo," Williams, an experienced counterterrorism investigator, wrote that on the basis of his investigations, he believed that there was the "possibility of a coordinated effort by Usama Bin Laden to send students to the United States to attend civil aviation universities and colleges." Williams went on to suggest the purpose of this was to position them to conduct terror activity on civil aviation targets. Shari, who was one of the NSLU lawyers who, along with Malcolm, determined there was not enough intelligence for a FISA, declared in her substitution for testimony that Rosa never told her about the Phoenix Memo. Rosa should have alerted not just NSLU about the memo, but also our team in Minneapolis, since the information it contained was chillingly like the facts learned in the Moussaoui case. It is impossible to know why Rosa did not do so without an explanation from her.

continuing to try to persuade, cajole or somehow incentivize Martin to move the FISA request forward, and I was standing nearby, listening intently to his side of the conversation.

I could tell Martin, as usual, was finding one excuse after another. At one point, he clearly accused Greg, as Rosa had accused me, of trying to make more out of the case than the situation warranted. That is when Greg, ordinarily so even keeled, lashed out with his comment about the World Trade Center. It was not, as he had to explain to numerous inquiries after the 9/11 attacks, that we had any specific information to indicate the Twin Towers were the target, it just came to him as an example in the heat of the moment.[9] Like so many arguments before, this one failed to motivate Martin. Greg shook his head at me as the call wound down.

Although neither Greg nor anyone else in Minnesota had any idea of the plot's targets, all of us working on the case understood that there was a strong possibility the plan included a suicide attack using a commercial aircraft. The reason we believed this was the lengths to which Moussaoui had gone to acquire sufficient knowledge to fly a 747–400 aircraft. He not only paid thousands of dollars for the training, but according to Clancy he actually studied the manuals provided to him *before arriving at the school!* Now, I myself love airplanes, but paging through those binders of endless technical language and schematics of electrical and hydraulic systems was boring in the extreme, however Moussaoui had done it. And according to Al-Attas, he was planning to sign up for and pay for more of the same after his first round of training ended.

We did some research and learned the first hijacking of a commercial aircraft had occurred in 1931 in South America. In the 70 years since, criminals, terrorists, revolutionaries, and mentally ill

9 By this point, so great was the gravity of what we viewed as an increasingly urgent situation, that Greg was keeping contemporaneous notes of all his conversations with Martin. Using these notes, he was able to show the date and time of this call and provide the context for why he made the statement about the World Trade Center when facing the numerous post-9/11 inquiries.

people had all seized control of airliners in flight. Sometimes the intent was to escape from a country, sometimes the goal was to steal the aircraft and ransom it back. Other times it was to extort money or to win the release of other terrorists held in prison. We could find no instance where any of the hundreds of actual and would-be hijackers put in the time, effort, and expense to learn to fly a complicated airliner. It was simply too easy for the hijackers to get the pilot to do what they wanted by threatening to shoot a flight attendant or a few of the passengers. Make that threat and the pilots will fly you to Cuba or North Korea or wherever else you want to go.

So why the flight training?

There was only one answer, and it was grim: *Moussaoui and his co-conspirators planned to do something with an airplane that they could not make its actual pilot do, no matter what they threatened.* That "thing" had to be a suicide crash. What else could there be?

During the many hours of reflection following the attacks, I concluded the fatal flaw in our pursuit of the case was the fact that from the second he was arrested, Moussaoui was subject to nearly immediate removal from the U.S. I believe Martin, ever risk-averse and deathly afraid of going to the FISA court, decided early on to "run out the clock" on Moussaoui. He therefore resolved to turn down each request from us, one after another, or to suggest diversionary busy work until our time was up, and INS was forced to remove him. This was a win from Martin's perspective since Moussaoui would then be some other (foreign) agency's problem.

CHAPTER 34

OUR BIG SHOT

Whatever Martin's strategy, by this time the team in Minneapolis concluded that there was no argument sufficient to persuade anyone at RFU to assist us, at least at our level. We therefore decided one of our last remaining options was to go to Ray, our acting SAC, with a request for him to elevate this as high up the chain of command in the Counterterrorism Division as he felt comfortable. I was with Greg when he went to talk to Ray as I had the most knowledge of the case.

As usual Ray was supremely approachable and always gentlemanly. When we arrived in the "executive area" and stood at his door, Ray looked up and smiled. Ushering us to the couch in his office, he took a seat in a chair opposite us across a coffee table. In contrast to many SACs before or since, he listened with great interest as we described the results of our investigation. We informed him we believed the information provided by both the French and the CIA was sufficient to justify a FISA search warrant, he nodded. "That seems good to me."

"We agree. The problem is that Martin keeps raising one objection after another."

"What should we do?"

Greg replied, "Ray, we would like you to elevate this. Martin seems to be making a bad call for the wrong reasons, and we need someone above him to reverse his decision."

As we discussed this, Ray professed himself willing to go to Martin's boss, Unit Chief, Devin. While I would have liked our argument taken higher, I understood Ray's reasoning. For starters, Ray was an *acting* SAC, not a real one, which meant he was really an ASAC, or GS-15 in grade. Therefore, etiquette-wise in the uniquely dysfunctional FBI management world, it would not be appropriate for him to reach upward too many levels. Ray also pointed out that the Unit Chief, Devin, who also held the same GS-15 rank as him, might be in the dark on this. After all, it was Martin who seemed to be the problem, maybe he was not being briefed appropriately or completely on what we were reporting.

As Ray explained this, he walked over to his computer, unlocked it with his password and pulled up his e-mail. Smiling at me, Ray gestured at the computer and said, "Send Devin an e-mail laying out our case." Ray was handing me a blank check to communicate with headquarters in his name. I realized whatever I wrote would carry some weight, far more than my own e-mails, or Greg's since Ray was the acting SAC.

I complied quickly, sitting in Ray's chair, and beginning to type as if I were him. I knew this was a golden opportunity to advocate for this investigation as the SAC and I intended to make the case, strongly, that what we needed was a means of obtaining a warrant to search Moussaoui's property. Because I was writing as the SAC, I was conscious to just hit the high points of the issue without delving into excessive detail. I had learned in both the military and later the FBI that senior officials tended to confine themselves to "big picture" perspectives and so made sure that I kept the scope broad and high level. However, I made sure the voice I used for the e-mail was that of a senior manager who was deeply concerned that his investigators in the field were not being well supported on an important case. Finally, I was conscious of the fact that Ray had hopes for his career and that in turning his e-mail account over to me, he trusted my discretion. Therefore, while the adolescent in me wanted to scream out (in writing) at the injustices and indignities heaped upon me, and Greg, and Joe by Martin over the last two weeks, I kept the email professional and clinical.

When I finished, I looked up at Ray, sitting on the couch in his office, since I was at his desk. He was reading some documents and looked back at me over his reading glasses. "I'm finished. Do you want to read it before I send it?"

"Nah, go ahead," Ray said. Thinking better of this, he added, "Wait. I'll just read it real quick." Stepping over to the computer screen, he scanned what I wrote. When he was done, he nodded, "Looks good." He clicked "Send."

With genuine gratitude, I said, "Thanks very much, Ray. I appreciate that." He smiled.

The following day, September 1, 2001, we had our answer. Ray forwarded Devin's response to my/his e-mail. Without addressing any of the specific concerns, Devin's reply assured Ray that RFU was doing all it could to advance our case. After including the usual meaningless headquarters platitudes about all the fine work we in Minneapolis were doing, Devin went on to parrot most of Martin's assertions that the intelligence we provided did not meet the foreign power standard. It was more of the same and showed clearly headquarters had closed ranks.

Reading that e-mail all of us on the team understood, once and for all, that we were not going to get our search warrant.

At least now we could focus on "Plan C," which involved deporting Moussaoui to France along with all his property. The groundwork for this had been carefully prepared by Jay in Paris, in the wake of the increasingly outlandish claims from RFU that our case did not meet the standard for a FISA. Experienced Agent that he was, Jay's efforts kept our options open and through his liaison work made sure the French Government would search Moussaoui's property when he entered the country. If we wanted to see what connections were there, it was now going to happen in France.

Because it was still early in the day in Minnesota, I called Jay in Paris to advise him our emphasis now was on removing Moussaoui and his property to France so we could conduct a joint search. Jay confirmed this was still of interest to the French and signed off to get the process started with them.

The next step was calling Martin to shift gears and let him know our decision now was to accept the French offer to receive Moussaoui and search his property. I handled that chore, believing it would be a relief to him that we were punting the case overseas. I was partially correct. Martin was fine with the Moussaoui going to France, but when I told him of our plan to accompany him, his annoyed tone returned. "And why is that?" he snapped.

Trying to control my tone, I said, "We will be there to assist the French with fully understanding the case. And we will be there to immediately receive the results of the search and set leads for additional investigations which results. We expect to find evidence of other co-conspirators. Also, if we just hand Moussaoui his property and put him on a plane to France, he'll have a solid 9 hours to destroy everything of use to us."

"That's not our problem! This is an INS case."

"No, it's not, Martin," I replied. "This is an FBI full field investigation. The file number is 199M-MP-60130. It's been open since August 15th. It's an FBI case!"

Martin retorted, "Well, it sounds like you guys are looking for a vacation in France."

I did not take the bait. "Not true. We're following this to a logical conclusion. We will be traveling with Moussaoui."

Knowing Martin seemed to have the full support of his Unit Chief, Devin no matter how irrational or indefensible his position was, I changed gears, "I prepared a letterhead memorandum yesterday for the FAA. It lays out what Moussaoui was doing, and the threat that poses to commercial aviation. I will send it to you for dissemination to the FAA..."

"No need for that," Martin interrupted. "Hold on to your memo. We are preparing an assessment from this unit for the whole intelligence community."

"Ugh," I thought. "Martin will surely understate the threat to keep things under wraps." Recognizing there had never been any advantage to arguing with Martin and realizing I had gone 0 for 2 on this call, I quickly ended the conversation.

For the next few days, developments on the case remained relatively quiet. Jay was working with the French on when, where, and how they preferred to receive Moussaoui, while in Minneapolis John and I were working on making removal arrangements to France and preparing to assist them with the search of his property on arrival. We deliberately did not engage Martin for fear he would mandate some action that would distract us or derail the plan. And these fears were justified since, much to my fury, the focus on deporting Moussaoui heralded the beginning of a new battle with Martin, who somehow decided this was now just an INS case and that any further participation in it by FBI Agents (me) was unnecessary since he was being removed to France.

CHAPTER 35

THE FAA

Sometime in the first few days of September I obtained a copy of the cable Martin drafted and sent to the intelligence community, including the FAA. Reading it I was disappointed to see that although he used much of the information (and wording) from earlier communications written in Minnesota, he completely removed any reference to a threat posed by Moussaoui's activity. It was obvious now why he instructed me to hold my memo: he wanted to control the narrative and, to use Rosa's words, "...try to keep people from getting spun up!"

This was a concern. Not only had Martin stripped the conclusions out of the memo, but he also omitted all the aviation-specific analysis I had intended to communicate to the FAA. I wanted to convey to aviation experts that the original complainants in this case were highly experienced pilots and flight instructors, not crackpots or alarmists. I wanted to let them know Moussaoui had already received an introduction to the 747–400 aircraft, including its critical systems, *and* been provided with 747–400 flight manuals. I also thought it was important for the FAA to know that Moussaoui's physical training and martial arts would be of use in seizing control of an airliner in flight. Of course, none of this was in Martin's memo.

The weakness of Martin's document made us decide to go to the FAA directly. There was a small aviation security office near the airport in Minneapolis and although none of us knew anyone there, the Agent in our office who was assigned as the Airport Liaison Agent (ALA) at Minneapolis-St. Paul International Airport did. In this job, he knew everyone connected to aviation in the Twin Cities.

From the ALA we obtained the number for Vicki, an FAA security expert in Minnesota. Our ALA spoke highly of her, noting he found her aggressive and dedicated to her job. Aggressiveness was good enough for us, so I called Vicki and explained who I was, also being careful to drop the ALA's name. I told her we were working on a case and informed her that John and I would like to come brief her in her office at her earliest opportunity. She agreed to meet.

At the appointed time on a sunny fall day in the first week of September 2001, John and I went to the FAA Security Office, located in a nice commercial building not too far from the airport. Both of us noticed the FAA had beautiful offices by government standards. Vicki greeted us professionally, handing each of us a business card which proclaimed her to be a person employed in aviation security. With her was an older gentleman, Jospeh, who Vicki described as the local manager of aviation security. "Perfect," I thought, "the boss."

They ushered us into a conference room and closed the door. Once we were all seated around the large and equally nice conference table, I began. "John and I are assigned to the FBI JTTF. We have a case that impacts aviation security. Our findings have been of such concern that our headquarters in D.C. put out a cable explaining what is going on."

At that, I placed my hand on the brown envelope containing a copy of Martin's cable. "I don't want you to read this yet, until we add some additional details." I then pulled a copy of my LHM out of a separate folder and placed it on the envelope.

John and I went on to describe the case, noting all our concerns. I explained that I was a pilot and with my training and experience had found Clancy's suspicions compelling and accurate. As the case progressed, our experience as international terrorism investigators compounded our fears. We tried to leave no doubt with the FAA that what we uncovered pointed to a plot to seize and use for terrorist purposes a commercial aircraft in flight. We also made it clear that although Moussaoui was in custody, we were aware he had associates who remained at large. These associates were free to continue advancing the plot. Vicki and her boss listened attentively. When we were finished, I slid the two documents across the table to Vicki.

Joseph asked, "What would you like us to do?"

"We would like you to pass this amplifying information to your headquarters. While the whole intelligence community should certainly know about this, it is most pertinent to FAA given your responsibility for aviation security. The cable from our headquarters is pretty vanilla and does not, in our opinion, convey the gravity or the imminence of the threat. Please pass up your chain that you met with the case Agents on the Moussaoui matter and received a more detailed briefing which raised concerns. Specifics and our reasoning are in the LHM we just gave you."

Cutting to the chase, John added, "In short, we'd like you to sound the alarm."

Smiling, Joseph stood up and extended his hand, "It was nice meeting you."

Vicki stood as well, holding both the headquarters cable, and my LHM. She promised to read both documents and appeared appropriately concerned at what we said. Joseph's face was more neutral, and it was impossible to tell what he thought.

When John and I were outside, we both breathed a sigh of relief. There had been no skepticism from either of the FAA officials and both appeared receptive to our request. At least FAA would be on the alert. We did not know exactly what that meant in terms of actual security measures, but both of us felt confident that *something* would be done.

Our confidence was misplaced. Following the 9/11 attacks, we learned that the Minneapolis Aviation Security Office took no action to notify FAA Headquarters about the briefing they received from us. When I read the testimony of Joseph and Vicki in one of the inquiries into the attack, I was disappointed to see they closed ranks and said under oath that although John and I had been there, we conveyed no threat information. My guess is they decided that having been briefed on this threat shortly before the 9/11 attacks and done nothing, they concluded the best course was to deny they received any threat information at all. Years later, our Airport Liaison Agent told me Vicki informed him that she felt guilty because, after John and I departed, she wanted to do exactly as we asked and notify FAA Headquarters of the threat. Instead, her boss Joseph told her they had already been notified. He then took both documents and placed them in a safe, presumably never to emerge again. No action was taken. When Vicki spoke to the ALA about our visit, she acknowledged we had in fact conveyed serious threat information and were "passionate" in our wish to get the word out.

During the week of September 3–7, 2001, there were numerous phone calls and e-mails between Minneapolis and RFU. There was absolutely no movement on the FISA or criminal search warrants, and Martin remained staunchly opposed to John and me traveling to France to participate in the search. As far as he was concerned, FBI involvement in the case was over.

On September 6, I received the translation of Al-Attas' Will. Like everything about that sinister little guy, it worried us. Al-Attas began his Will, which was addressed to his parents, by informing them "death has approached." He goes on to reassure them with the hope that "Allah will reward him with paradise and keep him with the prophets, martyrs and pious." He closed what he believed would be his last message ever to his parents by urging them to make their daughters, even the very young ones, wear the veil. This official document confirmed James' on-the-fly translation of the highlights of the Will had been spot on.

Pretty alarming stuff for a healthy 22-year-old. Why would Al-Attas state with such assurance death had approached? How could he also be so sure God would reward him with paradise, especially that area of paradise reserved for those who martyred themselves for the religion? This seemed like further confirmation Al-Attas, like Moussaoui, was an Islamic extremist who intended to carry out something soon and that *he did not expect to survive.*

No wonder Al-Attas grew concerned when he believed I was reading that document during our interview back on August 16th!

As we rolled into the weekend of September 7–9, 2001, we were still battling RFU for permission to accompany Moussaoui to France. I left the office that Friday hoping we would have a resolution on Monday, since by then the arrest had occurred more than three weeks before. We reasoned that any co-conspirators had by now had plenty of time to destroy evidence, flee or, worst case scenario, readjust their attack plans to go forward without Moussaoui. Because there was not much more to do until we got a ruling from RFU on whether we could go to France, I allowed myself the luxury of a whole weekend off, the first since the arrest. I know my family appreciated that. I sure did.

Although I had fun with my wife and kids—it was a nice early fall weekend and we spent a lot of time in our yard and on our newly renovated deck, a gnawing anxiety about what the future held never left me all that Saturday and Sunday. I would only just have forgotten about the rage-filled, malevolent man sitting in the Sherburne County Jail, when thoughts would come flooding in to intrude on my fun: "What is the plot? Who else is involved? Where are they now? What is coming next?" It was not just that weekend, it now seemed every waking moment was spent thinking about the case.

The morning of Monday, September 10, 2001 brought no movement on the case. On that last day of a forever gone era in America, Greg again spoke to Martin about granting permission for me and John to travel to France. As soon as we had permission our plan was to ask the Deportation and Removal Section of INS to get the ball rolling to deport Moussaoui to France. Martin remained noncommittal and reiterated his nonsensical position that this was an INS matter and there was no need for the involvement of the FBI or the JTTF. The call ended in stalemate, as had each of them before.

I had been keeping an ear on the conversation from my desk, keenly aware from Greg's side that he was making no more progress than any of us had since August 16th. When he hung up, Greg was frustrated, as usual. Looking at me, he shook his head and told me what I already knew: "Martin is continuing to stonewall us."

I am sure I said something unkind about Martin in response. My stress and frustration were at an all-time high.

Greg continued, "Please draft another EC to RFU. List all the requests we have made of them since the case was opened, starting with asking for permission to go to the U.S. Attorney's Office for search warrants. Then list everything else. Once their management sees how many requests they turned down or flat out ignored on this case, maybe they will change their mind. Put Ray on to sign the EC out."

I nodded.

Greg stood up from his desk. "I'm going up to talk to Ray to see if he'll call Devin again. I don't see what the big deal is about sending the two of you to France."

Turning to my computer, I started to draft what amounted to roughly my 71st communication to FBI Headquarters on this case, counting ECs, LHMs, and e-mails.

Before I had gotten too far, Greg returned. He informed me Ray completely supported our position and would be putting in a call to Devin. That was positive.

Feeling that this EC might be our last chance to influence this case in our favor, I decided to include something in it about how deporting Moussaoui to France would have the effect of putting a terrorist back on the street and "forestalling" rather than preventing an attack. And, on top of that, Moussaoui obviously now knew we were on to him, and could warn his friends. Unless we learned more, a cell of terrorists would remain intact. Deportation, even if it resulted in a search of Moussaoui's property in France, was just delaying an attack. We needed to do something to stop it altogether.

As I was typing, I noticed I received an email from Cathy, the FBI detailee to [Redacted by the FBI]. I had not heard from her since our initial exchange soon after Moussaoui's arrest, so I opened her e-mail right away. I have included our exchange here, because Cathy's words were uncannily prescient on the eve of the most devastating terrorist attack the U.S. has ever faced.

"Harry,

Did you ever get back anything that you use to get the search warrant? I didn't hear back from you and figured you were okay."

That was nice of Cathy. As described above in the long, sad catalog of refusals from RFU, we were *not* okay and had not gotten back what we needed. I felt like Cathy deserved an answer, so I stopped working on my EC and took the time to respond:

"Cathy,

ITOS/RFU SSA Martin has determined that we do not have enough for either a criminal search warrant or a FISA search warrant of Moussaoui's computer. We did not pursue this further because they have directed that this is an INS matter and that the "FBI does not have a dog in this fight". Of course, I strongly disagree.

The current plan is to deport Moussaoui to France. [Redacted] has advised that they have the legal authority to hold Moussaoui and search his effects. This search was a distant third in my list of desired outcomes, but at this point I am so desperate to get into his computer, I'll take anything.

My big fear is that the French will determine that most, if not all of Moussaoui's criminal activity occurred outside France and they have no ability to convict (he's lived in the UK since circa 1995). In that case, he walks. I don't know if they'll have to return his property in this case (including the 747 flight manuals), but it seems possible.

The current wrangle with ITOS/RFU is over whether John (our INS co-case Agent) and I can go to France to be present for the search. LEGAT Paris relayed a [redacted] request for FBI personnel to do just that, but RFU is opposed.

I'll keep you posted, but I am not optimistic. Thanks for your help and assistance.

Take care,
Harry"

I had three reasons for writing this e-mail to Cathy. One was to explain our thinking at this stage of the case. Two, I knew Cathy was a senior Agent with connections to the JTTF in New York. I was hoping that if she had the facts, she might call someone at headquarters senior enough to make RFU do the right thing. Three, even though she had not really helped the investigation other than to hear me out, I owed her an answer to her question.

What I did not realize as I wrote this e-mail on 09/10/2001, was that Cathy, counterterrorism professional that she was, *had* helped! Although I did not see the result until long after the 9/11 attacks, Cathy's request to [Redacted by the FBI] on my behalf caused them to search their databases. These searches located references to Moussaoui, and they drafted a cable to FBIHQ on 09/05/2001. This cable named Moussaoui as being someone who used a facility frequented by Al Qaeda operatives.[10] It was more information linking Moussaoui to Al Qaeda and it came, not from the FBI or from a foreign ally, but from the [Redacted by the FBI], a member of the U.S. Intelligence Community known to have very reliable sources. So, why did I not see this reporting? It is still not clear to me. The cable

10 This cable was highly classified and remains so to this date as far as I am aware. For this reason, my description of its contents is vague. In early September 2001 when it was passed from [Redacted by the FBI] to FBIHQ, the relatively recent information it contained would have shown another significant connection of Moussaoui to Al Qaeda.

was sent by [Redacted by the FBI] to FBIHQ, it referenced a terrorism case, and it had Moussaoui's name in the body of the message. It therefore would have been routed to RFU, since they were the unit which oversaw the Moussaoui investigation. The facts in this cable would have been a good example of information not available to me in the field which RFU should have used to strengthen the FISA request. Why Martin and Rosa did not do so, or even alert me to the cable at all, remains a question only they can answer. Like so many other opportunities, Cathy's considerable assistance should have been decisive, but it was ignored.

Cathy took only a few minutes before responding to my email, with the final, chilling, and prescient foreshadowing of the following day's events. Her e-mail was sent at 3:45 p.m. on 09/10/2001:

> "Harry,
>
> Thanks for the update. Very sorry that this matter was handled the way it was, but you fought the good fight. *God help us all if the next terrorist incident involves this same type of plane* (my italics).
>
> Take care,
> Cathy"

I was switching back and forth between the EC I was typing and my e-mail when I saw Cathy's last reply. I nodded silently to myself at her fear, one which I shared. It spurred me to make this final EC my most persuasive yet.

"SA Samit." I looked up to see Greg standing at my desk with a rare smile on his face. "Success! Ray just got an e-mail from Devin. You and John have been approved to go to France."

I looked at Greg, excited to have finally won one. After weeks of being told "no" in response to the most reasonable of requests, it was a relief to have received a "yes." I also saw a glimmer of hope that we might yet have a chance to stop whatever Moussaoui and his friends had planned. We just needed time.

I consoled myself that whatever the difficulties of the last few weeks, soon we would have additional information on Moussaoui, his associates, and his plan. When I got home, I was happy to see Terri and the boys were outside, playing in our cul-de-sac as the sun slowly set. That night, I had the first semi-relaxed evening since August 15, 2001. It would be the last for a long time to come.

And for nearly 3000 innocent Americans, it was their final night on earth. Our time had run out.

CHAPTER 36

CATASTROPHE

8:15 a.m. (CDT) 9/11/2001, Twin Cities, Minnesota

After a fast shower and hurriedly throwing on clothes, I got into my FBI car feeling a mixture of rage and sadness. Having seen footage by then of two airliners smashing into the towers of the World Trade Center, I knew with certainty that what the world had just witnessed was the plot moving forward without Moussaoui.

My first call was to Chris. He answered his cell right away. I asked him where he was, and he replied that he was in his office. "Have you heard?"

"Heard what?"

"Two planes just crashed into the World Trade Center!"

"What? Hold on! Let me turn on my TV!" After a short pause, "Oh, God! Where are you now?"

"On my way in."

As usual, Chris, who had been keeping up on the case even though he was no longer our boss had the answers. It was why I called him. "Ok. When you get here, get to the U.S. Attorney's Office. Bring your documents and have them turn them into a search warrant for Moussaoui's stuff!"

"Right, makes sense. Wait! We still need permission to go to them. Martin still hasn't given us that!"

Chris sounded grim. He could see on his TV what was happening in New York. "I'll handle it. Just go!"

Chris later informed me that after hanging up he immediately called Devin to discuss these events, and to obtain authorization for Minneapolis to apply to the U.S. Attorney's Office for a criminal search warrant. He was able to reach Devin immediately. To Chris' surprise and intense anger Devin, who was also watching the news, remained unconvinced that the two plane crashes in New York had any connection to the Moussaoui case! Devin's conclusion, a stance which can only be described as self-serving in the extreme, led to an argument. While that was happening, Chris saw it reported live that a third plane had just hit the Pentagon in Washington, D.C. He relayed this to Devin, asking something to the effect of "How many is it going to take?"

Chris told me that upon hearing news of the third crash, Devin granted Minneapolis verbal concurrence to obtain a criminal search warrant.

He was 3 ½ weeks too late.

My next call was to Greg, who was in the squad area. Because there were no TVs there, I was not surprised he had not heard either. Relaying the news, I told him about my call to Chris and Chris's instructions to head for the U.S. Attorney's Office to get the warrant. Greg stayed calm, and with good logic informed me he planned to call John and ask him to bring Moussaoui's property to the FBI Office from INS's evidence room. That made sense too. Greg's plan ensured that as soon as the warrant was signed, we would have the items and be ready to begin the search. We hung up.

Chris' idea of using the information in the documents I had already drafted as the basis of a search warrant affidavit made the most sense. Those documents contained all the FBI knew about Moussaoui in one place, so there was no point in trying to reinvent the wheel, especially when time was a factor. I was sure U.S. Attorney's Office would quickly push a warrant to a judge so we could begin the search as soon as possible. This was as important now as before the attacks since we still hoped to uncover additional co-conspirators or offshoots of the plot. Lives might still be saved.

As soon as my car was parked in its spot in the secure garage, I began running. I ran up the stairs from garage level to the tunnel which ran under Washington Avenue. I ran towards the guard desk at the beginning of the tunnel, quickly flashing my plastic building ID to the guard without slowing down. I picked up my pace and sprinted through the tunnel which connected the two buildings. When I reached the elevator bank, I impatiently pushed the up arrow. After 3 ½ weeks of sitting and waiting while people at headquarters declined to allow us to advance our case, the time for action had arrived, in the most terrible way imaginable. I was impatient, bordering on frantic to begin doing something to help.

When the elevator reached the 11th floor, where Chris' office was, I quickly used my ID to enter the FBI space and jogged down the hall to his office. As I approached, his secretary called to me that he was on the 9th floor in the JTTF squad area, presumably waiting for me. I abruptly about-faced and ran to the internal stairway, hurrying down the steps two at a time. As I exited the stairwell and burst into the squad area, Chris and Greg looked up from the conference they were having at Greg's desk.

Without speaking, I sat down at my desk and fired up my computer. My emotions were running high, and I did not trust myself to look at them or to say anything. I was afraid of what might happen, so I relied on completing the assignment Chris had given me on the phone 15 minutes before. Once I logged in to my computer and could access my documents, I hurriedly selected a floppy disk from a caddy to the right of my desk and inserted it into my computer. Onto that disk I saved the opening EC, the FISA application LHM, and the two documents we received from the French which linked Moussaoui to the Chechan mujihadeen and Al Qaeda. Ever since August 17, only 25 days before but seemingly a lifetime ago, I believed we had enough information for a warrant. Now we would have our chance before the judge.

As I ejected the disk with the documents on it and placed it in an envelope, Chris and Greg came to my desk. Chris began, "I spoke to Devin, and we have verbal concurrence to go to the U.S. Attorney's Office to obtain a criminal search warrant. Do you have what you need?"

I nodded. "I have the opening EC, the FISA request, and both ECs from LEGAT Paris containing their info linking him to Al Qaeda. That should be enough. Once I get there and the AUSAs get started on the warrant, I'll call Jay in Paris to ask him to see whether the French are willing to let us use their info in a criminal warrant."

Greg said, "Good luck. I called John and he is bringing Moussaoui's property up to our office so we can get started on the search as soon as you have the warrant signed. Also, I spoke to Brian and Matt. ERT is standing by to process the evidence once the judge signs."

All of that was great thinking on Greg's part. ERT stands for Evidence Response Team. It is made up of Agents and support people from the office who volunteer to receive extra training in handling evidence and processing crime scenes. ERT is called in when special expertise in the collection and cataloging of evidence is needed. It existed precisely for times like this since I could not imagine a case being any bigger. Brian and Matt were two Agents in the office who were senior members of ERT. I knew they were professionals who would ensure the evidence was processed correctly.

"Greg continued, "We also have Jerry and Chris standing by to do the CART analysis of the laptop." CART stood for Computer Analysis Response Team, a group of Agents and computer specialists with extra training in collecting digital evidence. I knew from working with them in the past that they would do a thorough job, and the laptop was sure to have important evidence on it.

"Thanks, Greg," I stammered. Cooler heads were prevailing and Chris and Greg between them had covered many of the bases which I had been too excited to consider. However, because it had by now it had been over an hour since my first glimpse of an airliner hitting the World Trade Center, my initial emotions were subsiding. Time, plus the fact that I was now doing something productive, allowed me to begin thinking clearly again. "Ok, I'm off."

Chris leaned in, "Oh, one more thing. Celia is over at the U.S. Attorney's Office. She came to see me right after you called and realized our case is connected to New York and D.C."

"D.C.?" I had not heard about the attack on the Pentagon yet.

"Yep. A third plane hit the Pentagon a few minutes after you called me."

"Oh." I looked down at my feet, wondering if anyone I knew from the Navy was assigned to the Pentagon.

Chris continued. "Anyway, Celia is over there now. She may be able to help with the warrant."

"Got it. On my way." And out the door I went, clutching a folder containing the all-important floppy disk and paper copies of all the documents.

As I trotted, the Nextel on my left hip beeped. Pulling it from the clip on the left side of my belt, I saw it was John. Before answering him on the direct connect, I made sure the speaker volume was at 0, making the walkie talkie act like a phone. When I pushed the button to respond, I held the Nextel to my ear so only I could hear John. Given what we were going to discuss, it would not have been appropriate for everyone within earshot to hear our conversation.

"Hey, John."

"Isn't this some shit?" I could hear the wailing of a siren in the background and the roar of John's engine as he sped to the FBI office with Moussaoui's property.

"Yep. It sucks. I am trying not to think about it. I am on my way to the U.S. Attorney's Office to get a warrant for the stuff."

John replied, "Bringing it up there now. Where do you want it?"

I thought for a second and realized I did not know where ERT planned to process the evidence. "Please call Brian or Matt. They're heading up the ERT effort and will be able to tell you where they want the stuff."

"Got it, amigo. See ya!" John ended the call. He was a good man in a storm. And today was the worst storm we would ever face.

CHAPTER 37

FINALLY

When I reached the U.S. Federal Court House in Minneapolis, I was directed to the conference room where the prosecutors assigned to help were assembled. I was disappointed to see that Peg was not among the several AUSAs present. Upon asking for her, I learned she was not available that morning, but that several other prosecutors would be assisting with the drafting of the warrant for our subject. As Chris had told me, Celia was there too. Although the assembled team knew in very general terms that we had a subject in custody who was almost certainly connected to the disaster unfolding in New York and D.C., they were lacking details. I handed over the documents to them and provided a short briefing so they could begin drafting the affidavit.

I also learned the "duty magistrate" for the day was the legendary J. Earl Cudd. This was good news for us because Judge Cudd was pro-government on any normal day. On a day like this, my guess is that he would have signed just about anything we put in front of him if the facts connected the subject to the tragedy on the East Coast.

Because I realized what that whatever affidavit we drafted that day would need to include information provided by the French, I put in a call to the LEGAT Office in Paris and within a short time our staunch allies in the French Government granted permission for us to use whatever we needed in our affidavit. They had been dealing with Islamic extremism for decades and could see for themselves what was happening on TV. I was then and will always be grateful to the French for their support on this case.

Time dragged on, and still the writing and discussion continued. I was growing very impatient and frustrated with what I saw as foot dragging by the prosecutors. In hindsight, I should have realized the AUSAs were facing a situation for which their legal training and experience had not prepared them. Most criminal cases with which they dealt were reactive in nature, meaning the crime had already been committed and there was usually little urgency in getting a search warrant to uncover the evidence. AUSAs were therefore accustomed to taking days or weeks to draft affidavits to ensure they were letter perfect to prevent evidence being suppressed later. That day, with a subject connected to the most prolific mass murder in U.S. history, some Agent had shown up in their office demanding an instant search warrant.

Fortunately, salvation came from an unexpected direction, and one which the AUSAs would not dare to ignore. Sometime earlier that day, someone in the U.S. Attorney's Office had called Magistrate Judge Cudd's chambers to give his secretary a heads up that Agents would be coming to get a warrant signed. This is a normal courtesy and just made good sense. No one likes to be surprised, and it was unwise to spring something on a judge whose goodwill you were seeking. It also seems certain that given the enormity of the events, whoever called the judge's secretary also told her the subject of the search warrant was connected to the attacks on the East Coast.

Around 2:30 that afternoon, one of the AUSAs' secretaries came into our conference room and announced that she had just received a call from Magistrate Judge Cudd's secretary.

Now, I will never know for sure, since I was not a friend of J. Earl Cudd, but I think that wily old former federal prosecutor realized the AUSAs down on the sixth floor were trying to make the warrant perfect, even though it was taking all day. Given what I do know of Judge Cudd, I am 100% convinced that with innocent people dying at that very minute and him knowing there was a search warrant on the same case being drafted for his signature, there was *no way* he was going home at 2:30 p.m. He had his secretary call to hurry things along!

And it worked. The message kicked things into overdrive, as even the boldest and most cavalier AUSA will *never* ignore an angry judge. The pressure seemed to concentrate their efforts and shortly before 4 p.m., six agonizing hours after I arrived at the U.S. Attorney's Office, I stood in front of Judge Cudd's beautiful oak desk in his chambers on the 13th floor as he invited me and the AUSA to sit while he read the affidavit.

We sat. The investigator in me had to look around the office. There was no evidence Magistrate Judge Cudd was in a hurry to leave. His computer was logged in, his coat hung on a hook, and he was reclining in his chair as he looked at my affidavit. He also did not make any comment at all about wanting to go home or being impatient in any way. When we got up to leave at the conclusion of our business, he remained seated comfortably, a slight smile on his long, lean face. No, I will be forever convinced that old friend of the FBI knew what he was doing when he jolted those AUSAs into hurrying the affidavit along.

Nor did Judge Cudd take too long to read the document. In fact, there was no way he could have in the short time he took before he signed. He certainly skimmed it, and I am sure hit the high points, but in no time at all, he took up his pen and asked me to stand while he swore me in.

"Ok, then." He signed the order and handed it to me. "Go get 'em!"

"Thank you, your honor. We will!"

As soon as we were out of the judge's chambers and in the elevator bank, I connected with John. "Judge Cudd just signed the warrant for Moussaoui's personal belongings and his laptop. Please tell ERT and CART to start the search."

"Got it."

CHAPTER 38

ANOTHER DELAY

When I arrived back at the office John met me at the door and informed me ERT was set up and ready to go. With an apology for keeping them waiting so long, I handed a copy of the signed warrant to Matt, an Agent on ERT. The team was already laying items out to be photographed, and I asked him to start by taking photos of the laptop so I could get it down to CART to allow them to begin their work. Brian placed the laptop case on the ground, laid a ruler next to it for scale, and began photographing it and its contents.

When they were finished with the laptop Matt handed me the case and its contents and I took it around the corner to the CART room, also located on the 9th floor. Inside Agents Jerry and Chris sat at desks with multiple monitors in front of them. Their workstations contained the FBI's most advanced equipment for retrieving and preserving digital evidence and I was hopeful the case I was carrying contained some. With Jerry and his team starting their searches, time would tell.

Greg flagged me down and I explained to him that CART had Moussaoui's laptop and a copy of the warrant. Although we knew Moussaoui had numerous notebooks, memo books and scraps of paper among the property we had, and even now ERT was preparing them to be photographed, I was still banking on the computer having the most data on it. It made sense since that small laptop could hold as much information as a library.

I observed as I came in on the 11th floor a few minutes earlier that our office had activated a 24/7 command post. In the wake of the attacks, all 56 field offices immediately did so, and these were manned 24 hours to handle the enormous number of investigative leads which would need to be handled. I was eager to begin blasting leads to other FBI offices worldwide as well as friendly foreign services based on what we would find in the searches.

Greg nodded as I spoke, "So, since the computer will take a few hours, my plan is to take all of the documents as ERT finishes photographing them and to go through them for possible leads to other plots or other attackers..."

Greg jumped in, "Yeah, good idea. Except, first you have to send copies of all of those documents to Martin...tonight."

"What? Why?"

"He's been calling me all day. Seems RFU wants to run all the names, numbers, etc. through their system to help make connections to any other people or attack plans."

I blinked, stunned at what I was hearing. Instead of having the sense to just go away and leave us alone after what he did, Martin was inserting himself in the process, again, and doing so negatively. "After that guy prevented us from getting a warrant, which the judge just signed in about three minutes, by the way...now he wants to help?"

"Yep. And orders are orders. RFU is still in charge."

The emotional momentum I had built up was gone. Instead of following my plan to review the documents and set immediate leads on them, I had to fax copies of each page to Martin first. Given the sheer volume of material and the fact ERT was meticulously photographing and cataloging each one, faxing the stuff to Martin would take all night. Greg and I looked at one another for a second. I did not say what I was thinking, and neither did he, but I was sure Martin had no intention whatsoever of "helping." While I do not know for sure what Martin did with the materials, I can say that not one tiny bit of assistance ever came from him or anyone in his unit out of the 156 pages John and I faxed him, one-by-one that night.

I walked back to the ERT room, feeling the old intense frustration welling up. John looked up when I walked in. "What's wrong?"

"Before we can start drafting leads on this stuff, I need to copy it all and fax it to Martin."

"Why?"

I shrugged, "He told Greg they'll run the names and numbers at headquarters to help make connections."

John smiled, "Yeah, right."

Just then, Matt walked up and handed me a small stack of notebooks and loose pages from Moussaoui's stuff. "We're done with these," he said. We could get started.

John and I walked around the corner to the copy room and began copying each page. I noticed Moussaoui was an inveterate note taker, scribbling, mostly in English, on everything from aircraft navigational procedures to grocery lists. There were also phone numbers—lots of phone numbers. Also present among the papers were disposable phone credit calling cards. We also noticed there was financial data, including references to bank accounts, money being wired, as well as numerous receipts for hotel stays and the purchase of many retail items. I longed to dig into that info, but I remained disciplined and methodically photocopied each of the pages so they could be faxed to Martin first. When we finished, John scooped up the pile of documents and returned them to the ERT room. He was back in a second. "It'll be a few minutes before the next batch is ready."

I decided to take a few minutes to call Terri. She had been home all day, no doubt watching the news and certainly taking care of Matt and Jake. I was sure she would appreciate an update. I tried to sound neutral, or slightly upbeat, but she knew me better than anyone. "It's pretty bad, huh?"

"It is. We have our search warrant now, and that's started, but headquarters wants the take sent to them first. That is just going to delay what we do with it."

Sympathetic as always, Terri listened to me and let me vent. When I was finished complaining, she added, "Matt learned to ride a two-wheeler today!"

I was simultaneously happy at my 5-year old's accomplishment—we'd been working on that for a while, and sad that I'd missed it, probably while waiting for the lawyers to finish drafting the affidavit.

She continued, "We were out in the cul-de-sac and George and Sherri saw us trying to get it. They came over and gave Matt a few pointers, helped him a little and then he did it all on his own!" George and Sherri were our neighbors from across the street. They were terrific, salt of the earth-type Minnesotans in their early 50s who were nice to us from the day we moved in. They had two sons in their late teens so of course they'd done the two-wheeler thing long before. I am sure they knew why I was not outside with Terri and the boys that afternoon like I usually was and came over to be with them. It was very kind, and I am eternally grateful.

John appeared at my desk with a new stack of notebooks. "Sweetie, I have to run. I don't know if I'll be home tonight."

"Ok. Please be careful." No complaints, no questioning, just solid support from Terri, always.

We returned to the copy room and added the new batch of copied pages to the now rapidly growing stack from the first batch. There were more lists, phone numbers and notes on aviation there. When we had a stack of around 30 pages, we decided to send the first fax to Martin. It was after 7 p.m. in Minnesota, so after 8 p.m. at the J. Edgar Hoover Building in D.C. I had Martin's fax number, but I wanted to make sure someone was there to receive it, so I called his desk first. He answered.

Keeping my voice dead neutral, I asked if he was ready to receive a batch of faxed documents from our search warrant. His annoyed tone remained, and he insistently indicated he would need *all* the "pocket litter" from the Moussaoui search. "Tonight. It all comes here tonight."

That was it. I held Martin completely responsible for what had happened and was in no mood to take any more from him. All pretense of respect for his position as a supervisor was gone, not that he deserved any. "Martin, as usual, you haven't been paying attention! What we are wading through now is not 'pocket litter.' It is pages and pages of notebooks we brought from Moussaoui's hotel room. I am copying them now, and rather than setting leads on the information contained in these documents, I am faxing them to you. Now, is someone standing by the fax?"

"Yes. Send them here and we..." I hung up while Martin was in mid-sentence.

Turning to the fax machine, conveniently located in the copier room, John filled out a cover sheet and prepared to send off the first batch. Our plan was to send Martin these documents as quickly as possible to forestall any more phone calls to Greg. Once he had these, we reasoned, he would presumably begin running checks on the information and would be too occupied to keep bothering us. John and I fed in small groups of papers at a time to make sure the machine did not jam. When we finally received a "fax complete" message, it was close to 9 p.m. and there were more documents coming from ERT as they finished photographing them.

John and I repeated the cycle, copying, stacking, preparing to fax, until we had a second pile of documents—this time 126 pages, ready to go. I filled out a second cover sheet and we spent over an hour making sure the fax went through. By the time we finished, it was after midnight, and I had not written one lead on the results of our search. I was determined to get started that evening, no matter how late it was, and I scooped up both packets we just faxed to Martin and took them with me. It was 156 pages containing information which might stop future attacks, and which would hopefully link Moussaoui to the ones which had just occurred.

CHAPTER 39

HIS BELONGINGS

When I returned to the squad area, I dropped the copies of Moussaoui's documents on my desk and sat down. I noticed my message light was on, so I listened to my voicemails. A number were from Martin, alternately requesting and demanding the materials from our search warrant be sent to him immediately. So, it had not been just Greg who Martin was calling all day. I deleted each message from him without listening to them. He had the materials now, so as far as I was concerned, our business was done, forever.

With a deep breath, I dug into the pile of copies in front of me. I began flipping through the pages until I came to names or phone numbers. As I found a notation written in Moussaoui's scrawling and sloppy cursive, I ran it through the FBI database. There were no hits in the FBI system for the numbers I ran, so I then wrote up a Rapid Start lead sheet asking for some type of investigation, like an interview of a person whose name and phone number appeared, or a records check on a business. Anything overseas was directed to the appropriate LEGAT. Once a lead was written up, I attached a post it note to the page in the bundle of copies so I knew it was completed.

After I had written five or six leads like this, each on a separate Rapid Start form, I looked at my watch and saw it was 2 a.m. I could feel my concentration slipping and decided to call it quits for the night so I could come back strong the next day. I could see there would be dozens, maybe hundreds of leads that would need to be set on the documents alone and reasoned those would be a fraction of the leads generated by the information on the laptop. I shut down my computer and ran upstairs to the command post on the 11th floor.

The team I was looking at in the command post now had been sent home as soon as the attacks happened or were called and told not to come in for their normal workday. Their shift began at midnight, and they were fresh. I walked over to an Investigative Assistant (IA) named Jan and handed her my stack of Rapid Start forms to enter. The leads were important, and I knew Jan would do a great job of entering the requests into the system.

Once I was sure Jan had what she needed and that I had filled out the forms correctly, I headed to my car. I walked back through the dark tunnel to our underground garage, where just that morning I sprinted in desperation to get to the office to finally begin the search for which the team had worked so hard for over the last 3 ½ weeks. That sprint seemed like it had been weeks ago now. The nervous energy was gone, and I dragged myself along, driven only by the thought of sleeping in my own bed so I could come back tomorrow to resume writing leads.

When my car emerged from our garage onto a now-deserted 2nd Avenue, I rolled down my windows and felt the cool air of the early morning. As I had on the way in, I kept the radio off and drove in silence.

Just when I pulled into my driveway, my phone rang. "It's 2:30 am," I thought, "Who would be calling now?"

"Harry, this is the ALAT in London," the voice said when I answered.

"Uh-huh," I responded, realizing it was 8:30 am there. My tone was cold because I was unhappy with him since I had heard nothing in response to my e-mails following Moussaoui's arrest. Unlike Jay, he'd shown no interest in helping our quest for search warrants. I was aware he sent two documents to the British Government in response to my lead and my e-mails, but he had taken his time in doing so and had not made the requests a priority as Jay had. In fact, a review of the second document he passed to Her Majesty's

Government showed he had not even asked them for information. The document simply ends, "The above is being provided to your service in the event Moussaoui is eventually deported to the UK." It was therefore no surprise that I had heard nothing back from the UK—we never asked the Brits for a response.

The ALAT then asked, "Do you remember the conversation we had a few days ago where I told you the Brits did not have anything on Moussaoui?"

"No." I said flatly. "We have not spoken since this case began."

"Yes, we did. We spoke a few days ago. Anyway, the British have some information now. I will send it to you as soon as I receive it."

"Ok." He hung up.

I admit I do not remember every conversation I have with people, but I certainly would have remembered one with the ALAT in London telling me the Brits had responded by saying they had no information on Moussaoui. I would have had a million questions for the ALAT about how the Brits would have had no information on a guy who lived in their country for the last decade while the French seemed to know all about him. Anyway, now the Brits had information for us, but it was too late.

I went inside the house, where everyone was obviously long asleep. When I kissed Terri, she murmured, "I love you." That little phrase made a huge difference and lifted my completely crushed spirits just a little. I tossed and turned for a few minutes before falling asleep, fortunately without dreaming.

The alarm went off at 6 a.m. on September 12, 2001. Despite getting only 3 hours of sleep, I was surprisingly ready to go back to work. I showered, shaved, and grabbed a quick breakfast. Just as I was ready to leave, my kids woke up, so I spent a few minutes with them while they ate breakfast. Of course, I made a huge deal about Matt learning to ride a two-wheeler.

I swung by the command post on the way to my desk and made sure the leads I wrote the night before were set. Jan had done a great job, and those requests were on their way.

I then swung through the CART room and saw Jerry and Chris, who were also in the office early. Jerry informed me the image of Moussaoui's computer, which had been purchased in the UK was complete. From a quick review of the image Jerry concluded Moussaoui did not have much on the hard drive. In fact, the drive appeared to have been erased or overwritten sometime earlier in the year. Despite that, it still made sense to do a keyword search and to look at the files on the laptop, but his assessment was that there was unlikely to be a smoking gun there.

When I got to the Squad area, I told Greg I had made a start on setting leads on the information in the documents and that was what I planned to do until there was a complete investigation of every name, company, telephone number, e-mail address and telephone calling card in that pile of documents. "Since the laptop now seems like a lower priority, I think the documents become job #1. I want to keep hammering away at that."

Greg nodded again. "Sound good," he said.

Returning to my desk, that is what I did for the next two days. September 12 and 13 were occupied with setting leads, one after the other in Rapid Start while sifting through the information among Moussaoui's papers. At this stage of the case, and with over a hundred and fifty pages of documents, I did not know what was most important or what would lead us to other plots and other terrorists. Making a series of educated guesses, I prioritized obvious things like Moussaoui's email address and his telephone number, because of the possibility he used these to communicate with other co-conspirators. Once leads to acquire call records and e-mail logs were set, I moved on to things like telephone calling cards. These were also a priority [Redacted by the FBI]. I wanted the numbers Moussaoui called and understood getting this data was time sensitive.

CHAPTER 40

LOSSES

As the hours of those two days rolled by, news of investigation by other Divisions slowly trickled into our office. New York, Boston, Washington Field Office, and Pittsburgh were beginning to identify the subjects who carried out the hijackings. They seemed to all be Arab males from Saudi Arabia or other countries in the Middle East. We also heard rumors there were recordings of radio transmissions from the airliners or cell phone calls from terrified passengers which told of horrible, unspeakable acts committed aboard the four jets.

At some point that first day, we learned two of our own were missing at the World Trade Center. Special Agent Leonard W. Hatton Jr., Lenny, to his friends, was a New York Agent who, like so many police officers and fire fighters, rushed into hell to save the innocents at 1 World Trade Center. Members of his squad heard from Lenny over the radio that he was at the World Trade Center, and he reported what he was seeing. Witnesses later saw him helping people evacuate the South Tower until it collapsed, killing him. Lenny's name is on the FBI's Wall of Martyrs, as tried and true an American Hero as ever lived.

Also missing was recently retired Special Agent in Charge John O'Neill, formerly of the New York Office. O'Neill was a famous counterterrorism manager, many of whose investigations targeted Usama Bin Laden and Al Qaeda. O'Neill retired from the FBI earlier that summer and had ironically assumed the job of Director of Security for the World Trade Center only a few weeks before the attacks. Like Lenny, O'Neill left a position of safety to enter the south tower and was last seen inside by witnesses helping to lead people out when the building collapsed. Another FBI hero who lost his life trying to save others.

Word also reached us that the Agents investigating hijackers on each of the flights continued to make progress identifying the subjects believed to have carried out the attack. Using passenger manifests and video of airport security checkpoints and other areas of the terminals, a picture was emerging of who did this. We learned a "major case" had been opened on the attacks. A major case was just what it sounded like: an investigation so large that it had its own funding and a separate team of Agents to run it. The events of 9/11 certainly qualified, and we were not surprised when the case was opened as a criminal terrorist matter, a 265A, just the kind of criminal case we sought to open on Moussaoui 3 weeks before. We were also not surprised when we learned the New York Office had the case. For a short time, it looked like the case might go to Washington Field Office, but ultimately New York won out. None of that changed what we were doing in Minneapolis. We were setting leads on everything found in Moussaoui's property.

On the afternoon of September 12, I was in the command post dropping off a stack of Rapid Start sheets so they could be entered in the computer, when an overhead page told me I had a phone call. Picking up a nearby phone and dialing the appropriate number, I heard Martin's voice. If I had expected Martin to provide some assistance on the Moussaoui leads (and I did not), I would have been disappointed. What he was calling about was surprising, however. It seems someone at FBIHQ decided in the wake of the attacks to re-initiate FISA coverage on all subjects who had recently been under surveillance. Since I had two subjects in that category, neither of whom were Moussaoui, Martin told me I needed to draft requests for each of them and get them to him immediately. He would take them to the FISA Court so we could begin listening to their calls again.

"That makes no sense," I responded. "Just a few months ago you insisted that the coverage be allowed to lapse on those subjects. Besides that, I have a subject who *was* involved in the attacks, and I am busy setting leads on the materials we obtained in our search warrant. If I stop doing that to write those requests, the leads will not be set, and additional bad things could happen. Speaking of which, how are the checks coming on the 150 pages we faxed you?"

Ignoring my question, Martin snapped, "That doesn't matter. What does matter is that you are being ordered to re-initiate FISA coverage on two of your subjects. Get the requests to me immediately!" He hung up.

The irony of Martin ordering me to apply for FISA coverage on anyone would have been funny under other circumstances, but in the wake of the tragedy, it was, like nearly every interaction with him, infuriating. His insistence that I stop investigating someone who almost certainly was involved in 9/11 to resume investigating two subjects who definitely were not was as off base as anything he said in the previous three plus weeks. One thing was for sure, I was not going to stop generating leads to do what Martin asked. I was done listening to him.

Therefore, I swung by Greg's desk to tell him about my call with Martin. Greg chuckled when I pointed out the irony. "Don't worry, we'll get someone else to draft the requests for Martin. You head back to the lead writing." I was grateful Greg saw it that way. One of the strengths of the FBI was that they can bring significant investigative manpower to bear when needed.

I stopped by the ERT room a few times on September 12, as Matt and Brian and their team finished photographing the rest of Moussaoui's property. Among his effects was a tape recorder, an aviation radio, a pair of boots identical to those Al-Attas had, protective gear for sparring, the two knives we located on the day he was arrested, and clothing. With a smile on his face Matt, who had a great sense of humor, pulled a T-shirt from among Moussaoui's possessions. Holding it up, we could see it said "World's Greatest Grandpa" in fancy script. With a twinkle in his eye, Matt said, "I don't think your guy did his research before he went undercover." It was a rare laugh during a sad time.

Later that evening, as John and I had just finished eating dinner, Greg came up to see us. "New York is aware of your guy," he said. Glancing at his notepad, he said, "They want you to call a Brian on the Al Qaeda Squad there to discuss what we have."

"Terrific," I thought sarcastically. Now New York will ride to the rescue." What I actually said was, "Ok," and held out my hand for the paper with Brian's number on it.

Greg continued, "Apparently New York's phones are not working well since their main Nextel repeater was on the roof of one of the towers. Also, all the landline phones to their main office are down because of the damage in the area. Keep trying until you get him."

That sure brought it home to me. New York might have been the bully when it came to counterterrorism cases, but they'd lost an Agent as well as their recently retired SAC and had their phones knocked out by a terrorist attack. I was sure it was personal for them.

I dialed Brian's number right away. The voice that answered was faint, as if we were speaking on an old-fashioned landline with a bad connection. "Brian?"

"Yes."

I explained who I was and that I was asked by my supervisor to call. Brian was expecting my call and thanked me for taking the time to make it. Not only was he courteous, but I detected a hint of a Philadelphia accent when he asked, "What do you have?"

Because I had been telling the story of the Moussaoui case for over 3 ½ weeks by then, I was able to quickly deliver a coherent summary. Brian listened without interruption. When I got to the end, I explained we tried obtaining a criminal warrant, a FISA warrant and finally a French customs search, all with the goal of preventing what had happened. "But they didn't believe me," I said.

Without hesitation, Brian responded, "Yeah, well I would have believed you, Har." In calling me "Har," Brian clearly marked himself as someone from Philly—now I was sure. In fact, he sounded like the kids I went to high school with. Better, Brian was the first Agent outside of Minneapolis to acknowledge we might be onto something with the Moussaoui case, and it caused me to like him right away.

Brian informed me he would talk to his management and some AUSAs in the Southern District of New York, but he guessed they would probably want our team to come there to brief them. If Moussaoui was connected to the attacks, New York would want to have details as soon as possible. I responded that we were ready. We ended the call on a good note. Brian sounded like a real Agent and someone we could work with.

John and I went back to lead writing. At the next break, I ran down to the squad area to inform Greg that New York was probably going to request we go to visit them with a team able to brief them on Moussaoui. Greg pointed out a fact that Brian and I had overlooked, "Commercial aircraft are not flying right now." Greg was right. However, he added, "I think they will be back in the next day or two, so we can go then."

And he was correct. Within a short time, the FAA permitted a resumption of commercial flights, and we were able to travel to New York.

CHAPTER 41

A NEW THREAT

On the afternoon of September 13, John and I ventured downstairs to the CART room. Jerry reiterated that the user directories on the hard drive of Moussaoui's laptop did not have much in them except for some old emails and a few PowerPoint presentations about the 747–400 from Northwest Airlines. Jerry found the e-mails the day before and confirmed they were associated with the pilotz123@hotmail.com account—one we already knew about. In fact, seeking information on the contents of that email account was one of the first leads I wrote two days earlier.

As John and I were discussing how the laptop might not have been the key piece of evidence we believed it might be, Jerry came over with a floppy disk. "By the way, this is a copy of a disk that was in the laptop case. It has stuff on agricultural aviation from some school in Louisiana on it."

"Agricultural aviation," I almost shouted. "Crop dusting? Why is he studying that?"

Jerry shrugged, "Take a look." He slid the disk into a spare review computer and opened one of the three or four files on the disk. "Here ya go. This is it."

As soon as I looked at the file, I realized Moussaoui had downloaded multiple chapters of a manual on agricultural aviation published by a university in Louisiana. There were more than a dozen chapters to the complete manual, and they all appeared to be there. From a quick review, the document seemed like a legitimate academic discussion of the nuts and bolts of delivering pesticides from aircraft. I did not know anything about crop dusting, but I could tell the person who wrote what I was reading was obviously a highly experienced agricultural pilot. A quick internet search also confirmed the university in question did have an agricultural aviation department, one of only a few in the U.S. In fact, we were able to find the same manual on the school's website.

The manual was a detailed guide on how to safely apply chemicals to farm fields using fixed wing aircraft. The pilot in me was curious about the kind of precision flying needed to do so safely and efficiently while spraying *only* in the precise location the pilot wanted to hit, so I sat there reading. I quickly realized as I read the document that chemicals being sprayed from an aircraft could spread vertically and laterally, meaning much larger areas would be covered by the spray pattern. There were even illustrations to go along with the very complete textual descriptions. While the manual obviously explained these conditions and flight maneuvers as those *under which pilots should not spray,* someone wanting to contaminate a large area using an agricultural aircraft only had to wait for these weather conditions and then fly in the manner prohibited in the manual. If read that way, *the document was inadvertently a guide to applying poison from an aircraft to an area target on the ground.*

When I had read enough, I looked at John. "Anyone with this manual would know how to contaminate a large area using a crop duster. And Moussaoui went to the trouble of downloading the whole thing, chapter by chapter. Correct me if I'm wrong, but that guy never once mentioned an interest in crop dusting."

"No, he didn't. 'Zac' was all about flying the 747."

"It's like *Goldfinger,*" I said, referring to the James Bond movie where Pussy Galore and her flying circus planned to use aerial spraying to kill everyone at Fort Knox so Goldfinger could get into the vault with the gold. John and Jerry nodded, having obviously seen the Bond classic. Only this was real life, and Moussaoui was an actual terrorist. What possible legitimate reason could he have had for researching crop dusting?

John and I swung by the squad area to grab Greg and then we headed up to talk to Chris about the crop duster find. Chris had previously been in the Weapons of Mass Destruction Operations Unit (WMDOU) at headquarters so he would probably know something about this. As a pilot, Greg understood right away the incongruity of Moussaoui having a crop duster manual while simultaneously paying big bucks for training in a 747–400 simulator. The two types of flying could not be more different. It was ominous.

Chris was not surprised to see us. One or the other of us had been checking in to update him several times a day. When we were all seated in his office, I held up the floppy disk. "This is a copy of a disk that was in Moussaoui's laptop case. Someone, probably him, downloaded multiple chapters of an agricultural aviation manual from a university in Louisiana that has a program to teach crop dusting. We reviewed the manual, and all a terrorist needs to do to use a crop duster as a weapon is to violate a few of the safety procedures explained in here. It lays out very simply how *not* to crop dust. Ignore or reverse some of the instructions and you have a weapon capable of contaminating a pretty big area, and fast."

Greg added, "It really does not make sense for someone training on the 747–400 to be researching crop dusting. The flying is so different."

Chris got it. "Yep. A crop duster attack was discussed at some point at WMDOU in the past. We need to call someone back there to loop them in." He looked in his rolodex, pulled up a number and dialed a supervisor he knew in WMDOU.

After the usual greetings, Chris put the phone on speaker, so we could all hear the conversation, and chime in. Chris explained to the supervisor that Agents on his squad arrested a subject involved in the attacks before 9/11. He added that during a search of his belongings, we found a crop duster manual. One of us added that the subject had been doing training on a 747–400 simulator, making his possession of this manual a serious concern. We passed him the web address of the university in Louisiana. While the supervisor was still on the phone, he found the site and informed us he would pull up this manual and take it to some of the scientists and HAZMAT technicians in the unit to see what they thought. That seemed like the right thing to do, so we ended the call with a promise to stay in touch.

In between making travel plans, assembling what we needed to brief New York and getting our team together, John and I continued to write leads. Around this time, we also learned from Scott in Oklahoma City that they took some aggressive steps in Norman, to include arresting Al-Attas on 9/11 and executing the long wished-for search of the apartment he shared with Moussaoui. Agents also located Moussaoui's 1989 Ford Tempo and searched that, as well. The searches in Oklahoma revealed Moussaoui left behind documents and other items in his car and apartment. They were also interviewing people who knew Moussaoui, including roommates, associates from the mosque, and students, staff, and instructors at the flight school. It sounded like they were on top of things, and I asked Scott to send us copies of the documents, reports of interviews and anything and everything he thought we should see. He agreed to do so.

CHAPTER 42

NEW YORK

After learning the FAA was allowing resumption of flights, we booked our travel to New York for Friday, September 14, 2001. We coordinated with Brian, and he generously offered to pick us up at the airport and get us to our hotel as things in lower Manhattan were still "a little messed up." Included in the Minneapolis team were Greg as our supervisor, Peg as the prosecutor, Joe, and I as the case Agents, and John as a case Agent and INS representative. We were going with the idea that New York was going to be taking over the Moussaoui case. While no one is ever happy about turning over an investigation, especially a big one, we realized the venue for prosecution of subjects involved in the attacks was in New York, Washington, or Pennsylvania, since that was where the crimes had been committed. It also made sense because New York had the manpower and other resources to dedicate to the case that Minneapolis did not.

Brian also let me know New York wanted Moussaoui there, so around this time, a special aircraft was arranged to transport him. Even before our team left, the FBI Minneapolis SWAT team took Moussaoui to the airport for his flight. As they came into sight of the airport, members of the team saw him looking out the window of the Suburban at the grounded airliners. One of them later informed me Moussaoui looked happy and made a few remarks about how it had been expected that the airplanes would all stop flying afterwards. This was later documented in a report by the SWAT team leader and provided to the prosecutors. At around this same time, Al-Attas was also being sent to New York from Oklahoma City where he had been held in custody since his arrest on 9/11.

Because I would be in New York for a few days, I came home in time on the 13th to say goodbye to the boys at bedtime. Terri and I prayed with Matt and Jake in their bedroom and gave them their usual reassurance that there were no such things as monsters. Monsters had been a bedtime problem for us for some time, and we found it best to front-load some anxiety-reducing statements while the lights were still on. Our usual catch phrase as we left the room was, "And remember, there are NO monsters!"

As we stood to leave, Matt, who was 5, looked serious, his little face hanging sadly over the rail of the top bunk. I asked him what was wrong. He voiced concern that I was leaving for a trip and asked why I had to go. From the bottom bunk Jake, who was a little over two, also looked at me, awaiting my reply. He was on his back, holding each of his little feet in the air and grasping them with his hands.

What I wanted to say, is, "I love you guys and mommy more than anyone, but I have to travel because there *really are* monsters out there, despite what we've been telling you. My friends and I are trying to keep more of them from coming here to hurt anyone else." Of course, that would have made for a scary bedtime, so I gave them some other reason. I also ended with the promise of presents when I came home.

We were on an American Airlines flight from Minneapolis to La Guardia that afternoon, one of the first to go following the limited resumption of service after the attacks. The airports were still eerily empty, as was the plane itself, and tensions were high among airport security personnel. When the pilots learned they had so many armed federal Agents on their flight, they asked the flight attendants to upgrade us all to first class, which was not difficult given the emptiness of the plane. Poor Peg had to sit back in coach, since she was not armed.

During that whole flight I studied and prepared for briefing the New York team. We had a cardboard printer paper box full of documents for them, backed with floppy disks with electronic copies too. I wanted to be sure Minneapolis looked squared away and that we were handing them as complete a case as possible.

As we began our descent, I started looking out my window. I could see we were heading southeast over central New York. The weather was good, and it was just starting to get dark. Within a few minutes the pilot announced on the PA that we would be passing over lower Manhattan and the site where the World Trade Center had been on our way into La Guardia. He added solemnly that it would be visible almost straight down from the left side of the airplane. Because the first-class section was nearly empty except for our group, I was able to slide over from my seat on the right so I could look out a window on the left. Almost immediately I could see the smoke from fires still burning. As we got closer, brilliant flood lights were visible, illuminating what seemed to be a scar in the middle of the city. It was terrifying in-person confirmation that the destruction of the site had been nearly complete, and I wondered how anyone was able to survive.

The first glimpse of the results of my failure.

If I thought security was tight at the airport in Minneapolis, what we saw when we landed at LaGuardia made that seem like nothing. Everywhere inside the terminal were police armed with rifles, backed by National Guard soldiers in full combat gear. As our group rode the escalator down to the baggage claim level, I saw to my left that there was a black railing with a swinging gate separating the main area of the arrivals' terminal from the baggage carousels. At the gate stood a police officer checking everyone's baggage claim check before admitting them to the area. Next to the police officer stood a tall, muscular, alert young man, about my age with longish hair. He was accompanied by an attractive woman, also in her early 30s. Even though they were dressed in casual clothes, I knew right away they were FBI Agents.

"Brian?" I asked, the man when I reached the gate.

"Yep. Har?" He asked.

"Hi," I said, setting the box down and extending my hand. We shook, and Brian introduced me to his partner, Janelle. I introduced the rest of the Minneapolis team to them, and we moved into the baggage claim area to get our luggage. We chatted while waiting for the bags to arrive. Brian and Janelle thanked us for coming. We learned they were on New York's I-49, the famous Al Qaeda Squad. Since it was looking more certain by the minute that Al Qaeda was the group behind the attacks, their squad was taking the lead on the investigation.

I added that we believed our subject Moussaoui was an Al Qaeda operative as well. I tapped the cardboard box I was holding and informed Brian and Janelle we brought some documents which explained how he was linked to the group. I went on to explain that since the attacks we had obtained a search warrant for Moussaoui's property with him in Minnesota and that Oklahoma City had done the same for things he left behind in Norman. Our priority in Minneapolis was reviewing these materials and setting leads to identify other co-conspirators or plots. We informed them Oklahoma City had also made at least one additional arrest since the attacks and that person, Al-Attas, was almost certainly able to shed more light on Moussaoui.

Brian and Janelle nodded. One of them informed us they would take us to our hotel that night and maybe get some dinner and a beer with us. That sounded like a good way to get to know our new teammates. Brian explained our first formal order of business was a meeting with their AUSAs the next day. We all understood this was a criminal case now, so our primary "customers" were the prosecutors.

In that sad, shocked, frightened city, we had AUSAs from the storied Southern District of New York who would be examining the evidence and deciding whether to charge Moussaoui. And in 2001 there were no prosecutors in the U.S. with more terrorism experience than those in the Southern District of New York. The Blind Sheikh and his group, along with the bombers of the U.S. Embassies in Kenya and Tanzania, and the murderers who attacked the USS *Cole* had seen to that.

We could see from our drive to Lower Manhattan that the city was on high alert. Just as at the airport, there were police officers and soldiers on every corner. When we were a few blocks from "26 Fed" as the New York Agents referred to their office, we passed a checkpoint manned by police and soldiers. Brian showed his FBI credentials before being allowed to proceed with our vehicle.

When Brian lowered his window to speak to the police manning the checkpoint, I smelled it for the first time. It was the odor of burning fuel and melted rubber and decomposing corpses and concrete dust and a million other elements that had been pulverized and thrown into the air by the impact of two airliners full of people into buildings full of more people. It was a terrible smell, as impossible to describe as it is to forget. I'd smelled that smell before, in places like Iraq and Pakistan, and the first time I did, I remembered my dad describing the smell of war in France as being a mix of dead bodies and ashes.

But never in the U.S.

I never smelled anything like that while at home. And the smell on that night triggered the rage-filled thought, "Finally the terrorists got what they wanted. They have turned a small part of the U.S. into the same hopeless wasteland they inhabit, complete with the smell." I was silent the rest of the way, until we pulled up in front of the office on Broadway.

As I climbed out of the car and looked up at the huge Jacob K. Javits Federal Building that was home to, among other agencies, the New York Office of the FBI, I realized I had not been back since my applicant interview five years before. That seemed like a hundred years ago now.

Brian popped the trunk and grabbed the box of sensitive materials which had to be taken to the office. He asked whether anything else needed to be run upstairs. No one else had anything sensitive, so that was it. Brian explained the JTTF was no longer in the Javits building but had grown so large it was instead housed in the Ted Weiss Federal Building at 290 Broadway, just to the south across

Duane Street. He informed us he would be right back. The rest of us stood with Janelle chatting about her experiences on the day of the attack, the smell of the devastation in our noses. I looked to the southwest where I knew the towers had stood but could not see anything unusual.

With that formality completed, Brian and Janelle got us to our hotel and arranged to pick us up the following morning. We were grateful, not just for the ride, but because we they whisked us through security. I knew from experience New York Agents sometimes came on strong, but our partners seemed terrific.

CHAPTER 43

GROUND ZERO

The next morning Brian and Janelle were outside our hotel to meet us. After a short walk through still eerily empty streets, we arrived at their office at 290 Broadway. Fall was beginning to take hold, and it was cooler, but the smell persisted in the gray air. We took an elevator up and entered the office space of the New York JTTF. Brian and Janelle ushered us into a conference room, where we were reunited with our box of documents. As everyone settled themselves around the table, I cut the tape on the box, pulled off the lid, and began laying out documents to hand to New York Agents and AUSAs as we told our story.

A few Agents from the New York JTTF drifted in to listen, but the guests of honor were two AUSAs from the Southern District of New York, Ken and Derek. Ken was dark haired with glasses and of medium height and build. He was casually attired in a button-down shirt and khakis. Derek was taller and more muscular, with dark hair and light-colored eyes. I thought he moved like an athlete and seemed more like an Agent than an AUSA. Both were a few years older than me—I guessed they were in their mid-30s and knew each of the New York Agents by name. They also seemed familiar with Bureau lingo and procedure. That was a good sign.

After introductions, we were asked to give Ken and Derek, who were experienced terrorism prosecutors, a summary of our investigation of Moussaoui. As the case Agent, I did most of the talking, rattling off the well-practiced description of how the case originated, the way John delivered us an arrest option, and how we made the decision to use this to forestall any advanced aviation training. As I described the interviews of Al-Attas and Moussaoui, we handed them copies of the reports so they could read for themselves what was said. I also described the French information linking Moussaoui to Ibn Khattab, Chechnya, and Afghanistan, and thus to Al Qaeda. Because I did not think it was hugely important to their decision whether to charge Moussaoui or not, I briefly summarized the fight with headquarters, without going into too much detail. I did not want to sound like "that" guy, even though I was. Others on the Minneapolis team chimed in to add facts I omitted.

As we spoke, I noticed Ken and Derek listened intently. They did not interrupt and did not look at any documents until we stopped speaking. When we finished, Ken and Derek asked a few clarifying questions, good ones which suggested they wanted to charge Moussaoui. After they were done with their questions, Ken and Derek skimmed over the documents we provided, especially the reports of our interviews and the ones from the French. When they were finished, both put down their pens on the legal pads upon which they had been taking notes. Smiling at us, Ken said, "This is a great case, and Minneapolis has done a terrific job. We're ready to indict Moussaoui today."

I felt a strong sense of relief. Although we in Minneapolis were convinced of Moussaoui's involvement, it was nice to hear it from an outsider, particularly an outsider who could decide to charge him with a crime. Greg echoed my thoughts perfectly when he said, "We're very glad to hear that!"

Ken smiled again. "Well, that's the opinion of two AUSAs. We have to talk to our boss, Mary Jo White, who is the U.S. Attorney here before we can commit to that. Then we'll need DOJ on board for terrorism charges. They'll also decide what the case looks like." Ken then used an expression I never heard before, but which, as it turned out, described the situation perfectly, "On any terrorism case, but especially one this big, we don't mix the colors. We just paint."

That all sounded fine to me, and I was not worried. I knew that with FBI New York and the Southern District on board, DOJ would do whatever they wanted. I was also happy we seemed to have highly qualified prosecutors. Looking at Ken and Derek I said, "So, we're a little over halfway finished going through the documents in Moussaoui's property and setting leads. We'd like to continue doing that."

One of the lawyers responded, "Absolutely. Keep it up."

Someone on the Minneapolis team added that Oklahoma City also made arrests of some of Moussaoui's associates following the attacks and were out doing interviews of others, including employees and students at Airman Flight School and people at the mosque. This also sounded fine to Ken and Derek, they just asked that we be sure to coordinate with the team in New York moving forward. We were happy to agree to that, as we now had the biggest office in the FBI assisting us on our case. It seemed unlikely Martin or his boss Devin or anyone at FBIHQ could derail this now. Even if I had not prevented the attacks, the combined Minneapolis-New York team could now at least ensure justice for the victims.

By the time we finished discussing the case with the New York Agents, the light was fading outside. We had talked nearly the whole day, with only a short break for lunch, during which we went together to get sandwiches at a nearby deli. By the end of the day all of us on the Minneapolis team had a great feeling about Brian and Janelle and were comfortable working with them on the case moving forward. I think we all understood that eventually we would be phased out, but we were relieved to see the investigation would be going to Agents who cared about it and about getting justice.

The following morning the team met for an hour or so to clean up the final details. As we were wrapping up, Brian and Janelle informed us they arranged a visit for us to the World Trade Center site to look around. It was already being called "Ground Zero." We learned the search and rescue effort was complete and that all the living had been removed and what we would now view was a cleanup and recovery effort. We were advised by someone on New York's ERT to wear clothes we could throw away because the whole area was a mess.

At the appointed time our group walked the few blocks to the perimeter around what had been 1 World Trade Center. As we got close, security increased. The area, which was a large crime scene, was guarded by police officers and soldiers. We noticed many of the cops were wearing jeans with their uniform shirts. We were told this was because the New York Police Department (NYPD) had been working its officers continually since the attack, with almost no chance when not on duty for anything other than rest and meals. For this reason, off-duty cops had not had time to do laundry and were running out of clean uniforms.

We stopped at a command trailer, where our credentials were checked, and we were asked to sign in. The smell of ashes and decomposition was strong, and we could, around the corner of a building, glimpse some wreckage in the form of twisted girders and concrete rubble. It was a preview of the devastation that awaited. The sky was overcast, and the day was rainy, making a gray, slimy mud under our feet. I had never seen so much mud in a city before.

Our group was asked to wait for the next safety briefing. These were given every few minutes and were a requirement before anyone was allowed into the area for the first time. While we stood waiting, I kept sneaking glances around the corner at the wreckage, understanding that what I was seeing and smelling occurred because I had been unable to solve my case and stop the attacks. The cold and bleak scene matched my mood and probably made me feel even more miserable.

When the time for the briefing came, an obviously tired official, maybe a firefighter, came out of the trailer wearing a hard hat and a fluorescent vest. Standing on the porch he gave us a short welcome, after which he informed us the area we were about to enter remained dangerous. There was the risk of collapse of many of the structures still standing because what was left had been damaged by falling debris and fire and was therefore completely unstable. There were also some fires burning. In addition to that, the scene was a hazardous materials site due to the presence of a large number of decomposing human remains. At hearing that, I looked away, feeling again the by-now familiar guilt. After a second, I looked back at the gentleman again, forcing myself to pay attention to his briefing.

After rattling off a list of dos and don'ts, the official referred to a map of Ground Zero zip tied to the fence running around the scene. The periphery of the site on the map was marked with some Xs. Pointing to the map, the man warned us, "If you hear a blast on a loud siren while you are at the site, it means a collapse or some other significant danger is imminent. Head for one of these Xs and rally with your party there. Someone get a count of the people you are entering with, and make sure everyone is together. If one of your party is missing, let one of the incident command staff know immediately."

Glancing quickly at everyone's feet, the official advised us to make sure we wore shoes in which we could run if necessary, since collapses or explosions might happen at any time. He seemed satisfied we were okay and moved on with his talk. As he did, I noticed Peg was standing near the back of our group, so the fire official had not been able to see her feet. As an AUSA, Peg came to New York wearing business attire, which meant high heels. That was all she packed and was what she was wearing that day, in contrast to the Agents, all of whom were wearing boots. As our eyes met, I wondered if Peg would opt out of entering the scene. I was about to suggest that when she whispered to me that she was going in no matter what. Peg was determined to see around the corner so she would be ever more motivated to bring justice to the victims. It was an admirable statement. She then asked us to be sure to get her out of there if things did go bad. Given Peg's spirit and determination, we all agreed we would make sure she stayed safe.

When the briefing was over, we were issued hard hats and handed off to a guide who would lead us through Ground Zero. As we headed through the fence, my heart began to pound. I was conscious that we were witnessing history, and a particularly tragic chapter. I wished then, as I have ten thousand times since, that we could have brought about a different result. I wondered how John was, and I shot a glance at him. He looked as grim as I felt.

When we rounded the corner, it was like entering another world. The view of the small pile of girders and few blocks of concrete did not tell the whole story. What we saw now was far worse—the devastation was complete, and it looked like a nightmarish scene from a bomb-destroyed European city during World War 2. It was apparent both towers had fallen into this relatively small area, crushing nearly everything beneath them, and scattering their contents around the site. Girders stuck out at extreme angles and irregularly shaped chunks of concrete, some as big as buildings themselves, lay all over the ground. Personal effects from the people who just last week worked at 1 World Trade Center were everywhere. There were fires still burning and water flowing from severed pipes and from the rain made the ground slippery with gray mud.

Crews were working everywhere around us. Heavy excavators and bulldozers moved rubble while teams on foot worked to map out areas for digging or pulling down portions of structures which still stood. While the efforts were not frantic, it was obvious people were working hard to restore order from the chaos which now existed there. We were informed the fire department was by this time sure the survivors of the attack had all been evacuated so there were no longer any rescue operations going on. Everything was recovery and salvage. We also observed teams wearing navy blue jackets emblazoned with the letters "FBI"—raid jackets. These were the Agents and professional support personnel of the ERT teams sent from across the country who were there to collect evidence of the monstrous crime which had been committed.

Our group stopped in front of what had been Building 7. This structure, although completely destroyed, still looked like a building. It had been crushed by debris from the towers when they collapsed and then charred by a fire, small offshoots of which were still burning. Furniture, pieces of the building and personal effects had spilled out onto the ground when the weight of thousands of tons of steel and concrete had flattened the steel structure. Pipes and wiring and girders and glass were everywhere. I remember looking down and seeking a small desk calendar lying on the ground. Although the pages were sodden, I could see it had been opened to Tuesday, September 11, 2001.

Our guide explained we were looking at the ruins of Building 7. She indicated that although not everyone had been accounted for yet, it was not believed that anyone had died in the building, as there had been time to evacuate completely before the North Tower collapsed. That made me feel a little better. Certainly, anyone who stayed in that building would have been killed by the collapse and I was glad to hear they made it.

As I looked around, I could see portions of concrete from both towers still stood. How these windowed shards of concrete survived the collapse, I do not know, but they were incredibly sad artifacts of what had once been the two tallest buildings in the city. We were told these swaying walls now posed a great danger to recovery crews at Ground Zero as they were unstable and liable to fall at any minute. In addition to the oppressive sadness and appalling filth and smell, there was still the very real danger of being killed and injured at Ground Zero, where so many had died already.[11]

After about an hour, it was time to leave. Our escort guided us out along the paths through the rubble, over what seemed to be miles of gray, unnatural mud. The entire time I was at Ground Zero, I felt an overwhelming sense of sorrow and guilt. I felt guilty in part because we were of no assistance to the hundreds of people we saw working to help. Mostly, I felt like I was trespassing at a funeral. Not only was it a funeral, but it was a funeral for victims whose lives *I had been unable to save*. Investigators sometimes come face-to-face with the results of their failure to solve a case, and that day those results were all around me. That feeling would never leave completely, even as I type these words. That day also shaped how I conducted myself as an Agent for the rest of my time in the FBI.

---

11 And first responders continue to die, including FBI Agents. At the time of this writing, shortly after the 17th anniversary of the attacks, 15 FBI Agents have died from cancers linked to their roles in the 9/11 investigation at Ground Zero and other 9/11 crime scenes.

CHAPTER 44

MORE CONNECTIONS

While this was going on in New York, things were happening in Norman, Oklahoma. In addition to the arrests of Al-Attas and some of his and Moussaoui's associates, the search team at Moussaoui's apartment at 209A Wadsack Drive found a duffel bag containing some clothing and documents. The documents in that duffel bag would prove to be highly significant and important to the investigation.

An examination of these showed Moussaoui had acquired sales brochures for several agricultural aircraft manufactured by the Air Tractor company in Olney, Texas, including the AT-402, AT-502 and AT-802 aircraft. The sales materials included price lists, as if Moussaoui were looking to buy such an aircraft. We also later learned from a search of Moussaoui's pilotz123@hotmail.com account that he had sent at least one email to an agricultural aviation expert asking for advice on buying an agricultural aircraft and running a crop duster business. It also became obvious from our continuing review of Moussaoui's documents that his research on the agricultural aviation industry had been extensive, and we saw he took methodical notes in his scrawling handwriting on names, phone number and web addresses likely to be of use to him. His interest in crop dusters was clearly not a casual one.

I do not know when the Oklahoma City materials reached WMDOU at FBI Headquarters, but sometime on Sunday, September 16th, there was finally action taken to address the mounting evidence of Al Qaeda's plans to use agricultural aircraft as a weapon. The

FAA grounded agricultural aircraft on that day, while an intensive investigation began to determine whether anyone associated with the hijackers had access to a crop duster or had gained the expertise needed to fly one. Given the importance of these aircraft to the food supply flights were resumed a short time later, though with increased restrictions on how and where these aircraft could operate. Specifically, they were required to stay clear of major population centers, not a huge challenge given their normal operating areas are mainly rural anyway.

We had been waiting for this development since our call to WMDOU and learned of the ban in New York on Sunday as we were preparing to return to Minneapolis the following morning. Greg and I discussed what seemed to be a long delay before the FAA addressed this threat since we had called WMDOU three days earlier. [Redacted by the FBI]. For this reason, WMDOU initially did not consider the threat a valid one!

Fortunately, someone in that unit eventually contacted the National Agricultural Aviation Association about this issue. [Reacted by the FBI]. Therefore, the threat *was* valid. Whether the Air Tractor materials found in Oklahoma on September 15 were added to the pile of evidence or not, the FAA grounded the crop dusters the next day and a large-scale investigation of the agricultural aviation industry began. What investigators learned quickly was that the ag aviation industry was a small and close-knit group, with pilots and maintenance personnel from across the country all at least loosely acquainted with one another.

They were also a patriotic bunch, quite inclined to assist law enforcement in tracking down terrorists attempting to use their aircraft or techniques to poison people. Within a short time, reports began coming in from interviews of crop duster pilots and mechanics in Florida that at least one other hijacker pilot, later identified as Mohamed Atta, also showed an interest in agricultural aircraft. This also began a dialog between the FBI and the National Agricultural Aviation Association that seemed to foreclose any future threat from this angle. People in the agricultural aviation industry were made aware terrorists had been interested in their aircraft and techniques and were now on the lookout for anyone suspicious attempting to intrude on their small circle of experts.

Our team landed back in Minneapolis late Monday morning. No one went home but instead picked up where we left off. John and I sat down and fired up the computer. The stack of copies of Moussaoui's documents lay open, just where we left them. And we dived in again, running names, numbers, and addresses and transferring what we found to Rapid Start sheets so Agents located elsewhere in the world could follow up with investigation.

After a few hours of that, Greg appeared. He handed me the fax from Oklahoma City which had come the night before. In the package were the brochures on the Air Tractor aircraft. Also included were copies of formally written business letters from a Malaysia-based company called Infocus Tech. Dated October 5, 2000, they were addressed to Moussaoui and stated that he would be acting as the company's marketing consultant. There seemed to be three versions of this letter, one for the U.S., one for the United Kingdom and one for Europe. In each case, the letters discussed salary and some operating instructions relating to the company's software, which apparently Moussaoui would be selling. The letters were all signed by a Yazid Sufaat, listed as the managing director of the company. Included with the letters were brochures for some of Infocus Tech's products. There was also a scrap of paper with e-mail addresses which were apparently associated with Infocus Tech, Yazid Sufaat himself and a place called "Greenlabs." There were also some overseas phone numbers on this piece of paper.

The Air Tractor information was interesting, but nothing seemed urgent in there since the FAA had grounded agricultural aircraft the day before. We planned to set a lead to Air Tractor to see what they knew of Moussaoui and the nature of his communications with them, if any, but those could wait. The Infocus Tech documents seemed much more significant and urgent. They appeared to corroborate

Moussaoui's statements that he had been in Malaysia the year before in connection with a phone card business. So why had he not told us the name of the company? And why had he not given us the name and phone number of Yazid Sufaat as someone who could vouch for his story?

These two questions made Infocus Tech and Yazid Sufaat our priority for the rest of the day. We ran the names, e-mail addresses and phone numbers in the FBI database, but got nothing back. I then wrote out a Rapid Start lead for LEGAT Singapore, which was the office that covered Malaysia in 2001. In the lead, I asked the LEGAT to ask the Malaysian authorities whether they knew anything about Sufaat, Infocus Tech or Greenlabs, and whether any of the e-mail addresses or phone numbers had come up in their investigations.

Within a few days or a week, we had information back on Sufaat and his company in response to our lead. He was under investigation in Malaysia for his support to Al Qaeda. This support included hosting a meeting in Malaysia in early 2000 attended by several Al Qaeda operatives.[12] The Malaysian investigation of his companies, Infocus Tech and Greenlabs revealed these seemed to be shell corporations. Sufaat's whereabouts in the fall of 2001 were unknown, as he left Malaysia before the 9/11 attacks, presumably for Afghanistan. He was a bona fide terrorist. Another associate of Moussaoui's who was connected to Al Qaeda.

12 It was later learned that two of the operatives who attended this meeting were 9/11 attackers Nawaf al-Hazmi and Khalid al-Midhar.

CHAPTER 45

MONEY FROM GERMANY

The days of September rolled sadly by, submerged in a welter of lead writing. As we continued, John and I found among Moussaoui's belongings a slip of paper which had been torn out of a small, flip-open pocket notebook, with ragged edges across the top. The page had been printed neatly in ink and was very unlike Moussaoui's own handwriting, so we knew he had not written it. It read, "Prof Amer Aziz; Tele: R 5712127; 570969; 60-A FCC, Gulberg IV; Lahore 54600 Pakistan; Fax 574419." We had not heard of Aziz and a check of FBI databases did not tell us anything, so we set a lead to LEGAT Islamabad and to the Counterterrorism Center to see what they knew of Aziz.

The response, which came in weeks later, was electrifying. Aziz was well known in Pakistan as a prominent physician, possibly the wealthiest in the country, who ran his own orthopedic hospital. He was also understood to have treated Usama Bin Laden on at least two occasions. That was certainly interesting. Moussaoui had the name, address, and telephone number of Bin Laden's doctor on a scrap of paper. Given what we knew of Bin Laden's security precautions we fully understood that his care would not be trusted to just anyone. Therefore, not only was Dr. Aziz a skilled and prominent physician, but he was also trusted by Al Qaeda with its most precious of assets: the leader of the group himself. And Moussaoui had Aziz's contact information.

John and I also discovered the name, Ahad Sabet in Moussaoui's handwriting on the bottom half of the right page of a small side opening notebook. Along with the name, were the notations, "10000" with an arrow drawn next to it, the word "Germany" and the word "code" with a string of digits after it that did not look like a phone number. At the top of this page, and separated by a hand drawn line, were written three phone numbers, the "0049" prefix for each one clearly showing they were German. A few minutes later, we came upon a second instance in the notebook of the name Ahad Sabet, this time with the notation "Germany," and two German phone numbers which were the same as two of the three numbers we found earlier. We ran the German numbers and the name Ahad Sabet through the FBI database. Nothing came up.

Moussaoui told us he received financial assistance from a friend in Germany. He claimed to have been unable to remember that person's name or to provide any means of contacting him, yet here was a clear German connection written right in one of his notebooks. Like Yazid Sufaat and the Malaysian connections which Moussaoui claimed he was unable to describe, Ahad Sabet seemed interesting, particularly because Moussaoui concealed this connection, too. John and I recognized the importance of Sabet, and one of us set a lead to LEGAT Berlin, asking them to enquire of their German partners for any information they had on the name and phone numbers.

Even though we understood Sabet was someone whose identity Moussaoui wanted to protect, we did not understand what role he played. That is, until we found a third document where Sabet's name appeared: a Western Union Customer Receipt dated August 4, 2001. According to this receipt, Sabet sent Moussaoui a total of $4063.25 via money transfer. The receipt showed Moussaoui picked up these funds at Pratt Foods #7 in Shawnee, OK. Since this transaction occurred less than one week prior to Moussaoui's departure for Minnesota, the timing was significant. We quickly set a lead for the field office where Western Union was located to ask them whether they had any more information about this transaction, including details about Ahad Sabet, and whether there were other transactions to or from him.

Oklahoma City also located evidence of Western Union transactions from Sabet to Moussaoui, their search warrants uncovering documents that showed Sabet transferred a total of just over $14,000 to Moussaoui on August 2, 2001. These funds were picked up by Moussaoui two days later. Oklahoma City also set leads to Western Union on their findings. We later pieced together that the receipt we found in Minneapolis represented a portion of the $14,000+ Moussaoui received in a series of wire transfers in early August. The timing of the money transfer suggested that the funds were sent from Germany by Sabet to support Moussaoui's trip to Minnesota. So, who was the mysterious Mr. Sabet?

The $14,000 transfer made is seem like Sabet was involved in the plot. Because information from Western Union showed the funds were sent by him from Germany using his U.S. passport as identification, we assumed Sabet was overseas, and that is where the leads were sent seeking more information on him. We figured it was very unlikely Sabet would be found, since chances were slim he would hang around Germany, having just sent $14,000 to a guy who was involved in the 9/11 attacks.

We were therefore amazed when we learned Sabet was found by Agents in Phoenix. We were told the Phoenix JTTF were planning to interview him and I was given the cell phone number of an Agent there and asked to call him to brief him on Sabet's significance to our case and to give him some idea of the questions we wanted asked, assuming Sabet would agree to talk.

Sadly, Ahad Sabet proved to be a dead end. It turned out he was a physician, and he cooperated fully with the investigation. Sabet was able to establish that he had not been outside the U.S. during the month of August 2001 when the wire transfers were sent in his name from Germany. He also explained his U.S. passport had been stolen during the summer of 1998 in Barcelona, Spain, while he was there for the World Cup. Someone obviously used his stolen passport to send funds in his name and whoever sent that money was an experienced operative, right down to being able to acquire a stolen U.S. passport. They did not try to travel using Sabet's passport, understanding the theft would have been reported, meaning the passport number would trigger alerts if the new owner used it to cross the U.S. border or that of a friendly country. However, flashing the passport to Western Union employees in Germany would raise no such alarm. If the person standing at the customer window looked like the photo on the passport, the funds would be sent, no questions asked.

Even though the real Sabet had not been involved, discovering his name and the Western Union transfers still proved to be extremely worthwhile to the case. This is because police in the German cities of Dusseldorf and Hamburg, the points of origination of Moussaoui's $14,000, went to the Western Union locations there and obtained the wire origination documents filled out by the sender. Fingerprints found on these documents came back to Ramzi Mohammad Abdullah Binalshibh. As the investigation progressed, it was learned Binalshibh, a citizen of Yemen, lived with Mohammed Atta (the hijacker pilot of American Airlines Flight #11) at Marienstrasse 54 in Hamburg, while both were students in Germany. Binalshibh was also linked to Ziad Jarrah (the hijacker pilot of United Airlines Flight #93) because Jarrah assisted Binalshibh with attempting to enroll at a Florida-based flight school.

Although Binalshibh clearly wanted to train as a pilot in the U.S. based on his submitting four visa applications to enter the country, these were refused because of his Yemeni Citizenship. However, on two of those unsuccessful requests, Binalshibh listed a German telephone number which was the same as one of the numbers we found in Moussaoui's notebook. Therefore, evidence from fingerprints and phone numbers showed the fake "Sabet" who sent Moussaoui $14,000 to pay for his flight training in Minnesota was Binalshibh, Mohammed Atta's roommate. By the time the investigation in the U.S. and Germany made this link, Binalshibh was long gone, having fled Germany on September 5, 2001, well in advance of the 9/11 attacks which he helped bring about.[13]

And to answer an often-asked question over the years: the link to Ramzi Binalshibh is one way in which search warrants, had they been granted before 9/11, *might* have led to our stopping the attacks. Binalshibh was Atta's roommate, and having his identity would have allowed the FBI to discover Atta was in the U.S. and had undergone flight training. The same was true of Ziad Jarrah, who was also connected to Binalshibh. Thus, among Moussaoui's property were links to two of the four hijacker pilots. Had the FBI known Atta's and Jarrah's identities before the attacks and acted, the neutralization of 3 of the 5 hijacker pilots (including Moussaoui), plus enhanced aviation security measures (as we advocated to the FAA) would have made it more difficult for the plot to advance. We will never know whether the investigation would have moved quickly enough for us to have obtained this information in time, but I am certain of one thing: *we should have been allowed to try.*

13 Binalshibh was captured by U.S. and Pakistani authorities after a gunfight in Karachi, Pakistan on September 11, 2002. He remains in custody at Guantanamo Bay, Cuba as an unlawful enemy combatant.

CHAPTER 46

BLAMESTORMING

I was at home on a Saturday in late October 2001 when my Nextel rang. A look at the screen showed it was a number at FBI Headquarters. When I answered, a woman's voice said, "Hold for Section Chief Roland, please." On hearing that, I got a shot of adrenaline. I knew the person I will call Roland was the Section Chief of the International Terrorism Operations Section (ITOS). That made him a senior official in the Counterterrorism Division, equivalent in rank to our SAC. I also knew Roland was Devin's boss and that Devin was Martin's boss. If I wanted to tell someone what went wrong, I was about to be talking to the right guy.

Having been condescended to by Martin nonstop for the last year, I expected more of the same from his boss' boss. I was wrong about that. When he spoke, Roland was even tempered and complimentary of Minneapolis' efforts in general, and mine in particular. He informed me he had been following the case closely and it seemed likely we had someone connected to the attacks. While I took this at the time to be a good sign that people at headquarters were finally coming around to our way of thinking, in hindsight Roland was simply bowing to the inevitable—no matter what he and his team wanted to believe, DOJ and the U.S. Attorney's Offices in New York and Alexandria were planning to charge Moussaoui and any nay saying now would be problematic for him.

Instead, Roland asked me a series of polite questions about how we in Minneapolis knew before the attacks that Moussaoui was part of a plot involving hijacking. I explained all of what we learned about the expensive flight training which did him no good as a pilot. I described the admissions, including a signed sworn statement by Al-Attas about Moussaoui's extremism. I recounted how Moussaoui had no convincing answers to questions about his travel, which included Pakistan, and his work history despite the large sum of money in his possession. Finally, I summarized the French information linking him to Chechnya, Ibn Khattab and Afghanistan. I concluded by explaining we in Minneapolis felt strongly that whatever Moussaoui was planning involved doing something with a commercial airliner which he would not be able to make the pilot do. A suicide attack was the obvious answer.

Roland was silent for a few seconds and then thanked me for my time. With a final compliment on the job we did, he hung up. As I stood there in my basement looking at the now silent phone in my hand, I realized that I had not had the opportunity to point out Devin and Martin's obstructionism. It had not been that kind of call, and I was not invited to offer an opinion on any subject.

I was to have the opportunity to meet Roland in person shortly after our call. On the morning of October 29th, Chris came down to the squad area to inform me and Greg that we had been summoned to FBI Headquarters for a meeting on the 31st. We would have to leave the next morning, and Chris would be going with us. Chris started to explain that we should compile all our documents to bring with us when the timing of the meeting registered on me. That was Halloween! Chris, Greg, and I all had little kids, and October 31st meant taking them out trick-or-treating. In the Samit family's case, my presence was even more crucial since Terri was six months pregnant with our daughter Anna. Taking a five-year-old and a two-year-old trick or treating by herself was going to be problematic, especially as far along as she was with her pregnancy.

Chris heard me out but refused to even consider requesting headquarters reschedule the meeting. Headquarters had called and FBI management culture was such that loyalty upward was paramount. Few if any managers in the FBI would consider pushing back simply because there might be an impact on their subordinates' (or their own) families. We were going.

I sat down at my desk to call Terri to break this latest in a seemingly unending series of bad news. As usual, she accepted it with her customary resolve. "No problem. We'll take the wagon in case Jake gets tired. We will be fine." Terri's outstanding resolve and great planning skills kicked in and solved the problem right away. Still, I got a lump in my throat when I pictured my pregnant wife towing my kids in a wagon through the darkened streets of our town alone, just so headquarters could have questions answered on their timeline, nearly 2 ½ months after the beginning of the Moussaoui case.

After I hung up, I started to get increasingly angry. The attacks had been something like seven weeks before. All the information we had on Moussaoui was uploaded to the FBI computer systems and instantly available to the people calling this meeting, as were my emails. Why did they need us to come there, and on Halloween, no less?

Chris answered my question as we sat in the airport the next day waiting for our flight, "Blamestorming," he said with a smile and a chuckle. "Blamestorming is something they do at headquarters when something goes wrong. They go around the room trying to decide who to blame the failure on." He shrugged. "It happens all the time, this one is just bigger."

Next to me on the bench sat a document box like the one I carried to New York. The contents were copies of all the communications I or others in Minneapolis sent to headquarters during the 27-day period between the opening of the Moussaoui investigation and the attacks. I spent most of the day before compiling these documents and counted them as I put them in the box. In addition to six official FBI communications (ECs and LHMs) each of which were marked "Immediate," there were also more than 70 emails, every one of which contained facts about Moussaoui, Al-Attas or their associates. There was no way headquarters could accuse us of not giving them everything.

Despite my confidence in the righteousness of our case, Chris was nervous. As it turned out, he was right to be. Although I did not know it then, the default conclusion that headquarters was never wrong was in full force now. It was likely that no matter what evidence we presented to the contrary, Minneapolis would be found wanting in some respect and RFU and NSLU would escape blame.

That concerned me too, but Chris had a plan. He informed us that the day before, he put in a call to Debbie, an FBI manager in the Inspection Division. More important than her senior position in a key division at headquarters, Debbie had been named as the next SAC Minneapolis. This meant she was due to transfer from headquarters to our office in the next month or so. When Chris explained to Debbie what was going on with the meeting, she agreed to attend and be our advocate. We were scheduled to meet and brief Debbie the next day in her office in the J. Edgar Hoover Building—FBI Headquarters, two hours before going up to the meeting with Roland and his staff.

Because of my inexperience with headquarters and my naivety about the way that insidious place worked, I was more annoyed than happy about this development. I could not see how Debbie's presence would help us at all. As I saw it, the downside was that we would need to spend the first two hours of our day getting her up to speed on the case. Still, it was not up to me and that was the plan.

CHAPTER 47

SMALL MEN IN BIG JOBS

The next morning, on Halloween, we arrived at the Hoover Building early dressed in business attire. It was starting to get cold in D.C. and the day was a gray one, matching my mood. When we reached Debbie's office she rose from her desk and greeted us warmly as she ushered us into chairs. Debbie was an attractive woman in her late 40s with auburn hair and blue eyes. She had the build of an athlete and was well dressed and seemed very sociable. After the introductions, we got down to business.

Debbie was an experienced bureaucratic warrior in the halls of the Hoover Building. As a senior official in the Inspection Division, she attended dozens of "blamestorming sessions" and knew the etiquette. That was good because my plan had been to come out swinging. Debbie nixed that right away. "We must tell our story professionally. Otherwise, they'll dismiss our claims."

That was irritating to me, but since this was my first meeting with the person who would be my new SAC, I kept silent. I was also unhappy to learn that our two-hour session was intended for us to brief Debbie on what had happened so *she* could tell the story. That made no sense at all. Debbie had not been in Minnesota during those critical weeks. Having her speak for us, new SAC or not, seemed to be problematic. My concern was that everything she would say about the case would be briefed to her by us in the two hours prior to the meeting.

My objections did not matter, so all of us took turns telling the story. Debbie listened attentively and took copious notes as we spoke. It took us the full two hours to run through the story and answer her questions, and then it was time to go. Although the entire process seemed odd to me, Chris later explained that from an FBI management perspective, what she did in helping us took courage. She used the pronoun "our," which told everyone Debbie was aligning herself with our cause, even though she could have just walked away. All the actions about which we were about to be grilled occurred before she was even named SAC Minneapolis so she could never be blamed for or even associated with them. Now she was voluntarily jumping into the bureaucratic tiger cage with us. Although sticking up for subordinates would have been a no-brainer for most military leaders, doing something like this was rare in the FBI.

It seemed to take a long time to reach the designated meeting room, which we entered promptly at 10 a.m. As I realized we were getting close, my pulse quickened like I was about to play in a big game. I could also feel my hostility grow as I realized we would soon be meeting the people responsible for allowing the worst terrorist attacks in the history of our country.

What I saw and heard when I entered the room did nothing to lessen my anger. As we stepped in and I set my document box on the conference table, a tall, thin older man on the far side of the room stepped briskly over to Chris, who greeted him with a friendly "Hi, Malcolm!" I realized this man was the head of NSLU. He had salt and pepper hair worn short and was dressed in a dazzling white shirt and tie, with dark suit pants.

Malcolm ignored the greeting and glared at Chris. "This meeting was supposed to start at 10! We are briefing the Assistant Director afterwards. You should have been early so we could start on time!"

My inclination was to tell him off. I stepped forward to do so, but Chris elbowed me back. "Sorry, Malcolm. We were meeting with our new SAC."

I was enraged that Malcolm, a non-Agent attorney who never arrested anyone or risked anything and who spent his entire time in the FBI in a nice, safe office at headquarters was talking to an ASAC that way. I resolved that he would not speak to me like that. The meeting was off to a bad start.

It got worse.

When everyone was sitting at the table, with the Minneapolis contingent at one end we went around for introductions. This was the first (and last) time I ever saw Martin in person, and I looked closely at him, seated as he was to my front left around the corner of a large rectangular table. Martin was in his late 30s, and thin, with a full head of light brown hair and a matching mustache. He wore metal rimmed glasses and was neatly attired in a tan suit—FBI management style. Martin appeared to be uncomfortable and irritated to be there, the same way he sounded on the phone. In short, he looked exactly how I expected him to—like an officious bureaucrat.

His boss Devin was seated to Martin's right. Devin was shorter and stockier than Martin with a receding hairline. He looked to be in his late 40s or early 50s and seemed much more aggressive than Martin. Not hostile to us, necessarily, but certainly aggressive.

As the introductions continued, I noticed NSLU brought a few attorneys in addition to Malcolm. Shari and a young woman about my age named Leslie introduced themselves as working in Malcolm's unit. Like Malcolm, neither were Agents.

At the far end of the table were seated Roland and Malcolm. They were clearly the audience and moderators for the discussion we were about to have. As one or the other of them began discussing why they called the meeting, I removed the lid to the document box and began arranging the 70 communications which Minneapolis sent to headquarters prior to the attacks. I am not sure what it was in the way Roland or Malcolm spoke that triggered this reaction in me, but when they ended with "...so obviously this Moussaoui (mispronounced) guy was involved in the 9/11 attacks. We're here to find out why you did not alert headquarters," I knew the "blamestorming" had begun.

Without saying anything, I stood and fanned out the six immediate communications on the table in front of them. Next to the fan of documents I placed the pile of 70 or so emails. Then, making eye contact alternately with first Roland and then Malcolm as I spoke, and said something like, "Didn't alert headquarters? These are six 'Immediate' communications not only alerting you in detail but also requesting concurrence for various sophisticated investigative techniques. None of those were granted and none of the leads were even responded to. In this pile here are the 70+ emails Minneapolis sent you, each one packed with more information than the one before. In my whole time in the FBI, I never once sent an EC marked with an 'Immediate' precedence, and in a two-week period I sent RFU six of them. You were alerted." I sat down.

The next person to speak was Leslie, the young female attorney. She slid a document across the table to me and accused me of sending an unauthorized National Security Letter (NSL). When I denied doing so, she said, "Oh, yes you did. Here it is, dated 9/11/2001." I detected a slight foreign accent.

Glancing at the document she passed, I realized what she was referring to was a National Security Letter we sent to Arvest Bank on the morning of the attacks to try to get Moussaoui's bank information as a means of identifying co-conspirators. She was right, we had done an NSL out of our office without going to headquarters during a time of crisis, but I realized she must have dug deep into the case file to get some dirt on us. "Blamestorming," indeed.

Glaring at her, I responded, "Oh, yeah, that's right. Since we were getting no support from headquarters, in the emergency situation that was 9/11, we sent an NSL to Moussaoui's bank trying to identify other terrorists to prevent follow up attacks."

Unfazed, Leslie responded, "Field offices are not allowed to issue their own NSLs. It's a violation." She smiled smugly.

I was about to respond, probably inappropriately, when someone, Debbie, or Chris, cut me off by suggesting that Minneapolis run through its timeline of events. They did so with that appeasing style and maddening courtesy which FBI management displays to one another. This suggestion was agreed to by Roland. I do not know whether Roland and Malcolm's opening strategy had been to come at Minneapolis with accusations in the hope of getting some admission from us, but that clearly was not going to work. Maybe they were now content to listen to our story in the hope of finding some hole in it which they could exploit to shift the blame off themselves and the units they supervised.

I am not sure why he did so, but around this time Devin spoke up. Looking at me and Greg, he complimented us on our work on the case. Without admitting he or anyone else at headquarters was wrong, he acknowledged "we ran a good case." Due to my newness in the FBI, I remained silent. In later years I would have pointedly asked him, "If you thought the case was so good, why didn't you give us any support?"

Debbie began running through the timeline with a smile. It was no fault of hers that she had to refer closely to her notes, essentially reading them verbatim with occasional glances at me, Greg, or Chris for confirmation. This took almost an hour. When she reached the appropriate point in the narrative, Debbie gestured to the documents still on the table and noted the aggressive efforts Minneapolis made to first obtain a criminal search warrant, and then to obtain a FISA search warrant. Venturing a comment, I added that the criminal search warrant we obtained after the attacks had already yielded evidence that Moussaoui was an Al Qaeda operative and tied him to the hijackers. Even before 9/11 the connections the French told us about were damning enough.

Upon hearing the word "FISA," Malcolm piped up, "You didn't have a foreign power for the FISA!"

Greg or I responded, "The French Government linked Moussaoui to the Chechen mujihadeen and CIA linked them to Bin Laden. We had a foreign power."

At that, Martin spoke, "The Chechans are not a 'named group.' It wasn't enough." He sounded as peevish and irritated as he had on the phone.

Hearing that argument repeated in person enraged me. Narrowing my eyes and looking at him, I almost shouted, “Really, Martin? Show me where in the FISA statute the law specifies a foreign power needs to be a ‘named group.’ For that matter, show me in the statute where they even use the term “named group!’ You made that term up to stop our FISA request!” My hostility towards Martin was palpable and I was barely using an inside voice. He remained silent, possibly under the same orders from his bosses to keep it cordial, which I had been violating since the meeting began.

At that point, Roland and Malcolm conferred quietly, and each reached into the pile of documents in front of them. Finding what they were looking for, they began reading. After a minute or so, Malcolm said, “See, here, you never even mention the Chechen Mujihadeen in your LHM requesting the FISA. You did not have a foreign power in your request.”

I realized what Malcolm was reading was Martin’s rewrite of my LHM—the one where he removed all references to the Chechens and Bin Laden over Greg’s written objections.

Flipping quickly through the fan of documents in front of me, I pulled out a copy of my original LHM. I held it up and said, “Yes, we did. What you are reading is the LHM drafted by Martin over our objections. He removed the references to the Chechens, Ibn Khattab, and Usama Bin Laden from his version. This is the one I wrote.” I slid it to Roland and Malcolm and indicated the relevant information was on page 5. Malcolm flipped the document open and held it so he and Roland could see it.

As they read, I stared at Martin, who shifted uncomfortably in his seat.

When they finished, Malcolm lowered the document.

I could see it on both their faces.

They knew.

These small, arrogant, patently unsuited men in big jobs knew that the people they supervised made mistakes. Horrible, bad faith mistakes which cost the FBI the chance to save the lives of thousands of innocent Americans.

In the FBI management context, for them this meant their next course was to distance themselves from their subordinates and figure out how to escape blame themselves. They need not have worried. In the military, and indeed in any rationally organized institution which understands basic leadership principles, those in charge are held accountable for the failures of their subordinates. Not so in the FBI. Roland and Malcolm went on to receive acclaim and prestigious awards for their work in counterterrorism. Even worse, Roland continued his ascent through the FBI ranks. Both were successful in leaving their subordinates behind, although, to be fair, even Devin and Martin did not suffer punishment and were promoted themselves.

When I pointed out how Martin changed the LHM, resulting in its fatal weakening, all the air seemed to go out of their efforts to pin failure on Minneapolis. I was not done, however, and raised the importance of continuing the investigation. Because no one interrupted, I explained the belatedly obtained search warrants in Minnesota and Oklahoma unearthed information which pointed to a separate plot.

Roland asked, "And what is that?" He looked and sounded skeptical.

I explained we learned Moussaoui was seeking detailed and operationally significant information on agricultural aviation, to include inquiries on buying a suitable aircraft. Greg or I informed the group this was a class of aircraft and a type of flying wholly inconsistent with the flight training Moussaoui and the other hijacker pilots received.

Someone asked, "So what was the plan?"

I replied that we did not know. I pointed out that the use of a crop duster obviously suggested the use of a chemical or biological weapon. Because the country was amid the mailed Anthrax attacks at the time that were being investigated under the FBI Amerithrax Case, I suggested that there was evidence to suggest there were people out there who were interested in using such weapons to attack the U.S.

I could see Roland was doubtful. Maybe not completely ready to reject the suggestion, but certainly not interested in listening right now. The meeting, after all, had clearly been to find out his and Malcolm's exposure, not to consider other plots.

As if to underscore this, Shari interjected, "It couldn't be Anthrax. They would need to weaponize it first." She finished by wrinkling her nose at me.

Meeting her gaze, I asked, "Really? Do you know what 'weaponizing' Anthrax involves? Can you say for sure Al Qaeda cannot do that?"

Shari looked away without responding. Like so many attorneys in NSLU, she clearly considered herself an expert in all things relating to terrorism. Even though her domain was the hallways of the Hoover Building, Shari felt qualified to comment on whether a plot using agricultural aircraft to deliver biological toxins was viable. Her arrogance was symptomatic of the issues that caused NSLU to make the wrong call on the Moussaoui FISA in the first place.[14]

The meeting broke up shortly after that.

---

14 Although I did not know it at the time, according to Defense Exhibit #951 on the EDVA website, Shari herself had a key role in hindering the case. She was one of the NSLU lawyers who, along with Malcolm determined there was not enough intelligence for a FISA search warrant to search Moussaoui's property, a decision later found to be wrong by all the experts which reviewed the case. As far as being held accountable for her failure, at the time of this writing 20 years after the event, Shari has been promoted numerous times and remains in a senior attorney position at FBI Headquarters.

CHAPTER 48

THE LEGAL TEAM

During Fall 2001 I first met the prosecutor who would ultimately be assigned to handle the Minnesota aspects of the case: an AUSA named David. Unlike Ken and Derek, who both worked in the Southern District of New York, David was assigned to the Eastern District of Virginia, or EDVA. As the case against Moussaoui gathered momentum and the decision was made to charge him as a co-conspirator in the attacks, legal strategists in the Department of Justice began to consider factors which would enhance their chances of a conviction.

I learned the decision was made soon after the attacks that Moussaoui would be prosecuted not in New York, but in the Eastern District of Virginia (EDVA) at the federal courthouse in Alexandria. Because hijacked American Airlines Flight #77 had crashed into the Pentagon on 9/11, there was venue to charge Moussaoui in Virginia. DOJ decided to exercise this option because EDVA handled many espionage and other national security cases, meaning prosecutors and judges there were used to the complexities of trials involving classified information.

Given the seriousness of the crimes and the appalling loss of life, DOJ also made the decision to seek the death penalty for Moussaoui, and that is where David came in. When I first met David, he told me smilingly that he was nicknamed "Dr. Death" by other prosecutors because he was one of the few AUSAs who had a successful prosecution which resulted in a sentence of death. David explained he prosecuted a drug dealer a few years before who committed several premeditated murders connected to his criminal enterprise. Because of the experience he gained through that case, the decision was made to involve David in the Moussaoui prosecution, particularly because federal death penalty prosecutions were not common and had rules and procedures different from those of normal criminal trials.

David was about ten years older than me with blond hair and blue eyes. He was short with a stocky build and spoke with a strong Pennsylvania accent. I was not surprised to learn he went to law school at Villanova in Philadelphia. David informed me we would be working together on this case. Because it was a death penalty case and one involving thousands of victims, David promised me he would be thorough and relentless in doing his job. I believed him. He also gave me a heads up that he would be a "pain in the ass" to work with, noting he never took anything for granted and "liked to run out all the ground balls" no matter how obvious an answer might be. David was as good as his word and worked extremely hard on this case, as we all did. My relationship with him had its ups and downs over the next four years, but I never doubted his heart was in the right place and that his goal was always to do his duty in seeing justice done.

Around this same time, I also met AUSA Rob, also from EDVA, who would be the attorney in charge of the prosecution of Moussaoui. Rob was tall and thin with dark hair. He was smart, very smart, and had a serious, almost grave manner which hid a dry sense of humor. Rob was in his early 40s and clearly had some significant trial experience to be entrusted with a case of this importance. He was obviously also well connected at DOJ because the lawyers and managers there listened to him.

Derek from New York was also staying on the case after it moved to Virginia. The three AUSAs worked together over the next four years preparing for Moussaoui's trial. I wish I could say I was a model case Agent and then witness as the Moussaoui prosecution moved forward, but I am sure Rob, Derek, and David would disagree. I created problems for them, for sure. Some of the tension came from the traditional friction between Agents and AUSAs. While our goal is the same: a successful prosecution, Agents and prosecutors frequently disagree on how to get there. Although the delineation of responsibilities should be clear: Agents investigate and prosecutors introduce the evidence they collect in court, it is a little more complex than that.

Agents, being naturally curious, want to learn all there is to know about the case, particularly when the crimes are serious. They therefore want to keep investigating to find additional evidence, identify more co-conspirators, and uncover additional plots. In short, Agents want to understand all there is to know both to ensure justice is done and to prevent others from becoming victims.

AUSAs, on the other hand, have the complex and nuanced job of presenting evidence to a jury who do not understand the law. And they must do so in a way the jury will find believable and compelling enough to convict a defendant. While the AUSAs are doing that, a team of equally competent attorneys on the defense team will work to undermine the government's evidence and present claims of their own which prove the defendant's innocence. For this reason, AUSAs usually like to have a cutoff date which dictates when the priorities change from gathering new information to preparing for trial using the evidence the government already has. More evidence is not always a good thing, as it can complicate the prosecution and confuse the jury.

In the case of Moussaoui, the only person who would ever stand trial in a civilian court for perpetrating the horrors of the 9/11 attacks, the stakes could not have been higher for the prosecutors, and for the defense. The AUSAs were entrusted with securing justice for a crime which nearly every American felt personally, while Moussaoui's attorneys were trying to keep him from being executed.

The FBI assembled a group of New York Agents to comprise an investigative unit known as the PENTTBOMB Team, after the FBI's nickname for the investigation into the attacks. The "PENT" in the name obviously referred to the Pentagon, while the "TT" in the middle of the name stood for the Twin Towers of the World Trade

Center. Whatever the symbolism of its name, this team was trusted with one of the most important investigations in the FBI's history. An important component of their mission was to bring much needed justice to the survivors of the attack, the grieving relatives of those lost, and the American people. Brian knew the initial group of Agents assigned to the team and was able to assure me they were experienced terrorism investigators.

Brian's assessment of the person appointed to lead the PENTTBOMB Team was much less enthusiastic. Someone in FBI New York management decided early on to name a supervisor from one of the office's domestic terrorism squads to head the PENTTBOMB team. Her name was SSA Marge. Since the attacks were carried out by an *international* terrorist group, I thought the choice was probably more a reflection of Marge's political standing in the New York office than her ability to lead a complex investigation. That turned out to be accurate. Marge was a catastrophe.

Marge was in her mid-40s with dark hair and glasses. She was always well dressed and made up whenever I saw her. Although she was cordial when John and I first met her, we could sense her insecurity and suspicion of us. Since we did not work for Marge and she did not control our assignments, she seemed a little uncertain about how to relate to us. That was a bad sign. Any FBI Agent who was not at ease talking to other Agents was missing an essential skill. If you cannot interact easily with your colleagues, how can you persuade a witness, an informant, or a subject to talk to you?

While the investigation continued throughout the rest of 2001 and into 2002, over time the AUSAs were ready to move from the evidence collection phase to the trial preparation phase. As Ken said back in September 2001 in that hot conference room in New York, "We're ready to indict today..." While Ken was just being nice then, it was true that we already had significant evidence by the time of the attacks. Before the fires were even out at Ground Zero, leads were being covered in the U.S. and overseas to find out all there was about Moussaoui. As evidence rolled in, it was sent to the PENTTBOMB team, based in the Federal Courthouse in Alexandria, Virginia, near Washington, D.C.

By mid-2002, six months after Moussaoui's December 2001 indictment, the PENTTBOMB team decided they had enough evidence and were ready to move to the trial prep phase. Some of the friction between us came about because I was not. I felt there was more investigation to do, and I was not ready to stop. As time went by and other subjects were investigated in Minneapolis, it was apparent PENTTBOMB had *not* identified everyone involved in the attacks, even though they believed they had. Worse, they had briefed the highest officials in the land on their version of events, and backtracking had become politically impossible. More on that later.

CHAPTER 49

CRIMINAL CHARGES

On December 11, 2001, a Federal Grand Jury in the Eastern District of Virginia returned an indictment against Moussaoui on six counts related to the 9/11 attacks. The man about whom who RFU said "there was no indication he was up to nefarious activity" was now formally charged as a co-conspirator of the hijackers and the men who sent them. He was indicted on the following charges: Conspiracy to Commit Acts of Terrorism Transcending National Boundaries (18 U.S.C. §§ 2332b(a)(2) & (c)), Conspiracy to Commit Aircraft Piracy (49 U.S.C. §§ 46502(a)(1)(A) and (a)(2)(B)), Conspiracy to Destroy Aircraft (18 U.S.C. §§ 32(a)(7) & 34), Conspiracy to Use Weapons of Mass Destruction (18 U.S.C. § 2332a(a)), Conspiracy to Murder United States Employees (18 U.S.C. §§ 1114 & 1117), Conspiracy to Destroy Property (18 U.S.C. §§ 844(f), (i), (n)). We in Minneapolis all felt vindicated because a Federal Grand Jury in Virginia agreed there was enough evidence to charge our subject with multiple criminal acts, including two of the statutes we listed in our paperwork prior to the 9/11 attacks.

Eleven days later, on December 22, 2001, someone else was acting too, only he was on the other side of the world, and of the law. And his plans, almost certainly in response to Moussaoui's indictment, were murderous. Richard Colvin Reid, a 28-year-old citizen of the UK, boarded American Airlines Flight #63 from Paris to Miami. Over the Atlantic a flight attendant saw Reid attempting to detonate explosives hidden in his shoes with the intention of destroying the airplane and killing everyone aboard. With the experience of the 9/11 attacks fresh in their minds, Reid's fellow passengers commendably showed zero tolerance for threats of this nature and immediately pounced. They not only severely beat and restrained Reid, but a doctor on board sedated him as well. The pilots diverted the flight to Boston and Reid was removed and interviewed by the FBI.

Within a short time, a counterterrorism case was opened and Reid, whose Al Qaeda affiliations quickly came into focus, was charged on multiple federal counts relating to his attempt to use explosives to destroy an aircraft in flight. The timing of this failed attack, coming 11 days after Moussaoui's indictment suggested some sort of connection, although we did not have confirmation of that yet.

The holidays passed quietly that year. I was certainly not in much of a mood for celebrating, especially after I came down with the worst case of the flu I ever had. It hit me about a week before Christmas and hung around for a full two weeks. I had never been so ill and felt sure the accumulated stress of the previous few months, combined with what was obviously a nasty virus, hit me hard.

By early January I felt well enough to get back to work.

And that was good because I had other priorities. In late January 2002, our daughter Anna was born. Thankfully, she was healthy and happy and brought us great joy. I was very grateful to my in-laws for hurrying out to Minnesota quickly, because the work tempo was so intense that I could only spare one day off from work for Anna's birth. Once Terri's parents arrived, it was right back to the office. Unfortunately, once I was back it was not just the investigation we had to contend with: senior people in Washington began looking into the handling of the 9/11 investigation and wanted to question me and others from Minneapolis—blamestorming on a bigger scale.

In early 2002, I learned I was required to be interviewed by congressional staffers as part of a joint inquiry being conducted by the Senate Select Committee on Intelligence and the House Permanent Select Committee on Intelligence. The process, known as the Joint Intelligence Committee Inquiry, or "JICI" (rhymes with Ricky), was seeking answers about the failures within the U.S. Intelligence

Community. I was also told the inquiry would have both open hearings and closed sessions. It seems DOJ was not pleased with letting me participate in the inquiry at all because I had already been identified as a witness at Moussaoui's trial in the future. That meant that *any* statements I made about the case were admissible during Moussaoui's trial, and prosecutors worried that could harm my potential as a witness.

I testified before a closed session of the JICI and told them everything that happened. I felt good about how seriously the knowledgeable team took the process based on the questions they asked. John testified too and had the same thoughts. This belief was reinforced in early 2003 when I read the report the JICI produced from their inquiry. Among many other conclusions, they agreed with my opinion RFU and NSLU failed to understand the FISA law and incorrectly shut down our chances to continue the investigation. They also identified other issues concerning the way the FBI structured terrorism investigations and made recommendations for improvement. I had not thought of many of these as problems until I saw the conclusions in the JICI report, but once I did, I agreed with those, too. Of course, the way the CIA did business was also examined thoroughly, and numerous recommendations were made to help them improve, as well.[15]

I thought the work of the JICI represented a real chance for improvement in the way the U.S. intelligence community in general and the FBI specifically worked to protect the U.S. against terrorism. Their conclusions were accurate and their recommendations, at least to improve the FBI, were right on target. Since such a powerful body as the U.S. Congress was urging change, I figured it would be a done deal. I was also hopeful the people responsible for the fatal lapses would be demoted and found jobs in less demanding areas where they were not in charge of others or could influence casework. Unfortunately, none of those things came to pass.

15 Although it is outside the scope of this book, mistakes made by CIA contributed greatly to the 9/11 disaster and constitute a major failing on that agency's part.

CHAPTER 50

15 MINUTES OF FAME

Unquestionably, the most famous person to testify before the JICI from the Minneapolis FBI Office was Celia. Shortly after I returned to Minnesota from my testimony, Celia called me at my desk. That was rare since we had no real interaction normally. She told me she had been contacted by FBI Headquarters and notified she would be required to appear before the JICI. Although I kept my opinion to myself, I wondered why Celia was needed because she had zero involvement in the case prior to the attacks. Everything she knew about the investigation, including all the facts about Moussaoui, and everything that had gone on with headquarters came from others. Celia's sole first-hand knowledge of anything that happened prior to 9/11 consisted of our 90 second conversation about the FISA (during which, she had not even bothered to hang up the phone) and her brief exchanges with Harold via email.

That is why she was calling now. Celia informed me she needed help with the timeline of the case. She understood the investigation was complex and was concerned about her ability to convey the facts accurately and coherently since public speaking was not her forte. Celia also informed me that because she was not going to be a witness at Moussaoui's trial, her testimony would be public, in front of members of congress as opposed to staffers. I was sympathetic to her, although I also thought it was ironic that the least knowledgeable person from our office would be the one appearing before

Congress. Still, Celia had been an Agent for more than 20 years and was an attorney, so my thought was she was qualified to handle this.

I agreed to help her get ready so she could accurately recount details of the intensive investigation which had been done in Minnesota and Oklahoma prior to the attacks. I also wanted her to be fully up to speed on all the roadblocks RFU threw in our path. While we talked, I could hear her taking notes.

Celia and I spoke for more than 45 minutes, by far our longest conversation ever, as I ran through when we opened the case and why, what we found during those three busy days of interviews, our battles with RFU, and what had been learned since the attacks that confirmed our fears and suspicions. Since Celia would be testifying before actual members of congress, I understood her statements would be harder to ignore than the ones the rest of us made in our private sessions with staffers.

One thing I did not discuss with Celia was any aspect of my own testimony. I did not tell her what I told the JICI, and I did not pass her any of the questions I was asked by them.

When we finished discussing the facts of the case, I offered Celia one final concern I had about the direction the wind seemed to be blowing at FBI Headquarters. Mindful of what I already heard about Director Mueller's mistakenly positive view of FBI management, I had been disturbed recently to read an account in the media where he seemed to be downplaying the idea the FBI had any opportunity to stop the attacks through the Moussaoui investigation. I also gathered from the tone of the Director's statements there would be no effort to hold accountable those responsible for stifling the investigation prior to the attacks.

I gave Celia my opinion Mueller was accepting the self-serving statements of his upper-level FBI managers uncritically and that this was wrong. I was sure to tell her that while I would never claim for certain that we could have stopped the attacks, what I did believe is that we could have tried. And by failing to acknowledge and examine how and why we failed to do our best and choosing instead to sweep things under the rug, Mueller was forfeiting any chance to improve the FBI.

I could hear Celia still writing. When she was finished, Celia again expressed doubts about being able to deliver a coherent oral account of all that had happened. I could hear in her voice that she was nervous. With a sigh, Celia thanked me for my help. Just before we hung up, she informed me she was planning to prepare a written statement which would help her keep the facts of the case straight.

I did not attach any importance to hearing Celia intended to draft a written document. She had not participated first-hand in the events, so it was understandable the many complex details were hard to remember in their proper sequence. Also, I had already observed firsthand how Celia's speech became a little disjointed when speaking to groups of Agents during legal training, so I believed it made sense for her to write things down. What I envisioned was that Celia would draft some prepared remarks or bullet points which she would read to the JICI to supplement her testimony when she became nervous or tongue tied. Even though the panel she would face were elected officials, the JICI testimony and the inquiry itself contained classified material, so I naturally assumed the document she drafted and her remarks would be kept secret.

That is not what happened.

Instead, Celia's prepared statement grew and evolved. I am not sure how or why it changed from notes to assist her with her oral testimony to a formal letter of more than 10 pages, but that happened sometime between our phone conversation and her testimony. Shortly before her appearance, Celia drafted a letter dated May 21, 2002 in which she summarized in considerable detail her concerns and those of others in Minneapolis, including me. Not only does this letter recount the actions by RFU prior to 9/11, Celia also decried the lack of any investigation to hold those in the FBI accountable for their errors in judgement once their actions became known. Finally, Celia expressed concern that Mueller himself had, since assuming his position as head of the FBI, been making statements minimizing or excusing the actions of RFU and NSLU by claiming nothing could have been done to stop the attacks, even with the information known about Moussaoui.

As I read the letter when it appeared in newspapers all over the U.S., my impression was that Celia's statements were accurate and fact-based. Even her opinions, all of which are clearly identified as such, are supported by factual and accurate information. It was also obvious that after our discussion Celia did some additional detailed study of Mueller's statements to the media, and she devoted a fair bit of space to pointing out where he misspoke and the possible damage this did. Finally, in a move near and dear to the hearts of street Agents all over the FBI, Celia pointed out the blatant double standard which exists in the FBI, where FBIHQ managers were allowed to remain in their positions or promoted despite mistakes, when low-level Agents in the field would have been removed from their positions immediately and subjected to a rigorous and thorough internal investigation by the Office of Professional Responsibility (OPR) in a similar situation.

I thought Celia wrote a good letter which was a fine example of speaking truth to power. I was hopeful it would bring some much-needed change. I was less clear on why it was that I had been able to read the contents of her letter in the Minneapolis Star Tribune and was concerned these details were aired publicly. Once it became public, I was worried the letter revealed exploitable cracks in the FBI's ability to defend the country and that our adversaries might find something of use in there. This concern was amplified by the fact news outlets in the U.S. and overseas picked up the story and ran with it, making Celia an overnight sensation and catapulting her to fame as a "whistle blower."

With these conflicting feelings, I called Celia on the evening the story of her letter broke. A man answered. When I asked for Celia, he countered by asking who I was and what I wanted. He was not rude but was very businesslike and direct. I thought that was a little odd, but I told him I was Harry from the office and that I worked with

Celia. He asked me to hold on, and I could hear him relaying my name to someone, obviously Celia.

A second later, Celia was on the phone and said, "Good evening, Mr. Samit."

I told Celia I was calling to see how her testimony went. She chuckled in reply, informing me things had "gotten a little out of hand." I certainly agreed with that. News outlets all over the English-speaking world were covering her letter, and her life story. That is why Celia's voicemail was full and why her husband was screening her calls. Reporters had been calling nonstop.

When I asked what happened, Celia explained that in the days before her JICI testimony, she remained concerned about her ability to verbally convey a coherent message. She was particularly anxious to hit all the points we discussed from Minneapolis' perspective. For this reason, instead of notes, she decided to write a formal letter to the JICI laying out what had happened and giving her opinions on why. Because the matter was very critical of the FBI, Celia decided to address the letter to Director Mueller and to send him a copy, as well. The letter was sent to both recipients in advance, so the JICI would have time to review it and question her about anything she wrote.

That all made sense to me.

The problem, according to Celia, was that someone on the JICI did what members of congress and their staffers do, even ones sitting on sensitive intelligence committees: they leaked the letter to the media. From there it became a lead story because it had all the ingredients American journalists love. First, it contained blow-by-blow allegations of government misconduct, or at best, incompetence. Second, it had detailed allegations of how the Director of the FBI covered these up. Finally, by pointing out in the letter that she was the sole breadwinner of a six-person family and invoking whistleblower protection for herself, Celia set up the classic David versus Goliath struggle of the little person standing up to the monolithic and impersonal government—a real modern-day "Mrs. Smith Goes to Washington" story.

I do not think Celia intended this to happen and it seems unlikely she anticipated someone on the JICI would leak the letter. However, whatever her intentions, the letter exploded on the scene once the media got a hold of it, revealing to the public in significant detail most of the essential facts about how the Moussaoui case was handled before 9/11. It also generated an intense interest in the whistleblower herself, eventually resulting in Celia being named one of Time Magazine's women of the year for her actions.

Unfortunately, the media interest was shortly to become an addictive intoxicant for Celia, leading her to make increasingly bold public claims as time went on. And not all these later statements were as fact-based as those in her May 2002 letter. The media also began to fill in the blanks and started to infer Celia had a role in the Moussaoui investigation, which simply is not true.

If Celia was expecting immediate action to be taken on the issues spelled out in her letter, she was disappointed. Robert Mueller, an experienced DOJ insider, did what any good Washington bureaucrat would do. He referred Celia's letter to the DOJ Office of the Inspector General for investigation, essentially washing his hands of the matter. In time, all of us involved in the case would be interviewed by DOJ/OIG and ultimately a report would be generated, but this was in the future.

CHAPTER 51

WHAT WAS HIS MISSION?

By Spring 2002, we understood much about Moussaoui's background and especially his almost six months in the U.S. One thing we did not know for sure was what Moussaoui's role in the 9/11 attacks would be. Those of us close to the case understood he was involved—he'd been indicted in the Eastern District of Virgina as a coconspirator on charges which carried the death penalty. But what was his mission? What did he intend to do on the Day? We discussed it quite a bit in Minneapolis and had our theory based on the facts we knew so far.

First, it was obvious Moussaoui was training to become a hijacker pilot and would not merely serve as "muscle" to seize and maintain control of the aircraft. Not only had Moussaoui been working for six months to obtain his pilot's license, but when that became bogged down by his inability to master the controls of a Cessna 152, he tried to short-circuit the flight training process and skipped right to buying expensive simulator time in the Boeing 747–400.

This confirmed that Moussaoui would be a pilot on the appointed day, and that the aircraft he would fly would be a 747–400. Since the attacks had been conducted using two hijacked 767s and two hijacked 757s, it followed that Moussaoui was slated to be on a fifth aircraft, and that this would be a 747–400.

Then there was the matter of Moussaoui's "muscle," the people who would seize control of the aircraft and keep the passengers at bay. A review of the four flights that were hijacked showed all the "muscle" hijackers but one were citizens of Saudi Arabia. In each instance these men were native Arabic speakers with varying degrees of ability to communicate in English. Since we knew from Al-Attas that Moussaoui's Arabic proficiency was poor, we reasoned that his prospective "muscle" crew would have had to speak French or English.

All of this told us there would be a fifth aircraft on the appointed day, that it would be a 747–400, and that Moussaoui's accomplices in the murderous venture would speak French or English well enough to communicate under conditions of loud noise, chaos, and the extreme stress generated during a hijacking. This meant there were other operatives out there since, aside from a small circle of people in Norman, Oklahoma, not many of Moussaoui's associates were even known to the FBI.

We considered but rejected the idea Moussaoui might have been part of a separate attack, possibly on a different day. We decided this could not be because Al Qaeda planners had proven to be nothing if not astute as regards Western security. We reasoned they understood that once the first hijackings occurred, we would quickly close the loopholes which allowed men armed only with short-bladed weapons to seize aircraft. They must have understood any prospective hijackers would in the future be immediately attacked by every passenger: man, woman, and child on the plane, as soon as they stood up to take control. No one would ever sit meekly by again while hijackers seized control of the cockpit of an airliner. Doing so invited certain death. Passenger and crew odds of survival would always be better attacking the hijackers than sitting and waiting to die and they would likely always outnumber the terrorists too. On this basis we concluded Moussaoui's role had to be the same day, different plane.

Finally, we considered Moussaoui's target. Since the 747–400 was the largest airliner then in service, it was a bigger and more destructive piloted missile than the 757s and 767s used on 9/11. Because this was the case, we reasoned the target must be large and one with the highest priority. Moussaoui himself might have given us a clue when he told John and me about his plan to visit the White House after leaving Minnesota. It therefore seemed to us the obvious answer was that Moussaoui's target must be the White House. Through many discussions, no one on the team in Minnesota could think of a higher-priority target than that. Moreover, someone raised the point that it seemed highly unlikely Al Qaeda would launch a large-scale coordinated attack on the U.S. and not target the White House.[16]

Therefore, at the end of our deliberations we concluded Moussaoui was training in coordination with the other hijacker pilots so that all would be ready at the same time. All planes would be hijacked and crashed the same day. Moussaoui's airliner would be a Boeing 747–400 which he would hijack using a different group of "muscle" hijackers who spoke French or English. Once he had control of the airplane, Moussaoui would pilot it into the White House. That was our working theory.

I was therefore surprised and frustrated by late 2002 to learn the PENTTBOMB team was floating a different theory, and that it was beginning to take on a life of its own. I am not sure where the idea originated, but we in Minneapolis learned about it when we saw a reference in the media to Moussaoui being the "20th hijacker." What is more, he was beginning to be associated with United Flight 93, one of the 757s that was hijacked, and which crashed near Shanksville, PA.

I waited until I saw AUSA David during one of his trips to Minneapolis during 2003 to address this issue. David was in town for follow-up interviews of some of the inmates at Sherburne County Jail. We were headed to the jail from our office in downtown

---

16 This theory was later proven correct following the arrest and interrogation by the Malaysian authorities of key Jemaah Islamiya (JI) figures who assisted Moussaoui during his mid-2000 visit to Malaysia. According to senior JI leader Riduan Bin Isamudin, aka Hambali, and Faiz abu Baker Bafana, a lower-level JI operative, Moussaoui told them during his time in Malaysia that he had dreams of piloting planes into the White House. A substitute for Hambali's testimony is Defense Exhibit#946 on the EDVA website. Moussaoui himself later also stated the White House was his target.

Minneapolis and I was riding in the back seat of a car driven by the Deputy U.S. Marshal who had been coordinating the interviews at the jail. David was in the front passenger seat. Since we had a nearly 40-minute ride, I figured now was a good time to broach the "20th hijacker" theory to see where that came from.

Because I am almost completely without tact, I dove right in by directly asking who came up with the idea Moussaoui was the "missing" hijacker on Flight 93. David, whose face I could see in the reflection of the side mirror, frowned. "We came up with the idea because the other three planes had four 'muscle' hijackers plus a pilot. Flight 93 had a pilot and only 3 'muscle' hijackers. Moussaoui was probably supposed to be the fifth guy on 93."

Now I frowned. "I don't think that's right."

"Why? It makes sense." David's reflection continued to look grim as he scanned the highway ahead of us.

"Well, for starters, Moussaoui was training as a pilot. He was going to great lengths not only to get his pilot's license, but when that fell through, he spent a ton of money to gain detailed knowledge on 747–400 systems. In fact, that is how we caught him. Ziad Jarrah was the pilot on Flight 93. Why would Moussaoui need flight training to be a 'muscle' hijacker? No other flight had two pilots."

David was silent. I saw he was thinking.

"Also, he was training on the 747. Moussaoui specified this model in advance. Flight 93 was a 757. If Moussaoui were slated to be on that flight, he would have asked Pan Am to put him in a 757 simulator."

David was still listening, so I continued, "Also, we know Moussaoui did not speak Arabic well at all. Al-Attas told us that. All the 'muscle' guys were native Arabic speakers. Moussaoui would have had a hard time communicating with them, especially with the havoc on that plane when all hell broke loose."

He shook his head, "They would not have had to communicate. Just take control of the plane and keep the passengers under control."

"I think they would have needed to talk. It would be a long flight with a plane full of scared and amped up passengers and the pilot might have had to give his 'muscle crew' instructions. I would want to be able to talk to them if I was the pilot. Look at the fight that happened on Flight 93. We could hear on the radio that Jarrah was speaking Arabic to his 'muscle' hijackers, right?"

"Yeah, but you don't know for sure the plan was for them to be able to talk. And maybe they could do it in English."

I nodded, "That's true. But the thing that convinces us here is the issue of Moussaoui's target. Can you imagine Al Qaeda putting together this big effort, the largest terrorist attack against the U.S. in history and *not* hitting the White House? Also, it's not theoretical because we know the JI guys reported Moussaoui informed them that *was* his target."

David shook his head, "You can't believe them, or Moussaoui either!"

"I agree. But the White House makes sense as the most symbolic of targets." David nodded, so I paused to let that sink in. "And all of what I am telling you means there was supposed to be another airplane, a 747–400 on attack day. That means there is a whole other 'muscle' crew out there."

We went back and forth like that for the whole drive. Where he was able, David pointed out when I was speculating as opposed to stating facts. After four dreary hours, we were done with our interviews in the jail and wearily climbed back in the car for the hour-long drive back to Minneapolis in rush-hour traffic. With seemingly undiminished energy David resumed our discussion. Like the outstanding prosecutor he was, David's command of the facts was terrific. But as we talked, I could tell he was coming to the realization that the neat mathematical symmetry of adding Moussaoui to the seemingly vacant slot on Flight 93 had too many holes. By the time we arrived to drop David off at his hotel, he seemed satisfied that the "fifth plane" theory at least had merit.

I watched David as he walked into the lobby and shook my head, realizing we had argued and discussed this topic for over two hours before David agreed to come off the original theory. As time went by, I gained a new respect for him and came to realize he was truly an honest broker whose only goal was to see justice done through Moussaoui's successful prosecution. That is why he argued so hard but ultimately allowed himself to be persuaded by facts. It was the mark of a good lawyer, but it made things challenging for me, and not for the last time.

CHAPTER 52

STAR WITNESS

As the prosecutors continued to prepare their case in Virginia, David made me aware one person they considered an essential witness was Clancy, the instructor who taught Moussaoui's ground school class at Pan Am before he was arrested. Clancy was important because he was the one who first noticed the odd behavior and inconsistencies in Moussaoui's story. David learned of Clancy's key role in the case from reading my opening communication and asked me and John what kind of a witness we thought he would make. We replied we found Clancy very credible and his information compelling when we first spoke to him and reminded him Clancy had been an airline captain for many years. I added that Clancy resembled and shared some mannerisms with the late actor Jimmy Stewart, who made a career of playing honest and decent patriarchs.

Clancy's obviously key role in sparking the case persuaded David to meet him shortly after 9/11. Since David wanted me and John present at the meeting, I called Clancy and asked him to let me know when he would next be in Minneapolis to teach at Pan Am. Clancy agreed to this and during the Spring of 2002 John and I arranged for him and David to meet.

At the agreed upon time, Clancy came to the U.S. Attorney's Office in Minneapolis where David, John, and I were waiting. It was the first time John and I had seen Clancy since our August 16, 2001 interview in the lobby of his hotel. That seemed like a century ago now. Thankfully, Clancy was as we remembered him: open, sincere, and willing to help. By now any doubts he had about whether talking to the FBI about "Zac" were gone. Clancy was on board for anything the FBI needed, including testimony at Moussaoui's criminal trial.

Using the report of Clancy's interview, David asked questions to determine how consistent his answers would be now, many months after the events. Clancy proved to be *very* consistent, describing his impression of Moussaoui and their interactions almost exactly as he had done before. Satisfied his recall would be sufficient, David asked a bunch of questions on aviation topics, as much to educate himself on the intricacies of what Moussaoui was trying to accomplish as to evaluate whether Clancy could explain complex issues in a way laymen on a jury could understand. Clancy came through like a champ, breaking down complicated subjects into simple concepts. This made sense: explaining aviation issues to passengers is something airline pilots do every day. Naturally, Clancy would be able to communicate clearly with a jury of non-aviation people. Plus, he was a flight instructor so he would have had plenty of teaching skills.

The one concern was that Clancy, whose name was circulating among media people as being involved in turning Moussaoui in, had been getting invitations to speak to TV and print reporters. These offers were clearly attractive to him, and while we could not order him not to speak to the media, we were careful at every stage to remind him that each encounter with a reporter ran the risk of diminishing his value as a witness at Moussaoui's trial. Any sensationalism or deviation from his original story would be seized upon by the defense and could become an issue.

For this reason, after the meeting ended David made a request of us, "Please stay in touch with Clancy and try your best to keep him from talking to the media. We promised to do our best. David then asked if we would not mind calling Clancy to put in a standing invitation to go to lunch whenever he was in Minnesota. It would be a good social opportunity to ensure he stayed engaged in the process of being a witness.

As it turned out, David's request to us that day about keeping Clancy free of the media began a 4+ year quest, during which John and I would have to periodically remind him of his importance to the case. It seems the drain on his willpower to remain out of the media spotlight came from his very vocal and determined wife, who became increasingly eager to see that her husband received "credit" for his actions.

When Moussaoui's trial began in the Spring of 2006, although Clancy had been in contact with numerous print and television journalists, he had only been quoted a few times in print. There were periodic lapses, probably encouraged by his wife, during which particularly charming and persuasive reporters would convince Clancy to tell them his story. But through it all, he'd remain consistent, and thus would be a viable witness come trial time.

CHAPTER 53

THE DEFENSE

In custody and on trial for his life, Moussaoui was proving to be anything but helpful to his lawyers, all of whom he seemed to regard as being on the side of the government. Before the trial he drafted numerous motions of his own, without consulting his defense team. These motions were handwritten and made outrageous claims and contained insults against the United States. It was apparent to anyone reading these that Moussaoui sought to make a mockery of the whole process. This was also obvious during court appearances, presided over by U.S. District Court Judge Leonie Brinkema, who would also be the judge at Moussaoui's trial. During these hearings Moussaoui would rant against the U.S., often for long periods. Judge Brinkema would allow him to continue, on the record, spewing his hatred against anyone who did not agree with his world view.

Also, during that busy summer of 2002, I was called by the Department of Justice Office of Inspector General (DOJ/OIG) to come back to Washington to be interviewed as part of their investigation into Celia's allegations. Two attorneys and one OIG Agent interviewed me in the Main Justice Building. Their interview covered some of the same ground the JICI had, but this time I was glad to see there was a focus on what exactly happened to derail our FISA request and why the case had not been allowed to advance. I noticed right away that none of the people who interviewed me had any of the expertise on FISA or counterterrorism work the JICI staffers had. Instead, they seemed well versed in what constituted employee misconduct, and gratifyingly their investigation seemed focused on that.

As can be imagined, I did not hold back at all and provided as much detail as possible about all that happened. I also backed up my allegations with documents, including some new information which had come to light since the attacks that showed Minneapolis was on the right track the whole time. I felt as if I received a fair hearing and had the chance to tell my story, but it remained to be seen what, if anything OIG would do with the information.

I had to laugh when, the day after I returned to Minnesota, I received a call from Marge, head of the PENTTBOMB team. It was a Saturday, and I was home mopping the kitchen floor when she called. I stood the mop against the wall and fished my cell phone out of my pocket to answer it. After her usual pleasantries and awkward efforts at building rapport, Marge got down to business.

"Harry," she said in a formal and insistent tone, "I need to know what you told the OIG about this case."

I smiled, "Oh, and why is that, Marge?"

"We briefed the Vice President on the extent of the 9/11 plot two weeks ago. I need to hear what you said about the investigation so I can be sure there are no contradictions.

I got it now. PENTTBOMB understood from their dealings with me already that I was not going to simply fall in line and parrot whatever they sold. "Contradictions? Like what?"

I could tell Marge was getting irritated, "Like, it's been more than six months since the attacks, and we told the vice president the FBI understands everything there is to know about this plot based on the investigation. It will be an issue if you said there is more to the plot than that."

"Well, Marge, that seems to me to have been a mistake. We *don't* know all there is to know about this plot. Were you able to explain the materials on agricultural aviation? How about naming the rest of Moussaoui's crew?"

A pause, probably while Marge was struggling to control herself, "You need to tell me what you said."

I smiled again. "Sure thing, Marge." I hesitated, "Only, the OIG attorneys and Agent told me *not* to discuss my testimony with anyone."

"Oh, they didn't mean internally."

Passive aggressive time again. "Gotcha. Ok. If you wouldn't mind getting the OIG people to release me in writing, I will think about telling you."

"That's not necessary..."

I finally laughed, but I was not happy, I was angry, "Marge, I am not telling you what I told them, and you should know better than to ask! It's an OIG investigation and I am a witness. And it was a complete mistake to brief the VP that you understand everything about the 9/11 plot. You don't. No one does."

I will give her this, she hung in there, alternately trying to persuade, then bully me. I was already mad, and getting tired of her, so I ended with Marge the way I stopped all such unreasonable requests, "Ok, Marge. Send me an EC with a lead and I will respond in writing with what I told the OIG. If it isn't necessary for me to get their permission, put that in writing and I..."

She hung up.

Sometime in late 2002, the Director of the FBI, Robert Mueller paid a visit to the Minneapolis Field Office. It was his first trip to our office, part of a year-long effort to get to each one to personally address the employees. I was suspicious of Mueller after reading the statements he made in the media where he seemed to be downplaying FBI's chances to stop the attacks through the Moussaoui investigation. Because of his reputation and background as a combat veteran, I was prepared to withhold judgement since it was likely he had not heard the whole story of what happened. After all, the upper-level FBI managers who surrounded him were still some of the same ones who committed serious errors or otherwise were derelict in their duty. They would obviously paint things in the most positive light possible. To do otherwise would be to admit they had failed.

On the appointed day, Mueller arrived in Minneapolis with relatively little fanfare compared to how large his entourage and security detail became later in his tenure. When it was 5 Squad's turn to meet with him just before lunch, we were admitted to the SAC's conference room where Mueller sat at the head of the table. He had his suit jacket off and the sleeves of his pristine white dress shirt rolled up. After greeting us Mueller spoke for a few minutes about his vision for the FBI, specifically how we had to transform ourselves into an intelligence agency to prevent things like the 9/11 attacks from happening again. As someone who was intimately involved the debacle that was the pre- 9/11 investigation, I did not see how it mattered whether we considered ourselves a law enforcement agency or an intelligence agency. Either way, the careerists at FBI Headquarters continued to believe they knew more than we did in the field about our cases, and as long as they were empowered to overrule us, bad things would be in our future.

When Mueller finished his remarks, he stopped and asked for questions. I did not want to go first and waited until the usual crop of aspiring managers asked their softball questions so they could get their names and faces in front of the high bureau officials in the room. There were a couple of those, and then a pause.

I raised my hand. Mueller nodded at me.

"I am SA Harry Samit. I heard what you said about the FBI becoming an intelligence agency. My concern is that whatever we call ourselves, unless we improve the quality of management at headquarters and change their role, we will continue to have failures." I could feel the tension increase in the room. "We in the field are closest to the cases. We know when something is significant and what needs to be done. The problem is, the way the current system works, a GS-14 at headquarters, most of whom are of dubious qualification anyway, can overrule us. We are required to report everything we learn to them, and then *they* make the decisions in Washington. I understand headquarters needs to know what is going on, but having these people make decisions on cases about which they know nothing is dangerous. That's why 9/11 happened."

Mueller frowned as I was speaking. One member of his entourage in the room cleared his throat. Before he responded, Mueller made a visible effort to return his facial expression to neutral. "Yes, you're right. I would like to see decision making more decentralized…" A pause, and then Mueller did what I have since seen him do a half a dozen times since when facing difficult questions from subordinates: he turned the conversation into a standup comedy routine.

Pointing a finger pistol at me, Mueller asked, rapid fire, "So when are you coming to headquarters?"

"I'm not. I am a street Agent. If I came there now, I would be one of the managers making questionable decisions on someone else's cases."

"Yes, but it's a nice place! People have fun there!" He drummed the table. Mueller's joking tone drew laughs, just what he was looking for. "Any other questions? From someone else?" And I was done. Robert Mueller in person proved to be as unable to address the problems in the FBI as his reputation indicated. What is worse, he had people telling him what was wrong, and he chose to ignore them and double down by enlarging headquarters and promoting only the most careerist and malleable of organizational politicians. In another decade and a half, the seeds sown by Mueller and his sycophants would jeopardize the very existence of the FBI and threaten our democracy. This would become apparent when FBI managers appointed and promoted by him would err so grievously in other investigations of consequence to the American People.

CHAPTER 54

EMBARRASSMENT

By late 2002 it was also becoming increasingly obvious that the U.S. was preparing to invade Iraq. The FBI tried to assist by launching a nationwide effort to locate and interview all Iraqis in the U.S. both to determine whether they posed a threat, and to see whether they had any intelligence which would be useful to the military in their upcoming campaign. For that reason, and because of the extensive media coverage, all of us in the FBI were aware of impending military action.

These preparations for war provoked a second letter from Celia to Director Mueller, only this time I had no warning it was coming. Also, instead of sending the letter through official channels, only to see it leaked, Celia, obviously emboldened by her status as an acclaimed whistle blower and clearly thrilled by the fame and adulation she received the last time, sent the letter to the Director and to the media at the same time. This was an obvious and egregious breach of Department of Justice and FBI regulations.

Of course, with the very public debate on the merits of war with Iraq swirling, Celia's letter was fuel on the fire. In her second letter, a multi-page missive dated 02/26/2003, Celia made some sweeping claims, taking aim at the FBI's counterterrorism program dating back a decade or more. Most troubling was her concluding passage, in which she publicly informed Mueller that he would find himself "a helpless bystander to a rash of 9–11s. The bottom line is this: We should be deluding neither ourselves nor the American people that there is any way the FBI, despite the various improvements you are implementing, will be able to stem the flood of terrorism that will likely head our way in the wake of an attack on Iraq."

I was shocked. The second letter is a masterpiece of egotism, written by someone who by this time clearly believed the media's reports of their own infallibility. Celia was never a terrorism investigator and had zero understanding of the dynamics of the situation or the threat. Without addressing her flawed logic point by point and to avoid a discussion of the controversial and consequential decision to invade Iraq in early 2003, I will simply say that I believe Celia suffered a break with reality around this time. I can think of no other reason why a serving FBI Agent would write a letter of this nature to the Director of the FBI and, worse, release it simultaneously to the media. For a U.S. Government Official to release such a letter on the eve of war is despicable, whatever their intentions or how correct they believe their opinions to be. I never spoke to Celia again after this.

It is fortunate indeed that most people began realizing shortly thereafter how unqualified Celia was, and her public star began to fade, even as her ego continued to drive her to ever more extreme behavior to gain media exposure. She ran for congress in Minnesota in 2006, suffering a disastrous loss because rational people by then could see the dangerous combination of ego, an unconventional political outlook, and a crippling lack of experience giving rise to outlandish ideas on foreign and domestic policy. Later Celia, to her everlasting shame, traveled to Moscow in 2013 to bestow a "whistle-blower" award on Edward Snowden. Sadly, this, like the rest of her post-FBI existence, seemed to be one in a series of desperate and increasingly sad attempts to stay in the limelight. I doubt there is a more pathetic example of someone trying to extend their 15 minutes of fame in the entire history of law enforcement and Celia will exit our story here, un-missed and irrelevant, especially when we needed her most during August of 2001.

It was around this time also when I received another surprise about how the U.S. Government functioned. I was in the office one day working when I heard from someone on the squad that members of "The National Commission on Terrorist Attacks Upon the United States" (also known as the 9–11 Commission) were in Minneapolis interviewing people about the events leading up to the 9/11 attacks. In fact, my friend told me they were working out of a conference room in our office.

I thought that made sense. Minneapolis was a logical spot for them to visit given the Moussaoui case, and it made sense to me now why I never received a summons to come to Washington, D.C. to be interviewed: they were planning to interview me in Minneapolis.

When I said that to my friend, he shook his head. "I don't think so. The staffer I talked to said they were all finished."

With that, I asked what room the 9/11 commission people were in and called up there. I asked to speak to a supervisor and was put on with a pleasant-sounding attorney. "Oh, yes. We know who you are. There are no plans to interview you."

I was stunned. "How can that be? I was the case Agent on the Moussaoui investigation!"

Still staying pleasant, she replied, "Yes, but you were interviewed already by the JICI, right?"

"Yes."

"We will be using the information you provided to them for our portion on you."

"Right, but that interview was more than two years ago. I have more information now."

A pause, "Oh, we will follow up on that and get back to you."

That is why I was shocked that July when I saw in the media the 9/11 commission was preparing to release its final report. I remember thinking, "But they still haven't talked to me or John yet, and we were the case Agents!"

And no one from the 9/11 Commission ever did speak to me or John. Without exaggerating our own importance to a study that looked at so many factors, I do have to comment that this omission leaves me wondering where else this study overlooked evidence or ignored witnesses with relevant information.

CHAPTER 55

OFFICE OF THE INSPECTOR GENERAL

And speaking of lawyers, in late 2004 one of the Agents who originally interviewed me from the Department of Justice Office of the Inspector General (DOJ-OIG) called me with an announcement. They were finally coming to the end of their three-year investigation of the FBI's handling of the Moussaoui case, an investigation triggered by Celia's letter to Mueller in May 2002, and they had some follow-up questions. This session was obviously less formal than the interview under oath in Washington since his questions were delivered over the phone.

That was not the only difference. The phone call felt a little like an ambush. The main question the Agent claimed the lawyers wanted me to answer was whether, after our FISA had been denied conclusively by FBI Headquarters, anyone in Minneapolis ever considered asking them a second time for permission to take the case the criminal route. I actually looked at the phone in amazement before answering, "No."

"Okay. Why not?"

"I don't know. Because RFU was absolutely unwilling to listen to any request from us. I didn't think there was a chance they would let us go to the U.S. Attorney's Office and we were focused on getting to France by then."

"But you didn't know for sure because you didn't ask?"

"Correct." I could feel myself getting angry. "Where is this question coming from?"

"Uh, one of the lawyers wanted us to ask."

"And just now, right before your results are released?"

"Yes." The person on the other end was deadpan, maddeningly so.

I ended the call before I said something I would regret. I was concerned because both the timing and the nature of the question suggested the OIG was "blamestorming." That is, trying to evenly distribute the blame for the failure so no one element would be hit too hard by their conclusions. It would seem more balanced if their report read that although the team at RFU had thwarted our FISA requests, no one in Minneapolis ever asked about the criminal option again.

Unfortunately, my misgivings proved accurate when I was provided with an advance draft of the OIG report in late 2004 or early 2005. This document, entitled "A Review of the FBI's Handling of Intelligence Information Related to the September 11 Attacks" laid out the OIG's findings on the Moussaoui investigation in Chapter 4. This document is available online, so I will not go into detail on specifics, except to explain my two biggest areas of contention with the report. First, the OIG found there was no misconduct by anyone, including people in RFU and NSLU. After an elaborate and lengthy recap of the facts of the Moussaoui case, the OIG drew the most favorable possible conclusion for them:

> *"At the outset of our analysis, we believe it is important to state that we did not conclude that any FBI employee committed intentional misconduct, or that anyone attempted to deliberately "sabotage" the Minneapolis FBI's request for a FISA warrant, as Celia wrote in her letter to FBI Director Mueller. For example, Celia argued that Martin edited the initial FISA request submitted by the Minneapolis FBI and omitted information to "deliberately further undercut the FISA effort." Celia also suggested that as part of the alleged sabotage, FBI Headquarters personnel failed to make Minneapolis aware of the Phoenix EC.*

As we discuss below, we believe that Celia's letter raised significant problems in the way the Moussaoui investigation was handled, and we criticize some of the actions of FBI employees. Her letter also alluded to broader problems that existed in how the FBI handled intelligence matters and FISA requests. But contrary to her assertions, we found no evidence, and we do not believe, that any FBI employee deliberately sabotaged the Moussaoui FISA request or committed intentional misconduct."

My first thought was that my pessimism about the OIG proved well founded. I could not imagine how anyone in good faith could conclude that the FISA request, indeed the whole course of the Moussaoui case was not sabotaged by RFU, and for precisely the reasons they highlighted. As I read on, I realized I had been right to be concerned about the last-minute question from OIG about asking again for permission to seek a criminal warrant:

"Failure to reconsider criminal warrant

We found it even more troubling that after the FBI Headquarters conclusion—based upon NSLU advice—that Moussaoui did not have a sufficient connection to a recognized foreign power for a FISA warrant, no one reconsidered whether to try to obtain a criminal warrant. As far as we could determine, neither FBI Headquarters nor the Minneapolis FBI initiated any discussion about pursuing the criminal warrant after NSLU Unit Chief opined that a FISA warrant was not feasible. After the FISA warrant was ruled out, the "smell test" was no longer a consideration. The FBI could have consulted with the Minnesota USAO at that point to determine whether it believed there was sufficient probable cause to obtain a criminal search warrant. If the Minnesota USAO agreed, one could have been sought. If the USAO disagreed, this consultation would have had no impact on a FISA warrant, since one was no longer being sought.

We asked Don (Chris), Henry (me), Celia, Gary (Greg), and Martin why a criminal warrant was not considered after the FISA route was exhausted. Don, Henry, and Celia told the OIG that they did not know why this was not done. Don said that looking back on the matter now, he wished it had been discussed. Gary told the OIG that he did not seek to pursue it again because he believed FBI Headquarters was not willing to support obtaining the requisite permission to approach the USAO. Martin told the OIG that because Minneapolis believed that there was sufficient evidence to support obtaining a criminal warrant, it was up to the field office to initiate pursuit of the criminal warrant.

We found it puzzling, and troubling, that no one discussed pursuing this option. It also showed that the FBI never fully evaluated the potential of the criminal investigation versus the FISA investigation. Instead, the FBI pursued the case as an either/or proposition, without evaluating the potential of each approach.

We also do not agree with Martin that it was Minneapolis' responsibility alone to consider this option. In our view, his position reflects the breakdown in communication between Headquarters and the field, and also shows a troubling lack of initiative and acceptance of responsibility by FBI Headquarters. While we cannot say whether a request for a criminal warrant would have been successful, it should have been reconsidered."

Chapter 4 of the report was as complete a job of evenly distributing the blame as I have ever seen, while also utterly failing to identify the actual problem, namely: the severe leadership crisis in the FBI.

That is why, when I read in the accompanying email that anyone mentioned in the report was invited to submit comments, I sat down at my computer and started to write my response. The email also noted that if people felt strongly, they would be invited back to Washington to give their input in person.

By the time I finished writing a few days later, I found that in my fury I had drafted a 44-page document. It was more than a rant. In it, I tried to make two related but separate points. The first, was that there very definitely *was* misconduct by FBI Headquarters personnel. Specifically, I strongly objected to their conclusion that in removing critical information from my version of the FISA request, Martin did not intentionally sabotage the request. Not only did I consider the suppression of the request intentional, I termed it "criminally negligent." The second issue I raised was that the current way in which the FBI selected, trained, and promoted its managers was in large part responsible for the failings in the Moussaoui case as well as numerous other investigations. I also offered my ideas on how to fix what I saw as a severe and pervasive leadership crisis. My suggestion was based on my experience with the military model, where promotions were based on a combination of tactical and technical skill, and leadership ability.

As to OIG's last-minute question about why Minneapolis did not reconsider seeking a criminal warrant once the FISA route was exhausted, something they found "puzzling and troubling," I replied:

> "My comment [on this finding] relates to a telephone conversation on the morning of 09/11/2001 between RFU Unit Chief Devin and ASAC Chris. The substance of this conversation was related to me by ASAC Chris later. The conversation occurred after AA flight #11 and UA Flight #175 had hit the two towers of the WTC. ASAC Chris was again asking UC Devin for authority to go to the U.S. Attorney's Office for a criminal search warrant for Moussaoui's belongings in light of the attacks, only to be told by UC Devin that we still lacked sufficient evidence to justify this course. While they were debating the issue, AA Flight #77 crashed into the Pentagon and this was announced on TV. Upon hearing this, ASAC Chris again asked UC Devin for authority, at which point UC Devin relented and gave verbal authority to do so.

> I would therefore submit that what was needed 'to bolster their argument for seeking a criminal warrant with the additional information that had been uncovered since the matter was initially discussed' as described by OIG was an event as horrifying as three airliners being used as suicide platforms. That is what was required before RFU would relent. I am certain anything less than those horrific circumstances would have been insufficient to move them because even after two aircraft had been used in suicide attacks, UC Devin asserted that 'it was a coincidence.' I maintain that nothing short of the disaster which befell the U.S. on 09/11/2001 would have caused RFU to give us the authority we so desperately sought, because we in Minneapolis witnessed this ourselves."

After taking three days to carefully write, review and edit my submission, as the instructions specified, I emailed it to Candice, who was the head of the FBI's Office of Professional Responsibility (OPR). A few days later, I received an email back from Candice "inviting" me to come to Washington, D.C. to discuss my concerns.

As with so many of my other attempts to "fix" the FBI from my lowly position, this came to nought. In March 2005 I ended up in a basement room in the Department of Justice on Pennsylvania Avenue arguing with a bunch of senior FBI officials and one DOJ Attorney whose careers had prospered under the system I was attacking. As a friend once put it, I was "calling their kid ugly," and no one takes that well, particularly those who owed their titles and large salaries (by government standards) to what I sought to tear down.

As I flew back to Minneapolis the following morning, I did not give a second thought to any of the enemies I might have made among the management ranks of the FBI. I had no career ambitions other than to remain a street Agent in Minneapolis and so, wanting nothing from them, I did not feel the slightest need to be political or conciliatory. What I did not realize and did not learn for several months is that I unintentionally caused additional problems for the prosecutors in Virginia working to prepare for Moussaoui's trial.

What happened was that the OIG or FBI Headquarters, I am not sure who, later turned my 44-page response over to the AUSAs on the Moussaoui case. That made sense. The submission contained statements by me about the investigation, specifically that the FBI had a chance to stop the attacks but squandered it through poor decisions made at FBI Headquarters. I wrote that in February 2005 and attended that acrimonious meeting in March. Because I was going to be a witness at Moussaoui's trial, whenever that took place, my written statements were discoverable, meaning they had to be provided to the defense.[17] This would cause me problems later.

17 This document was subsequently declassified and provided to the defense for their use at trial. Although they did not introduce it as a formal trial exhibit, Moussaoui's attorneys did use one portion of the document to question me on the witness stand.

CHAPTER 56

GUILTY PLEA

The following month (April 2005) I was stunned to read in the media "Moussaoui pleads guilty, plea accepted." Reading it twice to be sure I was not seeing things, I learned from this story that not only had Moussaoui acknowledged his role in the 9/11 attacks, but he also signed a 23-point statement of facts agreeing to all that the government would have had to prove at trial, specifically that he was a member of Al Qaeda sent here to participate in the attacks that occurred on September 11, 2001. As to one aspect of his involvement, in point #16 Moussaoui agreed:

"After his arrest, Moussaoui lied to federal agents to allow his al Qaeda 'brothers' to go forward with the operation to fly planes into American buildings. Specifically, Moussaoui falsely denied being a member of a terrorist organization and falsely denied that he was taking pilot training to kill Americans. Instead, Moussaoui told federal agents that he was training as a pilot purely for his personal enjoyment and that, after completion of his training, he intended to visit New York City and Washington, D.C., as a tourist."

As the headline proclaimed, Judge Brinkema accepted the plea, making it official. Moreover, the article also noted the government still planned to seek the death penalty because Moussaoui had not negotiated to have that taken off the table. I was sure the prosecutors would never have conceded that anyway. For this reason, the judge would schedule the "penalty phase" of Moussaoui's trial for the future. In the penalty phase, which is like a separate trial, the government presents evidence to persuade a jury why the now-guilty defendant should face the ultimate punishment of state-administered death. The defendant and his legal team, of course, present evidence to convince the jury why they should not.

I called Brian right away and he confirmed it. Apparently, Moussaoui agreed to plead guilty for reasons only he fully understood, though without cooperating with the government or showing any signs of remorse. Because of the lack of cooperation and the especially serious nature of the crimes, the prosecution team's orders from senior levels of government were to continue with the death penalty prosecution, so that is what they were doing. The trial would go forward.

Sometime later I learned David, the PENTTBOMB team prosecutor with whom I worked the closest, was unhappy with me. Although he did not contact me directly, he let FBI Headquarters know that he considered my 44-page submission in response to the OIG findings a serious problem for the prosecution. With his flair for the dramatic he termed my document "a dagger to the heart of the case" against Moussaoui. Always happy to find fault with me, one of their most vocal critics, someone at headquarters then called Debbie, who informed me of David's unhappiness.

Confused, I did what I always did. I called Brian. As usual, he had a much more balanced view of events, especially after I explained why I wrote the document in the first place. Like all non-supervisory Agents associated with the case, Brian had long agreed with me that people at headquarters were to blame for what happened and he well understood why I did what I did following the OIG's vanilla findings.

When I repeated David's phrase of "a dagger to the heart of the case," Brian chuckled, and replied, "No, it's more of a steel-toed boot to the nuts of the case, but it's not fatal." He went on to explain the problem was that my claims stood in direct opposition to the new theory which would be used by the prosecutors to persuade the jury to vote to end Moussaoui's life. Following Moussaoui's guilty plea in April, the government no longer had to prove what he did, since he admitted to it all. Now, they just needed to show that these crimes were especially heinous and serious enough to warrant the death penalty. The problem was it was a significant hurdle to convince jurors to vote "death" for someone who was sitting in jail on the day the attacks went forward.

For this reason, the prosecutors planned to argue that it was Moussaoui's lies to me and John on August 16 and 17, 2001 which allowed the 9/11 attacks to move forward. The idea was that if Moussaoui answered our questions truthfully about his connections and reasons for being in the U.S. the FBI would have been able to sound the alarm and stop the attacks. Instead, he misled us with false leads and sent the team off on wild goose chases by making up people like his friend the Dutch executive and Habib, his non-existent friend in Germany.

Once Brian explained that, I understood the problem. I spent a good bit of my 44-page submission claiming that it was FBI management's combination of incompetence and careerism which thwarted our investigation. This opened the door the defense to argue the 9/11 attacks were able to go forward not because of Moussaoui's lies, but because of the problems with FBI management as highlighted in my report.

Despite David's concern, I did not see a direct conflict between his argument and the fact that specific people at headquarters acted badly. The prosecutors' theory of prosecution *was* correct. Moussaoui's lies absolutely protected his Al Qaeda friends long enough for them to carry out their attacks. The missteps made by the FBI would not have happened had Moussaoui told the truth. One truthful admission by him about Al Qaeda and no one would have been able to stop us from sounding the alarm.

I called David and tried to explain that I wrote what I did to try to fix the problems still plaguing the FBI almost four years after the attacks. He was unconvinced and still unhappy with me. Even though I thought I was doing the right thing for the right reasons, he did not agree. We ended the call on okay terms, mostly, I think, because David needed me. Since I was the case Agent, I was connected to the investigation in a way no one else was. Although I am sure the prosecutors would by now have liked to drop me as a witness and move on to others, they were stuck with me.

And, though I was as stubborn and unyielding in my sense of righteousness at the time as David was, with the passage of years I have come to understand his position more. David was a very experienced and skilled prosecutor, and, I might add a complete believer in the federal criminal justice system. By that point he had lived away from his family in Richmond for more than three years working on the case in Alexandria. And unlike me, with other work to distract my attention, David was involved with 9/11 all the time. And the impact of that cannot be overstated. I had the luxury of shying away from the more heart-wrenching aspects of the thousands of individual tragedies that happened that day. I did and still do find it very upsetting to think about the lives lost and the dreams destroyed and so I simply insulate myself from knowing too much about what happened on the planes and at their targets.

That was not possible for David and the other AUSAs. On the contrary, they immersed themselves in each victim's story, experiencing a taste of the horror through listening to 911 calls, looking at gruesome crime scene photos, and collectively interviewing scores of family members. More than anyone else not personally involved in the tragedy, David, Rob, and Derek were daily face-to-face with the monstrousness of Al Qaeda in general and Moussaoui in particular. This was more than just another case. It was the largest mass murder in U.S. history, meaning the requirement to win was urgent and vitally necessary to ensure justice was served. I think that is why, no matter what my intentions, David viewed what I did as so wrong.

CHAPTER 57

TRIAL PREP

The months rolled quickly by, helped by the exciting and dynamic work on the Minneapolis JTTF. Cases came along, each requiring our sometimes-urgent attention to neutralize a dangerous subject. Two stand out as incredibly important in the fight to stop Al Qaeda from conducting any additional attacks in the U.S. The investigations into Mohammed Abdullah Warsame and Mohamed Kamal Elzahabi will be covered in subsequent books in this series, but for now it can be said that during 2003 and 2004, the race to stop these two extremely threatening Minnesota-based Al Qaeda operatives took up almost all our time and energy in Minneapolis.

And then it was time. Time to fly to Alexandria, Virginia for what would be one of the most watched and analyzed trials in U.S. history. Certainly, it was the most momentous and consequential proceeding in which I would be involved. John and I arrived in Alexandria, Virginia at the end of February 2006 for the death penalty phase of the trial of Zacarias Moussaoui. As he had from the beginning, Brian was there to pick us up and greet us with a smile at the airport. He took us to our hotel, located within walking distance of the courthouse, and we dropped off our luggage before heading out for beers and dinner.

The next morning, and for several days thereafter I met with David and Brian to get ready for my testimony in the large suite the PENTTBOMB team occupied in the U.S. Attorney's Office. As noted above, they had been living and breathing this case, but John and I had not and 4 ½ years had passed since our arrest and interviews of

Moussaoui. It had been a long time since we reviewed any evidence about which I would be testifying, and I needed to study. With the stakes this high I wanted to be sure I knew my stuff thoroughly. The pressure was even greater than usual because I learned that not only would a small number of family members of the deceased victims be present in the courtroom during testimony, but those unable to travel to Virginia would also be watching on closed circuit television from locations in Pennsylvania, New York, and Boston. I was keenly aware of their presence and wanted to be sure I did not fail them again.

As all good prosecutors do when preparing a witness, David put me through the ringer, raising many of the questions he planned to ask as well as aggressively posing questions he anticipated the defense team would on cross examination. It was exhausting for me, and that comes from someone who generally enjoys confrontation.

One area where David and I clashed again was when we discussed my 44-page submission to the Office of the Inspector General. A year later he was clearly still unhappy with me over that because it contained so many claims which he viewed as directly contrary to the prosecution's theory Moussaoui's crimes were especially serious and deserving of the death penalty. Anything I wrote which laid the blame for the attacks on anyone other than Moussaoui gave the defense fodder to cross examine me on the witness stand.

We never saw eye to eye on that document.

Even though we had an adversarial and acrimonious three days, I realized David was only doing his job. He was preparing me for all the questions I was likely to face on cross examination so I could think about my responses before I got on the stand. It was unpleasant for me, and probably for him, but it needed to be done, and I am grateful for it.

I should also say here that having John with me in Alexandria was critical. Even after the passage of so much time John remained as staunch, reliable, and capable as he had been during the moment when we first encountered Moussaoui in the parking lot of the

Marriot Residence Inn, and later when we interviewed him at the INS office. Although I tried to hide it, I was nervous about testifying and very aware many members of the PENTTBOMB team were hostile towards me. John helped more than he will ever know, not just with preparations for testimony, but by being my friend and remaining unswervingly in my corner.

After a few days I felt prepared, just in time for John and me to help Brian and David get Clancy ready too. Although Clancy had comparatively less on his plate as far as testimony went, he was a retired airline pilot and current flight instructor, not a professional witness like FBI Agents are supposed to be. For this reason, David wanted to be sure Clancy was ready for his time on the stand, especially because he was the guy who kicked the whole case off and was the witness whose statements persuaded me and John to move forward with the INS arrest. He would also be one of the prosecution's first witnesses, setting the stage for all who followed, including me. In short, it was critical that Clancy did well.

And almost immediately after we started, we had a little scare. Sitting in one of the conference rooms, David asked, "So, Clancy, how do you feel?" Over the years John and I relayed all of Clancy's concerns to David, so he was well versed in what worried him. Chief among these anxieties, likely stoked by his wife, was concern about testifying against a full-fledged Al Qaeda member.

On several occasions in the past David and I had to address this worry, but today Clancy seemed steely eyed and unafraid. He replied to David, "I am good. I'm ready to go!"

With that promising start, I could see David relax. He replied, "That's great, Clancy. We really need your help because you are a key witness. Now, do you have any questions before we start?"

"No. No questions." He paused, "Well, maybe one. How are we going to deal with the fact the government was involved in blowing up the Pentagon?"

David's face fell, and I could feel my own mouth pop open.

One of us choked out, "What?"

Clancy narrowed his eyes and cocked his head to the side before responding. He looked a little embarrassed, like he just caught two old friends in a lie but wanted to let them off the hook. "Well, you see, I am a member of a lot of retired pilot groups. In this one there is a guy who was at the Pentagon just after the explosion and fire. He said there was absolutely no sign a plane hit there. He also knows they didn't find any parts of an airplane in the wreckage. Not one. This guy has inside information the government blew up the Pentagon."

David glanced at me. I had explained Clancy was a nice guy, but also one who was easily influenced by others, not the least of whom was his wife. Obviously, someone else had gotten to him and filled his head with one of the hundreds of crazy theories surrounding the attacks, which he now clearly believed. If the defense on cross examination could get Clancy talking about a wild idea like that, it would be bad for our case.

Much to my relief, David handled this curve masterfully. I am not sure how he knew what to do so quickly, except that maybe some other witness or grieving family member had raised a theory like that before.

Whatever it was that prepared him to handle this, David said, "No, Clancy. That's not true. Hang here a minute."

David jumped up and left the room, returning in a few minutes with a small stack of photographs. Laying the first one in front of Clancy he asked, "Do you recognize what that is?"

Clancy nodded, "It's a main landing gear mount from a Boeing 757."

Dave replied, "Right. It's from American Airlines Flight 77 that crashed into the Pentagon on September 11, 2001." He placed the next photo in front of Clancy. I could see it was the same component, only photographed from farther away. In the two photos I recognized FBI evidence protocol which specifies not only taking a picture of an item up close but also capturing it from a distance so people later will be able to see where it was located relative to the rest of the crime scene. The far photo was not only obviously the same landing gear mount, but from that perspective it could be seen to be unmistakably embedded in a wall of the Pentagon. A few more photos of different aircraft components were sufficient to convince Clancy that his friend's theory was false and that there *were* airplane parts in the wreckage of the Pentagon, and lots of them. And from a 757.

With that behind us, David asked, "Anything else?"

Clancy nodded, "I've thought about it a lot and it's a pretty heavy responsibility giving someone the death penalty. I mean, I know this guy and sat with him in the classroom. I don't know..."

I nodded as Clancy spoke because I understood what he meant. Now, relying on the four-year relationship I built with him, I said, "Clancy, I get it. I am testifying too, but I am looking at the situation differently. You're not 'giving him the death penalty.' That is for the jury and judge to decide. Our justice system works because witnesses like you and I just sit on the stand and tell the truth. That's our whole job. And remember, I'll be up there right after you. My conscience will be clear, because all I am going to do is answer every question I am asked truthfully and completely. If Moussaoui is sentenced to death, it will be because of his actions."

Listening carefully to me, Clancy nodded. When I finished, he said, "That's fair. That makes sense. Okay." *Now* he was ready.

CHAPTER 58

PENALTY PHASE

Since this was about to be the one and only trial in federal civilian court of an Al Qaeda operative for the crimes committed on 9/11, the level of vigilance around the The Albert V. Bryan Courthouse in Alexandia, Virginia made sense. It also heightened my realization that this was some serious business about to start and that with so many people going to so much trouble, I had better get my part right.

I would be testifying in the first part of the penalty phase of Moussaoui's trial. In Part 1 the jury would hear evidence presented by the government and the defense on whether Moussaoui should be *eligible* for the death penalty. Rob, Derek, and David would be working to persuade the jury to vote "yes" for this portion. If they agreed and voted that Moussaoui was eligible for the death penalty, the trial would move to the second part, where more testimony and exhibits would be introduced by both sides. At the end of the second part, the jury would vote once more, this time as to whether Moussaoui's sentence would be the death penalty. It should not be easy for the government to take someone's life, and the rigorous two-phase process would ensure it was fair.

For that reason, John and I studied each day like we were about to face an important final exam, which, in a sense, we were. My testimony was a small part of the U.S. Government's response to Al Qaeda's attack on our country and its people. Sending Bin Laden a message that his operatives would be held accountable was important. I also felt a responsibility to see justice done. Moussaoui came to the U.S. where he was welcomed and allowed to attend fight training, just like anyone else. Instead of being grateful, he was here to learn skills to allow him to kill hundreds or thousands of innocent Americans. That deserved a response. I also wanted to show the American public that the Bureau was competent, particularly because the true story of the Moussaoui investigation had yet to see the light of day.

March 6, 2006 dawned cool and partly cloudy in Alexandria. On that first day of the trial, and every day thereafter that court was in session, the already tight security around the courthouse locked down even more. The plan was for witnesses to be transported to the courthouse from their nearby hotels by FBI SWAT teams who came to Virginia from surrounding field offices to help. The SWAT operators were in civilian clothes, as opposed to their tactical gear, but whatever they wore they were experts at smoothly and safely transporting people with a minimum of fuss or fanfare. Once a witness was in the back of one of their tinted-out Chevrolet Suburbans, they were safe from interference and from the prying eyes of the media.

When I got up to the U.S. Attorney's Office Brian was there to greet me. That was comforting too. As a former Marine and highly experienced undercover Agent nothing rattled Brian or shut down his sense of humor, so he was rock steady, as usual. John was there too, meaning I had as much support as I could ever ask for. I chatted briefly with David, who seemed a little keyed up, which was to be expected. After 4+ years of preparation, it was time for the prosecutors to perform, and the eyes of the nation were truly upon them.

Judge Brinkema convened court right on time, and the trial was underway. I passed the start sitting in the U.S. Attorney's Office, waiting quietly. As a witness I was not allowed to hear other witnesses' testimony, but once it got closer to my time, I would be moved to a witness room right next to the courtroom. No one was in the office now since all the prosecutors and other Agents were in the courtroom and I was truly alone with my thoughts. Because the opening arguments and prior witnesses were expected to take all morning, I would not be on until after lunch at the earliest. I was wearing my best suit and a new shirt, tie, and shoes. I picked the clothes I would wear that day conscious that I would be representing the FBI to the jury, so my suit was dark, my shirt was bright white, and my tie was red.

Around noon everyone returned. If David thought I might not get to testify on the first day of the trial before it started, now he was certain—no go. It ended up taking a few days, but on Thursday, March 9, it was my turn. That morning Brian told me it was time to move to the witness room because my testimony was getting close. David seconded that and estimated he would probably call me around 9 or 10 a.m., so we would have three or four hours of testimony from me that morning and afternoon, with more to follow the next day. As he said that, I felt a little shot of adrenaline.

My wait in the witness room ended up being longer than estimated. I was there with Scott and another Agent from Oklahoma City who were also slated to testify. We chatted while waiting to be called. One after the other, the two Oklahoma City Agents were called and disappeared. I was alone again. Around 11:30 a.m. one of the court security officers opened the door, looked in and said, "They're ready for you."

I thanked him and stood, exiting the room, and pushing open the frosted glass doors just to my right. I was conscious that I would be "on stage" from the second I entered, so I set my face in an appropriately serious expression and tried to look like an FBI Agent.

CHAPTER 59

DIRECT EXAMINATION

The sight that met me as the door swung open was intimidating, to say the least. In keeping with the importance of the trial, Judge Brinkema's courtroom was very large, and today it was packed full of people. As I entered, I walked down the aisle separating the two sides of the spectators' gallery, each row filled with the media, members of the victims' families and senior officials of the FBI and DOJ. Seated to my left in the front row was a sketch artist, drawing each of the witnesses in pastel chalk as they testified. I could see he had drawn in the room on his large pad, including the witness stand where I would be sitting in a second, but the spot where I would go was blank because he did not know what I looked like yet.

My one thought as I moved forward was to appear professional and present the judge, and most importantly the jury with an appropriate image of an FBI Agent. To that end I kept saying over and over in my head, "Don't trip, don't trip..." Since David had had the foresight to bring me up to the courtroom a few days before, I knew exactly where the witness stand was, and could go directly there with assurance. That was a smart move on his part since this courtroom was laid out very differently from those in Minnesota. Instead of being next to the judge, the witness stand was center stage, in front of the bench and facing the jury to my left front. The judge was seated to my left and the prosecutors and defense attorneys and their client were to my right front. It was a good layout for the ultimate audience, the jury, to be able to see and hear the witnesses while they testified.

When I reached the witness stand, I stood next to it looking at the judge's clerk with my hand raised as she swore me in. I agreed under oath to tell the whole truth, "So help me God," and was told to be seated. As soon as I sat, I looked for *him*. In less than a second, our eyes met. Moussaoui was seated on the far end of the defense table, to my far right and to the right of his attorneys. He was dressed in dark green prison scrubs and a white koufi. I saw right away that Moussaoui was a mess. The four plus years in custody had obviously done him no good. Moussaoui was bloated and his beard and hair were wild and untrimmed. He looked curiously at me, as if he did not remember where we met before, which surprised me a little.

I did not have much time to reflect on that because David stood and started asking me questions almost right away. I will not relate in detail the two days I spent on the witness stand at that trial since the transcript of my testimony is available online if the reader is interested in exactly what I said. Instead, I will give my impressions of what was happening while I was being questioned, first by the prosecution and later by the defense.

Because I was a witness for the prosecution, the prosecutors questioned me initially in what was called direct examination. David had done a solid job of preparing for this and after questioning me about my background and experience, started asking me specifics about the case. While answering, I split my attention between David, the jury, and the judge. At Quantico I was taught to address my most important replies to the members of the jury since they were the ones who decided on the verdict. I did so that day, responding to them what I thought was an appropriate amount. They appeared to be a representative cross-section of Americans, some young, some old, and with slightly more men than women. All of them were listening closely to my answers.

I used the pauses between questions from David to glance at the defense attorneys. I recognized Edward MacMahon, who I knew I would be facing when I was cross examined later. MacMahon was tall, handsome, and stocky, with neatly combed dark hair and wearing a suit that must have been expensive. He looked smart, competent, and self-assured. MacMahon met my gaze without looking away, a slight smile on his lips and I knew then and there I was in for a tough cross. To MacMahon's left was Gerald Zerkin, who was smaller and older, with a receding hairline and a bushy mustache. Zerkin stared back at me through his glasses, and I realized he, too, would be a very formidable opponent. It was obvious Moussaoui was getting the best defense available, and at taxpayer expense.

When David started asking about the investigation, I looked over at Moussaoui to see whether that might have jogged his memory about me. It seemed to, because when I looked again, he was staring at me through hate-filled, narrowed eyes. Now Moussaoui remembered where he knew me from, all right.

I received the gentlest of all possible introductions to testimony that day. Because I was called so late in the morning, I was only on the stand about an hour before the court adjourned for lunch. The judge excused me and ordered me to come back at 1:30 p.m. During the time I was on the stand, I had the chance to get comfortable and shake off all the pregame jitters and even to hear MacMahon object once, when David went too far into detail asking me about aviation-related topics. I caught my first glimpse of the feigned indignation so many defense attorneys assume when MacMahon rose dramatically and said, "Your honor, this witness is an FBI Agent, not an aviation expert!"

The judge nodded and looked at David, who replied that I was qualified to answer questions on airplanes too, based on my background and training.

The judge nodded again, but sustained MacMahon's objection, cautioning David to stick to questions concerning the case. With that over, she adjourned for lunch. I ate a light lunch with Brian and John and then sat and relaxed for a few minutes before heading back to the courtroom for the afternoon. The hour on the stand followed by the lunch break had been perfect for me. I was now ready for more.

David finished his direct examination of me around 5:15 p.m. that afternoon. His goal for my testimony was to build the record that it was Moussaoui's lies during John and my interviews on August 16 and 17, 2001 that allowed the 9/11 attacks to go forward. I absolutely believed this, so it was easy to answer David's questions truthfully in a way that showed Moussaoui's lies bought time for his co-conspirators to continue with their mission. Although I was confident David was making his point, we would not know whether we succeeded until the jury voted at the end of this first part of the penalty phase.

MacMahon objected numerous times that afternoon to try to derail David. The defense obviously wanted to minimize to the extent possible the jury hearing a long list of Moussaoui's lies and omissions which protected the other hijackers and allowed the plot to proceed. MacMahon was also intent on trying to limit the introduction of facts which linked Moussaoui to the leadership of Al Qaeda, figures like Usama Bin Laden and his military commander, Mohamed Atef. Obviously, these connections looked bad for Moussaoui. The judge sustained some of MacMahon's objections, meaning David had to ask a different question, but many she overruled, allowing me to answer. As judges sometimes do, Judge Brinkema also asked me a few questions herself, either to increase her own understanding or to make sure the jury was getting all the information they needed. Judge Brinkema ran her courtroom very well, maintaining a firm hand while simultaneously treating the witnesses and attorneys with courtesy. I have appeared in front of many judges in terrorism trials, though none with such high stakes or with intensity of media coverage. In my opinion Judge Brinkema was the best.

Toward the end of the day's testimony, David gave me a chance to repeat before the jury what I said to Moussaoui on August 17, 2001 right before he ended our second interview. At this point in the interview John and I were now committed to calling him out on his lies and so what we said then was particularly important for the jury to hear. David asked, "Can you tell us how it is the interview with Mr. Moussaoui ended?"

I replied, "Right before he, he invoked his right to counsel while we were talking to him, we informed Mr. Moussaoui that we were aware of his involvement in a plot, in a plot involving airliners. We reminded him that he was in custody and that if anything were to happen, that, in fact, *he* would be held accountable before the United States, before the American people." As I said that, I shifted my gaze from the jury until I was looking at Moussaoui. His black eyes narrowed, and he frowned at me, but he nodded slowly, still looking into my eyes. He clearly remembered being told that and now...here we were. He was being held accountable.

I held my stare until he looked away.

David asked dozens of questions, the answers to each of which linked Moussaoui to the plot or illustrated for the jury how his lies allowed the plot to advance. When those questions were complete, He wrapped up my direct examination by having me identify various items of Moussaoui's property which the Minneapolis Evidence Response Team found during the search on 9/11–12/2001. These items and all the aviation-related materials in Moussaoui's possession were important for the jury to see since the defense team was claiming Moussaoui, although he was an Al Qaeda member, was actually *preparing for a different plot when we arrested him*. As implausible as that seemed, Moussaoui's lawyers were claiming there was some separate plot being run by the group and that is the one for which he was preparing. The lawyers really did not have a whole range of options to mount their defense once Moussaoui, against their advice, signed the document stipulating to his role in the 9/11 attacks and his membership in Al Qaeda, so they must have believed the extremely thin "separate plot" theory was all that was left to them.

Understandably, MacMahon continued to object where he believed he could, but these were overruled by the judge, who gave David a good deal of leeway to have me explain the significance of various documents. By around 5:10 p.m., David was finished and as the last photo was admitted into evidence, he said, "Judge with that, I have no further questions of Agent Samit."

Judge Brinkema nodded and then looked at her watch. She said, "Well, I'll tell you what: It's 5:10. It's been a long day and, I think, a long week, and I expect this cross examination will go more than 20 minutes." She looked at the defense table.

Rising briefly, MacMahon replied, "It will, Your Honor." He looked at me and smiled and I held his gaze. I felt ready for him.

Judge Brinkema continued, addressing the jury, "All right. I think this is a logical time then to end for today, and ladies and gentlemen, as you know, you have tomorrow off." The judge then excused me from the witness stand, but not before telling me to be back on Monday at 9:30 a.m. and to be sure not to discuss my testimony with anyone else.

I replied, "Yes, Your Honor." I then stood and walked out of the courtroom, still silently repeating the mantra, "Don't trip...don't trip." Once I was out, I took the elevator down to the U.S. Attorney's Office to wait for Brian. When we got back to the trial prep room I sat down and cleared my mind. I could feel the tension of the day ebbing away, helped by the fact that I had three days before I had to be back on the witness stand. The direct examination was the easy part. David was friendly and we were on the same page. Cross examination on Monday would not be such a congenial experience. Like many defense attorneys, MacMahon was well practiced feigning doubt, indignation, or ever outrage when questioning facts that did not help his case. I had already seen him turn that on while objecting to some of David's questions. I knew an even more aggressive version would be headed my way Monday.

When I woke up in my hotel room on Friday my phone rang. I could see it was Brian calling and assumed it was about dinner. It was not. "Hey, buddy," Brian started, "So, you're not going to be testifying Monday." He went on to explain that he could not give me a reason for the delay, but that it had nothing to do with me or my testimony or anything involving the Minnesota aspect of the case. Brian informed me it would make sense for me to go home to Minnesota and he would let me know when to come back to Virginia.

Naturally, I was very curious, but all he was able to tell me was that there was a problem with some other witnesses and Rob, Derek, and David were working through that. Once it was resolved, testimony would resume. Brian passed on a warning from David not to watch or read any media coverage of the trial since I might get asked about it on the stand under oath when I was back. Of course I told Brian I would comply.

Hanging up, I called John and then we both booked flights to Minnesota for later that afternoon. Although I was concerned about the case, I was happy to be headed home to see Terri and the kids. I got home in time for dinner and even though I had been gone more than a week, was right back in the swing of things with my wife and kids within five minutes. The delay in the trial also meant I was home for my birthday, which was nice.

I stayed in touch with Brian each day during the delay, expecting that I was going to have to come back to finish my testimony at some point. Early on, whatever the issue was, it sounded serious, and Brian hinted that the trial might be finished. Thankfully, however, by the middle of the week he was confident things would resume and recommended I plan to come back the following Sunday, with the expectation that I would be back on the stand for cross examination early in the week. And that is what happened.

Once I was finished with my testimony and free from the sequestration requirements of a witness, I went back and read the press reports to learn why the delay happened. To my surprise I learned that a lawyer for the Transportation Security Administration (TSA) violated the judge's orders and legal ethics by coaching upcoming expert witnesses by providing them trial transcripts and advice about their planned testimony. This is obviously not allowed since doing so taints the witnesses and prevents unbiased and spontaneous testimony. As I read the news reports, I shook my head in wonder at how an attorney could be so misguided as to put a case of this magnitude in jeopardy with such thoughtless and unprofessional actions.

Although Judge Brinkema rejected the defense's motion to throw out the death penalty entirely, she did prevent many of the government's witnesses from testifying. These experts had been selected by the prosecutors to help the case by explaining to the jury what they would have done to bolster aviation security had they received a warning from the FBI about a terrorist plot involving airliners. Because I was not privy to the overall prosecutive strategy, I do not know how important these witnesses were to the case, but I assumed their testimony would have been helpful. For me, I was just relieved to learn things were back on track and I was determined to hang in there under MacMahon's cross examination that I knew was coming.

CHAPTER 60

CROSS

And so, on Tuesday, March 20, 2006 I was back on the stand being sworn in again, eight days later than planned. Although the pregame jitters were there again, I was far less nervous than on my first day of testimony. Once I was seated, I looked over at Moussaoui, who once again averted his eyes.

When given permission, MacMahon rose and walked to the lectern. In keeping with the polite and professional style that prevails in the federal courtroom, he introduced himself to me, "Agent Samit, I am Edward MacMahon. I represent Mr. Moussaoui there." He nodded to his left.

As hostile as I was feeling towards MacMahon, I pushed all of that aside. Smiling, I nodded and said, "Nice to meet you, sir." I learned early on that it was important, especially as a law enforcement witness, to appear professional on the stand and not to make any aspect of my testimony appear personal. That took an effort because I despised Moussaoui.

MacMahon brushed that aside with a "Yeah...well..." and then launched into his cross examination. As I had observed during his objections, MacMahon had mastered the defense attorney's quarrelsome, doubt-filled style of asking questions, as if the government witness on the stand was the one who did something wrong. I stayed neutral, ignoring this and the other provocations MacMahon used to goad me and kept my answers factual and my tone upbeat. I was not surprised MacMahon was mounting an aggressive cross examination.

As an FBI Agent, I was expected by both sides and the judge to be able to hold my own on the stand. Initially, I was following where he was going with his questions. He was seeking to unravel the prosecution's theory that it was Moussaoui's lies that shielded the hijackers so they could carry out their attacks. MacMahon's simplest and most direct way to do that was to point out that the FBI already had all the information it needed to stop the attacks and that it was bureaucratic bungling or infighting or plain old incompetence that caused our investigation to fail.

What surprised me was the way in which MacMahon went about weaving this narrative. His cross examination was confusing for me, and almost certainly for the jury because with one question he would try to paint me as a far-sighted hero, fighting against the uncaring and incompetent FBI bureaucracy, while with the very next he would accuse me of being a poor investigator. For instance, while asking me about the decision-making process which led us to decide to arrest Moussaoui to deny him access to the flight simulator, MacMahon abruptly pivoted, hissing at me, "You blew an opportunity to search ... without arresting him?"

Realizing full well that *not* arresting Moussaoui would in no way have enhanced our chances of searching his property, I looked at the jury and shook my head before responding, "That's totally false." I started to explain why, when MacMahon cut me off with another question, this time on an unrelated topic.

In fact, as the cross examination went on, I started adding little explanations onto my answers, just so the only narrative was not what MacMahon was trying to sell. After a while, that started to annoy him, so in his most indignant tone, he appealed to the judge to order me to stop.

Judge Brinkema, her face neutral but her tone kind, looked at me and said, "Agent Samit is reminded to just answer the question."

I nodded solemnly, "Yes, your honor."

Although I was feeling comfortable dealing with MacMahon's questioning, his style did prevent me from using one of my favorite tactics. When testifying on cross examination most Agents, me included, like to think a few moves ahead to see where the defense is going with their questions. Not only does this predictive analysis allow the formulation of the best possible answers but thinking ahead also allows an Agent to reply without hesitation, making him or her seem more credible to the jury. MacMahon completely thwarted that since it was not obvious to *anyone* where he was going with his questions. I later concluded his plan had been to come out like a boxer swinging wildly without a clearly defined strategy, but alert to any openings to land a punch.

Unfortunately, MacMahon *did* have some openings, simply because of the missteps of those at headquarters and the amount that dirty laundry was aired through all the inquiries. This allowed him to ask me questions about the approximate number of documents I submitted to RFU prior to 9/11 (including emails, there were more than 70) as well as Martin's responses shutting things down. MacMahon was trying to get me to testify that headquarters was so incompetent that even if Moussaoui told the truth about 9/11, the FBI would never have been able to foil the plot. That was clearly not the case, and I said so.

MacMahon then shifted his questions, asking me whether it was true that we in Minneapolis tried time and time again to get a search warrant. I replied that it was. Then, MacMahon stepped out from behind the lectern, clearly holding a thick document in his left hand. It was open to the middle, and I could see that it was my 44-page response to the OIG's findings that had so angered David. I swallowed, thinking, "Here it comes."

Once MacMahon was sure I saw and recognized my own document, he stepped back behind the lectern and resumed asking me rapid-fire questions about the actions of the people assigned to RFU. I think he sped up his pace because he sensed I would be emotional about being denied assistance by Martin and would be more likely to slip up in my replies. Realizing this and knowing he was right, I forced myself to slow the cadence of my speech, so I was answering deliberately and only after listening to each question and carefully considering my answer.

Even with my care in replying, facts were facts, and I had to give some answers which hurt the prosecution's case, just as David predicted. One reply which I know generated angst at the government table was when MacMahon asked me whether I was 100% sure we could have stopped the attacks if Moussaoui had been truthful. Although I felt very strongly that we could have stopped 9/11 had Moussaoui responded truthfully to our questions, I could not be 100% certain.

I know at least David was unhappy with my answer because I was looking at him when I replied, "No. Not 100% certain." He had been sitting with a neutral expression, gazing in the direction of the jury, but when I said "no" his head jerked ever so slightly. I did not want to hurt the case, but I was required to answer truthfully. There were just too many variables in any investigation, especially one as complex and far ranging as the 9/11 plot and there was no way I could swear under oath that I was 100% sure everything would have gone our way.

Sensing he had me finally answering the way he wanted, MacMahon kept hammering at the people at headquarters, and what they did to hurt the case. He asked, "But you didn't get the chance to find out, did you? Because the people at headquarters obstructed you, correct?"

"Yes."

"You also said they were obstructionists and careerists, correct?"

"I said I believe some of their decisions were guided by a wish to protect their careers."

MacMahon nodded. Still holding my 44-page document in an obvious manner, clearly as a signal to me that he knew what I wrote, MacMahon asked, "Did you ever say their actions were criminally negligent?"

I replied without hesitation, "Yes."

Glancing sideways at the prosecutors, MacMahon paused dramatically for a second, then asked, "Do you want to take that back?"

"No."

Obviously, none of this was good for the prosecution's case, and for that I was sorry. But it was also true, and what's more I had already declared it in writing. After the trial I went back and read some of the media reports from March 20, 2006 about MacMahon's cross examination of me. Many of the same journalists who a week before praised my testimony on direct examination now wrote I harmed the prosecution's case. Even while I was on the stand, I was aware my statements were damaging, but I also knew my thoughts on the subject were in the report MacMahon was holding, so to deny or minimize these statements would be to invite being discredited. As David predicted nearly a year before, I just had to sit there and take it.

However, I also knew David would have another chance to question me later, during redirect examination and was confident he would ask me questions that would allow me to clean up those answers and explain that although I believed headquarters obstructed our case, and badly, I also felt equally strongly that had Moussaoui told me and John the truth, we would have had a good chance to stop the attacks. And David did not disappoint. Like the rock-solid prosecutor he was, once MacMahon finished his hours-long questioning, David rose and proceeded to give me the chance to explain.

Despite my efforts to remain dispassionate and professional, I had one or two emotional reactions to his questions. The one I remember most vividly came during one of those confusing lines of questioning, when I could not tell whether he was trying to vilify me as an inept investigator or paint me as a lone hero standing against the FBI bureaucracy. MacMahon had just asked me about how I failed to uncover some obvious fact, and I responded, "No, sir. That is not correct. In fact, it is completely wrong."

Stepping out from behind the lectern, MacMahon abruptly switched gears. He looked hard at me and asked, "Agent Samit, you were working hard to find out about the plot, correct?"

"Yes."

"And isn't it true you would have done anything to stop the attacks?"

That got me. In an instant I thought of those who were lost and of their lives not lived and promises sadly left unfulfilled. And I thought of their families who were watching and how awful this must be for them. I felt a lump in my throat. "Yes," I choked out. I could feel the emotions welling up, but I was determined not to let MacMahon goad me into going beyond what I wrote in my submission to the OIG. He cracked the door, but I held it there and did not let him fling it wide open.

I am sure MacMahon heard my tone change. That is probably why he used what he saw as an opportunity to launch into another determined assault on the FBI's incompetence and obstructionism. Maybe he thought I was wearing down and would give him the statements he wanted. I did not. I stood firm and made a clear distinction between people at FBI Headquarters and the FBI employees in the field. I pointed out that at no time did I see anyone in the field display either of those qualities, or for that matter let up one bit in their efforts during the days leading to the attacks. Moussaoui's lies protected his associates and allowed them to move forward. They were the decisive factor.

And then, after several hours of my cross examination, MacMahon ended as abruptly as he had begun. With no fanfare or sign he was wrapping things up, he closed his folder, said, "Nothing further, Your Honor," and sat back down.

Then David rose for redirect, clarifying some things for the record, particularly where MacMahon cut me off on answers. When that was finished, MacMahon rose once more, for one final cross examination of a very few questions, and then I was excused.

As I rose and walked numbly through the courtroom and out the door, I realized that was it. Exactly 1678 days had passed from the time the Moussaoui case was opened at around 10 am on the morning of 08/15/2001 until my final testimony at his death penalty trial on 03/20/2006. During that time, the world had changed around us. Thousands of innocent people died on 9/11, the U.S. became involved in two wars where more were dying every day, and the threat of terrorism became a central focus of life in America. Whatever the jury decided, I had now done all I could on the Moussaoui case. And I hoped it would bring some closure for everyone.

CHAPTER 61

ELIGIBLE FOR DEATH

Determining whether Moussaoui was eligible for the death penalty was the part in which I testified, and I was eager to know whether the jury found me and Clancy credible and the prosecution's theory convincing. As discussed above, I was aware some of my statements had been helpful to the defense and I did not want to be the cause of the case being lost.

Before that verdict came, there was a long wait. Because I was scrupulously following David's instructions on sequestration, I knew nothing of the witnesses who testified after me in Phase 1. I avoided reading the paper or viewing news stories on the internet or TV. If some news flash came on while I was watching TV, I covered my ears and closed my eyes until Terri told me it was over. I wanted to make sure I could still testify if needed, and part of that might be having the ability to swear under oath that I had not been following the trial.

Of course, once the trial was over and the restrictions were lifted, I went back and read the news articles. One of the first things I learned is that Moussaoui himself testified a week after me, on March 27th. Because Moussaoui had been insistent on testifying at his trial in the numerous hearings leading up to the big event, I was not surprised.

However, I was so intrigued by what I read in the media about his statements that I obtained the complete transcript of his testimony and read his words for myself.

While being questioned first by his own lawyer, Gerald Zerkin[18] and later by Rob for the government, Moussaoui made sweeping admissions, most of which were consistent with information we had from other Al Qaeda members, like Minneapolis subject Mohammed Warsame, and Asia-based JI members Faiz Bafana, and Hambali. Moussaoui acknowledged being a member of Al Qaeda and admitted to being involved in the 9/11 plot. One by one he identified several of the other hijackers as people he knew from Afghanistan and described numerous conversations he had with operational planners of the attacks, like Mohmed Atef, Khalid Sheikh Mohamed, and Usama Bin Laden himself. Most compellingly for the purposes of this trial, he also acknowledged he was intended to be the pilot of a fifth airliner on 9/11, that another member of his crew was Richard Reid, and that his target was the White House. Moussaoui also told the jury he lied numerous times to me and to John to conceal the operation so it could go forward. Sickeningly, he said on the stand that he was "delighted" when he learned that the towers collapsed in New York and that the video and photos of the result were "gorgeous."

I do not understand why Moussaoui chose to take the stand and to say what he said. However, when I later read his March 27th testimony, my thought was that everything he said was consistent with what I knew about him.

Defense attorney Zerkin tried to paint him as delusional or mistaken during his questioning, but from what Brian said after listening to him, Moussaoui sounded composed and lucid on the stand. And, most importantly Moussaoui's statements were consistent with what we knew. The defense also introduced statements from five senior Al Qaeda detainees which likewise claimed Moussaoui was not part of the plot. I was not in the courtroom when these were

18 Obviously, Moussaoui forced his attorneys to call him as a witness. Seldom will any competent defense attorney make the decision to allow their client on the stand because no matter what he or she might say to exonerate themselves on direct examination, the cross examination which follows will be damaging, if not completely devastating.

put on the record, but I imagine the jury saw them for what they were: lies to protect one of their own.

That is why I was so angry to learn that members of an entrenched faction at FBI Headquarters went into the office in the evening following Moussaoui's testimony or the very next day and prepared a summary for FBI management *refuting his testimony about his membership in Al Qaeda and his participation in the plot* and calling him a liar. Most of the statements in the document were "assessments," shorthand for opinion, or at best educated guesses. Dana, the analyst who led this effort, was a prominent and vocal member of the Usama Bin Laden Unit, and this may have been a factor in her deciding to draft the document.[19] I am not sure why she and her colleagues prepared such a report, except to cover their own failure to detect the plot. I'm guessing their reasoning went that if Moussaoui was simply a crazy liar who made up his participation in the 9/11 plot as their analysis implied, then there really could be no way the Usama Bin Laden Unit or anyone in the FBI could have spotted the threat in time.

Naturally, this quickly came to the attention of the prosecutors, who were enraged. The reason for their anger is that this document, which sought to undo Moussaoui's sworn testimony, now needed to be turned over to the defense. Accurate or not, it could now be used by Moussaoui's attorneys to refute their client's own statements about his membership in Al Qaeda and role in the plot. To my knowledge this is the first (and hopefully the last) time in the long history of the FBI that current Bureau employees, acting in their official capacity, worked *against* the criminal prosecution of a mass murderer in the shameful interest of protecting their professional reputations. I do not know what the defense ever did with the document, as it is not among their exhibits, but it certainly had the potential to destroy the

19 The drafting of the March 2006 document was not Dana's first failure in the case. She also bungled several key chances to learn about the presence of hijackers in the U.S. before the attacks. At the time of this writing (April 2020) Dana is still employed by the FBI and has risen high in the ranks of analysts.

government's case. And it was drafted for no other reason than to further protect those whose job before 9/11 had been to detect the plot, but who failed to do so.

Careerism and obstructionism, indeed.

Two days later, on March 29, 2006, the first part of the case went to the jury of nine men and three women. They certainly did not rush to a decision. The jury received the case on a Wednesday and did not return their verdict until the following Monday, April 3, 2006. When they did, to my relief the jury found Moussaoui eligible for the death penalty. That meant the trial would move to its final phase, one in which the prosecution would argue there were "aggravating factors" which made Moussaoui's crimes so serious as to warrant the government ending his life. This time, if the jury voted for death, Moussaoui would be sentenced to die.

The relief I felt was mostly for the victims' loved ones. I strongly believed they deserved justice in the case, and the best way to get it would be to see the ultimate punishment handed down to Moussaoui. He was someone who in the weeks leading to 9/11 had the ability to save the almost 3000 victims of the attacks but chose instead to cover for the hijackers long enough to see the plot come to fruition.

Selfishly, I was also relieved for me. I felt tremendous guilt at the statements I made to those investigating the FBI's failures, especially once the theory of prosecution gelled around the idea Moussaoui's lies were the specific conduct which made him eligible for the ultimate punishment. With that established, every negative thing I said about FBI Headquarters was fodder for the defense. My sense of hopelessness was further increased after the March 2005 meeting at headquarters, when FBI management made me understand once and for all that my statements had been futile, and that the status quo would prevail. Had the Moussaoui case failed after I realized that no one in power cared in the least about that gaping hole in the FBI's capabilities, I would have been crushed. Thankfully, that had not happened. The trial would move forward.

It should also be understood that all my criticisms of FBI management were submitted through official channels and appropriately classified. Unlike others who voiced concerns, I took great pains to ensure my comments were submitted in a way in which they were unlikely to be leaked to the media. My reasons for keeping my concerns within house until now were two-fold. First, I wanted to privately provide my opinions in the interest of keeping our adversaries from finding any exploitable weaknesses in the FBI's capabilities. Second, as always, the Moussaoui trial was uppermost in my mind, and I wanted to balance reforming the FBI with preserving my ability to be the best witness possible when the time came to testify.

CHAPTER 62

VERDICT

The second part of the penalty phase now moved to the prosecution presenting what were called aggravating factors to persuade the jury to vote for the death sentence. The defense for their part would introduce evidence which constituted mitigating factors, that is information which explained why Moussaoui was not completely responsible for his actions. A review of their exhibits for Part 2 of the trial shows the defense introduced documents which they clearly hoped would persuade the jury Moussaoui's conduct was driven in part by witnessing the abuse of his mother by his father as a child or some associated mental illness. After his statements on the stand in Part 1 it is hard for me to imagine how the defense believed they might paint him in any sort of a sympathetic light, but they obviously tried.

However, during Part 2 it was the government's case that was so completely heart wrenching that it made me glad I remained sequestered. Brian gave me a little preview of what the AUSAs planned to introduce, including a nearly 46-minute video of the photos and names of all the deceased victims, as well as photos of surviving family members without their loved ones. One of the worst was the photo of the baby daughter of a Fire Department of New York Captain who was killed responding to the World Trade Center. Born in May of 2002 (four months after my daughter Anna), she never got to grow up with her father because of the attacks. Almost 20 years later I still carry tremendous guilt for the loss of every one of those victims, especially the fellow law enforcement officers and other first responders who willingly ran to their deaths. Seeing even a few minutes of that gut-wrenching testimony would have been difficult for me and I can only imagine how hard it was on the AUSAs and the Agents who helped arrange the exhibits and got to know the family members personally.

Nearly one month later, on the afternoon of May 3, 2006, someone came by my desk in the 5 Squad area and said, "Fox News just said they're about to announce a verdict in the Moussaoui case." I had been diligently avoiding any news of the case, but since the verdict was going to be final, I realized I could watch it on the news with everyone else on the JTTF. I jumped up and joined my squad mates in the breakroom and saw on TV a podium with a solitary microphone outside the familiar courthouse in Alexandria. Presumably, as soon as the verdict was reached inside, someone would come to that microphone and announce it to the waiting cameras. I could feel the adrenaline start to churn.

It was probably 40 minutes or more until Edward Adams, the court's public information officer emerged from the courtroom to make the announcement. In that time, the small breakroom next to the squad area filled up as people heard it was coming. Then, a hush fell over the room as Adams, clad in a gray suit, walked out the doors to the courthouse and up to the microphone. With an air of solemnity that befit the situation, Adams explained in lengthy detail that the jurors in the case weighed the mitigating and aggravating factors before deciding the appropriate punishment would be to sentence Moussaoui to life in prison without the possibility of release.

He had escaped the death penalty.

Although I was disappointed that we had not gotten the verdict we sought, I did not feel as upset as I believed I might. It felt less like the crushing defeat I imagined it would and more like losing a long-anticipated big game which of course, this was not. As people patted me on the back and consoled me, I was not sure why I did not feel devastated, but over time I came to realize it was because the justice system had functioned as intended.

Going back and looking at the case the AUSAs and the Agents presented, I realized they did their best, putting on damning evidence using compelling witnesses, including Moussaoui himself. For reasons known only to themselves, the jury saw the case otherwise and decided not to vote for death.

More than a year after the dust settled on the case and the members of the PENTTBOMB team returned to their normal lives, David told me he had been contacted by the foreperson of the jury, a woman the AUSAs had been concerned about during jury selection. The woman was a teacher, and prosecutors tend to fear teachers will be inclined to be more sympathetic to defendants. Whatever their misgivings, the prosecutors did not use one of their six challenges to have her struck from the jury, and she was eventually chosen as foreperson. Now this woman wanted to let David know what had happened in the jury room and how upset she and the others were about the final verdict. According to this woman, during an oral polling of the jury each member stated their intention to vote for death for Moussaoui. Despite a few jurors accepting some mitigating factors put forward by the jury, they were satisfied they had a unanimous verdict. It only remained to mark the ballots in writing, whereupon it would be official. When the ballots were anonymously marked and collected however, all but one of the jurors had voted for death, despite what they had just stated aloud. One juror voted for life in prison. That one vote meant the decision was not unanimous, as required for the death penalty.

To continue the foreperson's account, the more vocal members of the jury then invited the unknown dissenting juror to identify him or herself to allow the group to discuss that person's concerns. No one spoke. A second oral poll saw all jurors again voting for death. Unfortunately, the second round of written ballots returned the same result: one vote against. They therefore had no option but to return the recommendation of life in prison. The foreperson called because she wanted David to know what had happened behind closed doors.

The next day, Judge Brinkema sentenced Moussaoui. He received six consecutive life terms, with no possibility of release. During the hearing, the judge said, "You came here to be a martyr and to die in a big bang of glory, but to paraphrase TS Eliot, you will die with a whimper." She concluded, "For the rest of your life you will never get a chance to speak, and that is a fair and appropriate ending."

I appreciated her sentiment. For more than four years Moussaoui had ranted and raved at the West and the U.S. in general and the judge herself in her own courtroom, even as he was treated with great fairness and even indulgence. The justice system had given him a bully pulpit to push Al Qaeda's global jihadi propaganda. Now, that was over. Although Judge Brinkema did not control where Moussaoui would be sent to serve his sentence—that was the provenance of the Bureau of Prisons, it was generally understood he would be sent to United States Penitentiary, Administrative Maximum Facility, Florence, Colorado, more popularly known as "Supermax."

The judge's statement at the sentencing, although supremely fitting and appropriate given Moussaoui's offenses and his conduct in her courtroom, would create problems for me later.

There was a bizarre postscript on the trial, one which surprised all of us. Less than three weeks after the verdict, on May 23, 2006, a five-minute audio recording was released on an Al Qaeda associated website. The recording, which experts believed was the voice of Usama Bin Laden speaking in Arabic, stated Moussaoui "had no connection at all with September 11 ... I am the one in charge of the 19 brothers and I never assigned brother Zacarias to be with them in that mission ... Since Zacarias Moussaoui was still learning to fly, he wasn't number 20 in the group, as your government claimed."

I was stunned. Bin Laden himself, in hiding and at risk every time he communicated with the outside world saw fit to release an audio clip exonerating "brother Zacarias." I had never heard of Bin Laden doing anything similar. In addition to being an inveterate liar, Bin Laden had never imperiled his own security, before or since, to release a communication claiming someone in his organization *was not guilty* of a crime. That recording just reinforced for me that we had the right man in jail.

With the trial finished, I resolved to get back to working cases, and just cases. I hoped I was finished talking to committees investigating what went wrong before 9/11 and I no longer had any responsibilities on the PENTTBOMB Team, except one. At David's request I nominated Clancy for an award under the State Department's Rewards for Justice program. That process took over a year, and after considerable bureaucratic drama and angst, he was approved for a payment of $5 million for his role in reporting and then testifying against Moussaoui. Other employees who worked at Pan Am International Flight Academy during August 2001 who assisted with the investigation were eventually also nominated for smaller awards, a discrepancy which naturally led to hard feelings on their part, and on the part of others who also believed their actions warranted a payout. It eventually became an ugly scene, with numerous parties contacting members of Congress and pleading their cases in the media for payment.

CHAPTER 63

THE FINAL MEETING

And so, in time I and the Minneapolis JTTF moved on from the Moussaoui investigation, his trial, and the aftermath. There were other significant cases where our task force did some incredibly aggressive and cutting-edge investigation to protect Americans from the scourge of Islamic extremist terror. Many of the strategies and tactics we used on these later cases were developed and refined during the early days of the JTTF, during the 1999–2004 period. And the lesson we learned about never again letting people at FBI Headquarters hinder our cases played a role in our success.

On a personal level, of course I got older, and so did many stalwart members of the team. We had people transfer to other offices or retire, and new faces appeared in their places. But through it all, the mission remained the same and the investigators on the Minneapolis JTTF never failed to rise to the challenge of catching terrorists when we could and neutralizing them in other ways when we could not.

After his sentencing and placement in Supermax, I tried to forget about Moussaoui. Stories on him would occasionally appear in the media, usually around the anniversary of 9/11. Less regularly, he would also emerge in my nightmares, an ominous figure seemingly sent to remind me he was not gone from my subconscious. With frustrating consistency, the Moussaoui of my dreams was always just beyond my reach, and though I would run or climb or swim as fast as I could to catch him, he would always escape. It did not take Sigmund Freud to figure out what those dreams meant, and it was obvious some part of my brain was suffering because Moussaoui eluded me in real life when it truly mattered.

And then, in early 2015 while the Minneapolis JTTF was heavily engaged in working a case against members of the Islamic State, I got a call from SSA Jim from the now-defunct PENTTBOMB Team. Jim was calling now to ask whether I was interested in going with him to interview Moussaoui in prison in Florence, Colorado. Jim had been a long-time member of the PENTTBOMB team, and though I had frequently been at odds with nearly every member of that team except Brian, Jim was a nice guy. He also had an encyclopedic knowledge of the 9/11 plot and even when we were on opposite sides of an argument our exchanges were mutually respectful.

However cordial our relationship had been, Jim's call certainly caught me off guard. The last thing I was expecting almost nine years after the trial and 14 after our original encounter was to talk to Moussaoui again. But as Jim explained, Moussaoui was generating attention for himself in a way that was hard to ignore. That was typical of him. Here's what had happened: a group of families of the 9/11 victims were suing various entities for restitution connected to the murder of their loved ones. Because so many of the hijackers were Saudi citizens, there was a growing belief by them and their lawyers that the government of that country, and specifically its intelligence service might have had a role in the attacks, and they were named in the suit.

Somehow the families' attorneys were granted access to Moussaoui and during his deposition in 2014 he made statements which not only seemed to confirm Saudi knowledge and encouragement of the plot, but also outright participation through the actions of members of the Saudi royal family.

Jim explained that he was skeptical of Moussaoui's extremely inflammatory claims, the thrust of which served to put Saudi Arabia, a key U.S. ally, at the center the worst attack on America in history. For that reason, Jim wanted to do a thorough and detailed interview of Moussaoui, which we would record, to get his statements locked in.

Of course, I accepted Jim's request immediately. However, pushing my luck, I asked Jim whether he would object to my asking Moussaoui other questions as well, questions pertaining to the materials we found in his laptop case on agricultural aircraft and questions about other Minneapolis subjects. Because he is a fair-minded person and a curious investigator, Jim agreed to this right away.

And so, on a snowy day in February 2015 Jim, an NYPD detective, and I arrived in the cold and forbidding mountains of Florence, Colorado, and entered the colder and even more forbidding United States Penitentiary, Administrative Maximum Facility. The famed "Supermax" was situated in rocky and mountainous territory not far from the town of Pueblo. Built on a plateau, most of the structure of the facility is underground, making it even more ominous.

After passing through several checkpoints, each secured by a pair of sliding steel doors with armored glass windows more than an inch thick, we turned a corner and were faced with a long, sloping ramp down which we walked to get to the inmate area. When I say long, I mean long, and we seemed to be descending for more than five minutes, with each step bringing us not just forward, but also farther underground. In fact, as we walked, I could feel the air pressure change in my ears, so great was the difference in altitude from start to finish of that hallway!

In addition to its stark cleanliness with gleaming tile floors and immaculately painted concrete walls, one overriding sensation prevailed on this walk: silence. Our surroundings seemed to absorb the sound of our footsteps on the tile and our voices did not carry at all in the still air. It was quiet down there and I began to feel a creeping sense of loneliness and isolation, even though I was surrounded by people. I guess that was the idea. Clinically clean, cold, and silent.

Our trek ended, improbably, at a gym containing a basketball court, but one unlike any other I had ever seen before. It had the usual two hoops and a hardwood floor, but there were no bleachers, in fact there were no places for any fans to sit. There were no windows and like every room I visited in Supermax, the court was cold and silent. And there was more. Against the wall and out of the way were 8 or 10 dark box-like structures, constructed from riveted steel plates painted in government gray. Upon further examination I saw each of these was a mini cell, essentially a small desk inside an armored shell in which an inmate would be seated and locked so he could be safely interviewed through the small, caged screen where his face would appear. We were informed in fact, that when Moussaoui was deposed for the 9/11 lawsuit, he occupied one of those small cells as he was questioned by the plaintiffs' attorneys.

We had a quick conference and decided we did not want Moussaoui in one of the little cells. We wanted to sit across from the table from him so we could show him photos and look him in the eye. The BOP people obligingly agreed to that request but suggested he might stay cuffed and in belly chains. We demurred on that too, asking that he be allowed the free use of his hands and feet. We figured three FBI Agents, an NYPD detective, a BOP investigator, and a BOP attorney were more than enough muscle to handle even a rampaging Moussaoui. Besides, I secretly thought it might be fun to kick the living crap out of him if he tried anything.

But the reality was that I understood from my previous interactions with Moussaoui that the possibility of his becoming physically violent was slim. For all his posing and histrionics, Moussaoui was calculating. There was no way he could escape from Supermax and even assuming he somehow could overpower all of us at once and take over the gym, he was still in the very heart of the prison. No, his goal for all of this had to be to get someone from the FBI or the wider DOJ to listen to what he had to say to advance his own agenda. For that reason, I judged the chances of his attacking one of us as low. I was banking on being right, because if Moussaoui was going to go berserk on anyone, it was likely to be me.

Given the security protocols required to move an inmate like Moussaoui within Supermax, it was more than 45 minutes before a special team of corrections officers brought him to us. When the metallic "thunk" of the door into the gym being unlocked signaled his arrival, I was angry at myself because I felt a slight shot of adrenaline. I was ashamed Moussaoui's impending arrival provoked any emotional response in me at all, let alone one of nervousness. In hindsight, I think I was simply conscious of the historic opportunity we had before us. Moussaoui for so many years had been the one subject whose plot our JTTF was unable to foil, even though we arrested him. I wanted to make up for that now by learning all I could. Therefore, as much as I despised him, I wanted to talk to Moussaoui for as long as it took to get from him every single fact about the 9/11 attacks and other plots. I felt like the victims' families and the American people deserved to know. Here was what seemed like our last chance to do just that, and I did not want to mess it up.

Despite my pregame jitters, when the door swung open and I saw Moussaoui for the first time since the trial nearly nine years before, I had to stifle the urge to laugh. Moussaoui was much smaller than I remembered him, his narrow, sloping shoulders barely filling out the food-stained white T-shirt he was wearing over dark green prison Dickie trousers. He had a gray shapeless sweatshirt tied around his waist and still wore a white kufi on his head. Moussaoui had the wild, untrimmed beard he sported in the courtroom in Virginia, only now it was shot through with gray. His eyes were still hard and angry, lit by a fire now stoked not only by ancient Wahhabi hatred and modern Al Qaeda propaganda, but also through years of being incarcerated by a government he despised.

None of that was funny. But what nearly made me laugh out loud was the figure Moussaoui cut standing among the team of guards who brought him to us. Walking slightly behind and on each side of Moussaoui were two female guards, each of whom was holding one of his arms, which were secured in front of him by the belly chains he wore. The two guards were normal-sized women, meaning they were roughly as tall as Moussaoui. Directly behind the three of them was a very large and muscular male African American prison guard, who was obviously part of the team as insurance in case Moussaoui tried anything. He towered over the trio in front of him, his long stride curtailed by the shuffling pace forced by Moussaoui. Moussaoui could only walk with short, fast steps because he was wearing leg shackles which, like his handcuffs, were connected to the belly chain around his waist. The image of the four of them gave me a silent and private laugh and broke any tension I was feeling. I was ready for Moussaoui.

CHAPTER 64

DAY 1, AGAIN

Once in the gym, the trio of guards halted the procession and looked expectantly at the chief investigator for the prison. He indicated where Moussaoui was to sit, and they escorted him to the chair behind the table and unceremoniously sat him down. As his rear end touched the seat, the old, familiar Moussaoui emerged. Speaking angrily (I'd never heard him communicate any other way), Moussaoui looked at the chief investigator and said, "Ah, now, you see, Mr. Smith! You know I am supposed to be placed in one of these boxes when I am interviewed!"

I thought, "Wow, that didn't take long!" Moussaoui was still as ill-tempered as ever.

Because I wanted to get rapport going right away, I stepped into Moussaoui's line of sight and said, "Well, Mr. Moussaoui, we want to be able to sit across the table from you while we talk. Why would you want to be in that box?"

Moussaoui's looked at me for the first time and he held up his cuffed hands, "Because these hurt and I don't have to wear them in the box."

I nodded, "Well how about this? We will take the cuffs off and you can still sit here with us. Will that work?"

"Yes." He nodded. Once again, I heard the lisp and the French accent. I also got a whiff of his old but familiar smell of stale body odor, unbrushed teeth, and stained clothes.

One of the guards stepped forward and began removing the handcuffs and shackles. As she did so, Moussaoui's eyes searched my face. I looked back at him, not breaking his gaze. After a second, he said, "I think...I think I know you."

I nodded. "You do, Mr. Moussaoui."

Eyes narrowed, he said, "Yes...from Minnesota. You are ze pilot."

I nodded again.

The guard stepped back and there was now no one between us. After a second, I said. "And I am back to talk to you again."

Breaking my gaze, Moussaoui said, "Okay." He sat there in his chair and seemed ready to go, so all of us sat too.

Jim and his partner introduced themselves and Jim explained he was there to ask Moussaoui questions about his claim Saudi Arabia was involved in the 9/11 attacks. Moussaoui nodded. I chimed in and added I was there to ask Moussaoui about other issues.

Eyes narrowed, Moussaoui asked, "Like what?"

I replied, "Things in your background, other people you know, different aspects of the 9/11 plot."

Moussaoui shook his head, "I will tell you some things, things about myself. But others...no!"

I smiled, "Well, Mr. Moussaoui, why don't we just take it chronologically and we will see?"

Looking at me warily, Moussaoui replied, "Okay, but there some things I don't answer!"

Now that the surrealness of being back in front of Moussaoui had completely worn off, I got into the groove and started warming up by trying to build rapport with my most famous subject. I must say that in the 21 years I spent as an FBI Agent, I did some unpleasant things. There were disgusting things I had to do in meth houses I entered for SWAT operations, things involving dead bodies, sights and smells and sensations experienced in working my way through Red Lake High School in the aftermath of the carnage caused by the shooting there, and rapport building while talking to murderers and pedophiles and rapists and terrorists. But nothing was as disgusting and offensive to me as working that day to establish a relationship with Moussaoui. Talking to so hateful and twisted a person and trying to be ingratiating made my skin crawl like nothing ever has, before or since.

I quickly realized keeping Moussaoui talking was not going to be hard. He saw few people and spoke to even fewer, and even someone so fundamentally disturbed clearly craved conversation. This allowed us to ask him questions about his background, and more specifically about how in the mid-1990s a guy like him ended up in an Al Qaeda camp. Moussaoui explained that after he was denied advanced educational opportunities in France, he went to the UK to attend university and then obtained a master's degree. While he was there, "his eyes were opened" by Muslim brothers who told him about his religion, specifically his obligation to live strictly according to the Koran and to spread the word to others.

And it was here we hit our first roadblock with Moussaoui, one of many we encountered that day, and the next. When I asked, "And who were those brothers?" Moussaoui's face grew angry.

"Oh, no! I am not going to say about them. They, the Tooting Circle, they still there, so no!" He glared at me, a look I'd seen before.

I knew "Tooting" was a neighborhood in London, home to a mosque of the same name. I also knew the Tooting Mosque was not far from Southbank University, where Moussaoui obtained his master's degree. We learned in the years since 9/11 that there was a shadowy group of British and foreign-born Muslims in London in the 1990s who radicalized themselves and each other, fueled largely by what they perceived as the anti-Islamic violence in places like Bosnia, Chechnya, and Afghanistan. What we had not known is that Moussaoui was associated with them or that they gave him his start in jihad.

"So, is that how you decided to go on jihad?"

Calming down, and clearly considering that an acceptable question, Moussaoui shook his head. "No. It was not until after I won my master's degree that I learned about going on jihad." Moussaoui went on to explain that following graduation, he was having no luck finding a job, either in the UK or in his own country, despite his academic qualifications. According to Moussaoui, life seemed so meaningless until he attended a lecture at his former university at which the speaker explained it was the duty of all Muslims to fight in a jihad and that that best of them would die in that cause.

When we asked whether he attended that meeting with anyone else, Moussaoui nodded and indicated Masood Al Benin, his childhood friend also attended. Moussaoui told us that once he heard the speaker's words, he decided then and there that he too would die in jihad, and this became his life's goal. Clearly, whatever seeds the Tooting Circle planted, this unidentified speaker fertilized, because Moussaoui was sold on terrorism from that point on. As he described that lecture, which he estimated occurred sometime in 1993, Moussaoui's face lit up. We therefore had little trouble believing him when he said he was "so happy" as he left the lecture because he now knew what his life's purpose was. Moussaoui also noted that his friend Al Benin became enthusiastic about jihad at that lecture too, and that the two of them began working hard to become mujihadeen from that day on.

Since Al Benin had been dead 15 years by then it was not a surprise Moussaoui was willing to discuss him. It also confirmed that long-ago French reporting that attributed Al Benin's recruitment to Moussaoui. Although Moussaoui claimed Al Benin was as interested as he was in jihad, his explanation of the circumstances when both got their start in the movement was close enough to what the French discovered back in 2000 and reported to us during the dark days of August 2001.

It was a logical follow on for us to ask Moussaoui how he got from the idea of jihad to the reality, but he would only state that "some brothers" helped them learn how to get to Chechnya, which was where he said his career began. Moussaoui informed us that when he arrived in Chechnya, the mujihadeen were experiencing a low level of activity, and despite his ardent desire to fight the Russians, most of his time was spent training and then waiting for a chance to get into battle. According to him, that chance never came, because, one night after many months in Chechnya he and all the trainees were warned of an overwhelming attack by the Russians. Moussaoui explained that their leaders told the trainees to leave the country immediately to save themselves for another day because the expected Russian attack would be too powerful for the mujihadeen to resist.

Moussaoui went on to describe a hurried evacuation in which he and a group of his fellow trainees crossed rivers and mountains to leave Chechnya. At the end of his trek, Moussaoui found himself back in London, his desire to die in a jihad temporarily (he hoped) thwarted. Rather than return to Chechnya, Moussaoui was able to find his way to Afghanistan for his next jihad. Although equally unwilling to describe who helped him get there, Moussaoui informed us he trained at a camp, corroborating Warsame's information by describing the camp as being located near Kandahar. He also said that after training, he spent time on the front lines in combat.

Although what Moussaoui was saying at this stage seemed truthful, I mixed in some questions to which I already knew the answers to see whether he would lie. By 2015, I had interviewed many more Al Qaeda members than I had when Moussaoui and I last spoke in 2001. I also read the reports of interviews of dozens of other captured operatives or fighters who went through Al Qaeda's training system in Afghanistan in the 1990s so I had detailed knowledge of normal procedures for the group.

However, my best gauge of his truthfulness at this stage came from what I learned during some 2003 interviews of a Minneapolis subject named Mohammed Warsame, who had been with Moussaoui in Afghanistan. When I asked Moussaoui where he lived when he was not at the camp, he replied, "At a guesthouse, in Kandahar." I knew that was true.

"And did you have any duties when you were not fighting?"

Moussaoui nodded, "I was head of security at the guesthouse." He went on to explain that his primary duty was to check the belongings of people coming to stay at the guesthouse to make sure they did not have any forbidden items in their luggage.

"So, did people try to sneak stuff in?"

At that question, Moussaoui grinned, and chuckled, "No, but sometimes they would forget they had things from the camp with them. They weren't allowed to have weapons in the guesthouse." His smile and laughter made him seem so normal, and I tried my hardest to pretend like he was one of my buddies from the Navy telling stories about our time at sea. That technique helped me to temporarily forget how much I hated Moussaoui, or at least to suspend my emotions while interviewing him. This interview called for the ultimate poker face, or more difficult still, a convincing portrayal of empathy as a means of getting him to speak freely. When he displayed signs of his own sense of humor or humanity it made it easier for me to pretend that I understood his point of view, which, of course I didn't.

Because we were discussing Kandahar, I asked, "And how about the institute?"

Moussaoui frowned, "The institute?"

I nodded and said firmly, "Yes. There was an institute near your guesthouse where classes were taught. You attended there to study."

Seeming to get it now, Moussaoui said, "Yes. It was religious school. We learned about the reasons for jihad in Afghanistan and wars for God in other places."

"And they also taught you how to operate in the West."

Another smile. "Not me. I am from France and lived in the UK. I already knew how to live in the West."

I shook my head, "But others there didn't. What were *they* taught?"

Moussaoui deadpanned, "I don't know."

"What was happening at the medical clinic?"

In a measured and casual voice Moussaoui replied, "There were sick people from the camp there. And people who got injured."

I nodded, "But what else were they doing there? Especially once they closed it down and moved the sick people out."

Moussaoui's face clouded over. "They didn't move them."

Staying neutral, I replied, "Sure they did. That's when the other work started there." I was referring to the Anthrax development we knew Warsame had been a part of. Still looking angry and suspicious, Moussaoui stayed silent, so I continued, "That's why you did all that work on researching crop dusters. It's because you..."

Moussaoui interrupted me with a shout, "No! No! I will not talk about this! That is a separate plot! I will not discuss!" The mention of the agricultural aviation and linking it to the clinic in Kandahar was obviously too close to home for Moussaoui and I saw shades of his performance from August 2001, particularly with the histrionic yelling. As in 2001, when he was excited, Moussaoui made excited utterances, for example, referring to "a separate plot." That confirmed what I thought but sadly gave us no additional information about what the plot was or who was going to be involved.

It was obvious from the evidence amassed since 9/11 that there was a separate plan for Al Qaeda to use a biological weapon against us, and Moussaoui's slip seemed to confirm it, but he would not give any details, no matter how I pressed. By this point I felt comfortable ignoring his objections because we had not yet covered what Moussaoui wanted to discuss and because he seemed to be enjoying the experience of talking to us given his isolation. I was therefore not concerned he would end the interview, and I kept asking. He simply refused to answer.

"Okay then, what about your plot? Who else was on your crew?"

Moussaoui shrugged, "I only know one. Richard Reid was supposed to be with me."

"But you would need more than just him to take control of a 747."

He responded, "I did not know. They did not tell me yet. You arrested me first." We asked this question quite a few ways, but no luck. Moussaoui did acknowledge that his target was intended to be the White House. Nothing new there, either. And we were no closer to knowing who else was going to be involved.

Shifting back to Afghanistan I asked, "So how did you join Al Qaeda?"

Moussaoui responded that when he reached Afghanistan, he met Bin Laden and some of his senior associates, like Mohamed Atef. I believed Moussaoui when he said both took a liking to him because he was familiar with English and could use a computer. That he was a favorite of Bin Laden was corroborated by statements of other detainees and by the fact Bin Laden released that audio tape attempting to exonerate Moussaoui after the trial. We just did not know why this was. Therefore, when Moussaoui explained he did some computer work for the Al Qaeda leaders, compiling lists of members and doing budgets, it sounded reasonable. This brought him into regular contact with Bin Laden who probably saw for himself how fervent Moussaoui was in his hatred of non-Muslims. Moussaoui's fanaticism combined with his French passport and ability to operate in the West made him a useful asset to Al Qaeda.

It was at this point in the interview that Moussaoui started working in his Saudi Arabia agenda. He informed us that once he proved himself to the leadership, Bin Laden sent him on several trips to Saudi Arabia. The details of his story did not hang together well, since he claimed he traveled from Afghanistan to Saudi Arabia via private jet. Moussaoui said that he made at least two visits to Saudi Arabia this way and that he met with Saudi Government officials to exchange messages between them and Bin Laden. He also claimed he met a Saudi Prince in the U.S. prior to the 9/11 attacks, and that this prince, and a Saudi Princess who accompanied him were directing the plot. Moussaoui informed us this was proof the Saudi Government was controlling Al Qaeda.

None of this made sense and neither did his descriptions of how the Saudi Government participated in the 9/11 attacks. His story seemed so off, in fact, that by the end of the first day, we were convinced Moussaoui, who utterly refused to discuss anything I cared about, was simply pushing his own agenda on Saudi involvement in 9/11. Because I was still a big believer in the split interview and giving the subject a chance to worry about his lies from the day before, we were coming back the next day. Much like in 2001, we decided we would push Moussaoui even harder on day 2, although it is not like we held back much on day 1 this time. We told Moussaoui in no uncertain terms we believed he was lying whenever we did, which was often.

CHAPTER 65

DAY 2, AGAIN

The next morning, we repeated our long slog out to the prison and then back down to the dreary basketball court. Today, Jim led the questioning, aggressively focusing on the holes in the Saudi Prince story. It was no surprise to any of us Moussaoui was unable to convincingly explain why the Saudi Government would be involved in 9/11 or, even if they were, why they would take such a monumental risk as to meet operatives in the U.S. Also, his only counter to our reminding him he was the least suitable person in Afghanistan and among the 9/11 hijackers linguistically to meet with Saudi citizens of any rank, was to claim all conversations between him and the Saudis occurred in English.

Jim told him, "I do not believe you. You are obviously not telling the truth."

To attempt to divert and distract and hopefully take advantage of Moussaoui's emotions running high at being called a liar, I tried to ask him some more questions about the other topics. I started back slowly, again covering his time in Afghanistan, but trying to work my way around to the institute and to the clinic. He was not having any of that, and once more became irate, the motion of his long black beard, shot through with gray exaggerating the shaking of his bald head. "No! This is what I will not discuss!"

Angry myself now, I responded, "Then why did you ask us here? Did you expect we would just allow you to push your agenda without asking questions of our own?"

He started to respond, "Well..."

But then, I did something I tried not to do in subject interviews. I interrupted Moussaoui. "If you want this conversation to continue you have to expect to give us some information. Otherwise, we will walk out of here and go home to our families and our jobs and our normal lives and leave you here."

Jim added, "Forever."

Speaking slowly, Moussaoui responded, "I will not answer these questions. I am not going to discuss that."

"Why?"

"Because I am at war with United States."

I suppressed the urge to laugh bitterly, but keeping my tone neutral, I asked, "Do you still believe that? How can you possibly still honor the completely discredited rhetoric of leaders who hid in comfort and sent their followers out to die? Look at Bin Laden."

In possibly the most honest response Zacarias Moussaoui ever made, at least to a question I asked him, he shrugged and said, "I have to, or all this," he gestured at the walls around us, "would be for nothing."

"I think you're making a mistake."

Moussaoui considered what I said before responding, "Perhaps. But remember, I will not live long. I do my research and 65 is the average life of a prisoner here. Because of stress. And I have untreated illness." Gesturing at the prison investigator, Moussaoui continued, "He won't allow me medical care." He pushed on his upper stomach and grimaced like it hurt him.

Hoping to catch him off guard, I am sure, Jim asked, "So, Mr. Moussaoui, how do you feel about Saudi Arabia?"

His face contorted angrily, "I hate them. I hate them even more than United States."

"Why?"

"Because they pretend to be Muslim but aren't. They are apostates. Even America does not pretend."

"So, you are at war with them too?"

"Yes."

Jim continued, "And it's fair to say that you would do whatever you could to harm them?"

Moussaoui nodded.

"Like telling us that they were a part of the 9/11 attacks to harm their relationship with the U.S.?"

If Moussaoui realized Jim outwitted him, he did not show it and instead took the offensive as he so often did when backed into a corner. "I tell you that what I said is true..."

Quietly, Jim asked, "Then are you willing to take a polygraph?"

Moussaoui's eyes opened wide. "No!"

"And why is that?"

Indignantly, Moussaoui replied, "Because I have no wish to die."

"How will a polygraph kill you? We've all taken them, and we're fine."

Smiling slightly, Moussaoui responded, "They will kill me. They will find a way."

Jim shook his head, "No, Mr. Moussaoui. You don't want to take one because you're lying, and we all know it. And you know the polygraph will show that."

Moussaoui shook his head but no longer made any denials. After a few seconds, he said, "And this Islamic State, they are doing big things in the Middle East." When no one responded, Moussaoui continued, "I think they are on the right track."

As he was about to speak again, I interrupted him for the second time. "Mr. Moussaoui, the last time you and I spoke, a long time ago, you ended the interview. Well, today, I am ending it. We do not want to talk to you anymore. We're done." I stood.

Moussaoui smiled and shrugged. "Okay. But I think..."

I turned and started walking away and did not hear what he said. I stood looking on from a distance with the other Agents as the guards shackled Moussaoui's ankles and fastened his belly chains and handcuffs. We watched as the tiny procession shuffled off, through the door out of the gym. Once Moussaoui was gone, our group left the prison, convinced his claims about Saudi involvement in the 9/11 attacks were fabrications.

CHAPTER 66

THE LAST CHANCE

This is a good place to finish this story, but as with so much else in the investigation, it ends in disappointment. In late 2018, more than three years after I last spoke to Moussaoui so frustratingly at Florence, I learned he claimed to have renounced radical Islam. In addition, there were indications that he might be willing to talk, and this time, to tell the truth.

For me, that meant one more trip out to Florence to once again interview Zacarias Moussaoui. I knew in late 2018 that my retirement was fast approaching—I would become eligible in January 2019, and I wanted one more chance to ask Moussaoui about Anthrax, the other Minneapolis subjects, and the muscle hijackers scheduled to be on his flight. Although he was an inveterate liar, guys like him did NOT renounce their beliefs or loyalty to a group they swore allegiance to lightly. If Moussaoui was claiming he was done with Al Qaeda and willing to speak against them, I figured it was worth the cost of an airline ticket or two to fly out to Colorado to see if this was true. We might hear about those people and plots which had eluded us for nearly two decades.

Just when it seemed we might actually be able to close this chapter, Derek, one of the AUSAs from the trial team, made it known he was opposed to any interviews of Moussaoui. I asked Brian and then Jim to speak to Derek, hoping to persuade him of the merits of one more interview, but to no avail. In fact, when Derek learned we planned to go through with the interview over his objections, he called a meeting with DOJ to argue vehemently against it. I was disappointed in him but determined to fight for what was right at the meeting.

The meeting ended up being a video teleconference hosted by FBI Headquarters. I connected from Minneapolis and Derek logged in from Kansas City, where he was once again an AUSA after many years in private practice. Also on the call was George, a Deputy Assistant Attorney General in the National Security Division. I groaned inwardly when I learned George would be participating. The AUSAs in Minneapolis had a very low opinion of him as an extremely cautious lawyer, one far more likely to say "no" to any request than ever to agree. Even by the usually risk-averse standards at DOJ, George stood out among his peers for weakness, hand wringing, and vacillating.

I was asked to begin, and I did so by explaining I made the request to interview Moussaoui after learning about his softening allegiance to Al Qaeda. I acknowledged that I was convinced we had finished talking to him forever after our experience in 2015, but the new information seemed to indicate enough of an opportunity existed to make a second trip to Florence worthwhile. I was sure to explain we were not planning to offer Moussaoui anything in return for his cooperation. I was also aware of Derek's objections so I also added Moussaoui would not be given a public voice of any kind and that we were bringing Jim along to ensure we did not do any inadvertent damage to the cases against the terrorists awaiting trial at Guantanamo Bay. I thought I covered all possible reasons he might have had to object to the interview.

Derek was then invited to voice his objections. Nodding, he flipped open a legal pad and began reading from a list. As first Brian and then Jim had informed me, Derek was adamant that no one be permitted to speak to Moussaoui again, for any reason and under any circumstances. He began by saying that if we were to interview Moussaoui it would anger Judge Brinkema, who implied during sentencing that Moussaoui would never again have a chance to speak. He was anxious to avoid giving Moussaoui a "platform."

I responded, reminding Derek that we already interviewed Moussaoui in 2015. I also added that an interview by FBI Agents in the depths of ADX Florence about topics of investigative interest would not constitute giving Moussaoui "a platform." Finally, I also offered to meet with Judge Brinkema to explain to her why I wanted to interview Moussaoui, namely, to find out all we could about the crop duster threat, his unknown co-conspirators, and the full extent of the 9/11 plot. If she objected, I would drop the request.

I watched Derek on the screen as I spoke, and I could see he was not accepting anything I said. The only point he even responded to was about the 2015 interview. He said, "Yeah, I wasn't in government service then, but if I had been, I would have objected. I spoke to Rob and he also objects."

I did not see how that mattered. Rob had been out of government service for more than a decade and he had no standing in this or any other case—unlike the rest of us who were still serving.

Derek went on with his list of objections, including his concern that after an interview Moussaoui would have grounds to make a Rule 35 motion requesting a sentence reduction. I was aware this was a possibility. In fact, *any* defendant can make such a motion at any time. However, two things argued against this being a concern. First, Moussaoui had not done so after being interviewed in 2015, and second, motions of this nature long after the trial, even for substantial cooperation, are seldom granted, especially if the government does not also weigh in with the judge and ask for a reduction, too. It therefore seemed unlikely a Rule 35 motion, even if one were made, would make a dent in Moussaoui's multiple life sentences.

Derek also claimed that such an interview would anger the victims' families. He cited the despicable, hateful remarks Moussaoui made in court about enjoying the suffering caused by the 9/11 attacks. I got that. But I replied that what we were trying to do was to prevent there from being any more victims in the future. Love him or hate him (and I hate him), Moussaoui had information in his head about what Al Qaeda was planning to do with crop dusters, and I wanted it. If he was claiming he renounced extremism, then the crop duster information alone made a trip to Colorado worthwhile.

Derek scoffed, replying that nothing Moussaoui would say was likely to be of value.

"We don't know that, Derek. Not until we go and check it out."

Shrugging off that suggestion, Derek ended by lodging his strongest possible objections to a new interview of Moussaoui.

As I could have predicted, George merely concluded by saying he sided with Derek. DOJ therefore did not concur with our request to reinterview Moussaoui. Although it was pretty much a formality from there, the FBI official running the call said he would take what he heard to the Assistant Director (AD) of the Counterterrorism Division for a final decision. I appreciated his honesty, though, because he added that the AD would be unlikely to go against the recommendation of DOJ.

A day or two later, it was official. Request denied. And that is how my last chance to interview my nemesis ended, once and for all.

THE END OF THE CASE

Like nearly everything in the investigation of Zacarias Moussaoui, I believe this final decision was made not through the lens of what was best for the interests of justice, or for the American people, but to protect the reputations of a few government officials. However, unlike my feelings towards the managers at FBI Headquarters whose conduct cost us so much, I have some sympathy for Derek, who ended my last chance to interview Moussaoui. Back in 2001 Derek was part of the team of prosecutors who were handed the most consequential and emotional criminal prosecution in the history of the U.S. and told not to mess it up. Then, for the next four and a half years he and his fellow prosecutors were closely directed, watched, questioned, and second guessed by the highest levels of political leadership on the choices they made on the case. I know all three AUSAs were deeply involved with the survivors and the victims' families. As a result, they believed strongly that their mission was nothing less than getting justice for the fallen and each made personal and professional sacrifices in pursuit of that.

And even while under that pressure, they had to contend with me: defiant, angry, and unwilling to just toe the line and accept their decision to cease investigation and begin preparing for the trial. When what they sought was clarity for a future jury, I kept muddying the waters by continuing to investigate other subjects and offshoots of the main plot. I also spoke out against the errors made by FBI Headquarters, imperiling their theory of prosecution and once again complicating things for them. I understand the stress my actions must have created, and for that I am sorry.

However, what was done in 2019 to derail our opportunity to speak to Moussaoui was wrong. It is my opinion that Derek, and possibly others feared Moussaoui *would* tell the truth and that what he might say would show how much the PENTTBOMB investigation missed or worse, flat out ignored. By the time he claimed to have renounced extremism at the end of 2018, at least two other Minneapolis subjects (Warsame and Elzahabi) and likely other co-conspirators whose names we did not know had long since escaped American justice. Having Moussaoui discussing them freely at this late date would be deeply embarrassing to those who ran the post-9/11 investigation and prosecution. This is because in 2003, and again in 2004 Minneapolis alerted PENTTBOMB that other 9/11-connected subjects were out there and provided them pertinent evidence. *And they chose to ignore us.*

If you ask me, what will make the victims' families angry is not that we went back and spoke to Moussaoui. No, what will make them mad is the idea that others who were involved in the 9/11 attacks were never prosecuted for those crimes and were now free to live their lives at large, when so many of our fellow Americans died at their hands and those of their friends.

And just as we had a chance to take action to stop the attacks in those critical weeks leading up to September 11, 2001, we also had a chance to charge other monsters with 9/11-related crimes. Sadly, the decision was made by the PENTTBOMB Team to do otherwise. And so, in the final analysis, this entire account is a tale of what might have been. A who-done-it saga so unlike any to which the TV and movie watching public has become accustomed because the good guys did not prevail. Worse, we let some of those who were responsible go free when it was within our ability to hold them accountable.

But we did not.

ABOUT THE AUTHOR

Harry Samit retired from the FBI in April 2020 after a 21-year career as a Special Agent. During his time in the FBI Harry served as a case Agent and human source handler, while also performing collateral duties as a SWAT team member, SWAT observer/sniper, and Special Agent Aviator (Fixed Wing). Harry was assigned to the Minneapolis Division, working high-stakes international terrorism investigations of members of Al Qaeda, the Islamic State, and other violent extremist groups.

Before joining the FBI, Harry was an officer in the U.S. Navy for nine years. He was commissioned through the Naval Reserve Officers Training Corps (NROTC) at the Pennsylvania State University as a Special Duty (Intelligence) Officer. He is married and has four adult children.

This is his first book.